1

First Published Online in 2015
2<sup>nd</sup> Edition November 2015

ISBN 9781517032845

# Grandchild of Empire

## A British Life in Changing Times

David Tolliday-Wright

I have written my memoirs down
primarily for my family to read and retain.
I have had a good life and it has been full of stories.
I hope that my children and grandchildren will enjoy reading

# Contents

# 1. Oranges and Babyshit

On the day I was born, the 29th April 1943, the RAF carried out in the Baltic its largest scale mine laying operation of the war. Three days before, on the 26th, the mass graves of 4,000 Polish officers were uncovered in a forest at Katyn, near the Soviet city of Smolensk. The Germans blamed the mass murder on the Russians; the Russians blamed the Germans. We know today it was the work of the Russian NKVD security police. The poor Poles, what a great people, but so sorely treated by history. I remember my Londoner parents praising their fighter pilots, for the valour shown during the Battle of Britain. We certainly owe them our gratitude for their part in that joyful event of the 20th April. As the threat of invasion had been lifted, Winston Churchill was able to announce in the House of Commons: We have reached the conclusion that existing orders can now be relaxed and the church bells can be rung on Sundays and other special days, in the ordinary way to summon worshippers to church.

My dear mother would have been involved with my birth a week later at the Bradley Moor Nursing Home, Wellington U.D. Shropshire. She would have heard the bells from our home, at 10 Roseway, Wellington, with my young sister Jillian. I have little recollection of my time in Shropshire; I was barely 5 when we moved to London. I do have a picture however, of being claimed by my mother at the Blackpool Police Station, after being lost on the beach. I was happy to spend the hour or so with the Bobbies, with their big helmets, jolly faces, fizzy pop, and things to eat. I cried my eyes out on being taken out of custody. I attribute this escapade when I was just 3 or 4, as did my mother, to my desire to become a policeman.

Another event which took place in my infant days in Wellington and must have been mentioned many times by my parents to have remained in my mind to this very day concerned: the 'Wrekin Orange Disaster.' The whole country was on rations, it was war-time or just after. The whole family were on the Wrekin Hill, a delightful spot just above Wellington, for what went for a 1945/47 picnic. I hazard a guess: bread and jam. The centre-piece of the hilltop 'feast' was an orange. An ORANGE! Certainly not a Jaffa from Israel, as that place was not yet there and I can hardly imagine the British mandate of Palestine was then in much of a state to export oranges! Oranges from Franco's Spain hardly likely either! Outspan from the dominion of South Africa, well? In any event they were a luxury food and if they had come with the war still on they had to escape being torpedoed by German 'U' Boats. In the austere, immediate post war days, when the country was broke they were not for the lower orders! Although I hasten to add the government, as my dear Mum used to say, did a marvelous job keeping us all fed. There was orange juice and milk always available for all the children. No, this orange was one from food packages sent as gifts from the USA. Certainly at the time no shortage of good folk there.

I was given the orange but I, or perhaps it was Dad, dropped it! It rolled down the steep sides of the Wrekin Hill with Dad chasing after it, gathering speed as it got further and further away, to be lost hundreds of feet down and out of sight. Dad apparently returned after a considerable period 'orangeless' and downcast. The family were not to see a whole orange for years later. I never really got into eating oranges, was it because they were too much trouble with their skin and pips or was it this terrible incident from my childhood?

My parents, as I describe later, were hard working people. My father was an office worker involved in a number of jobs, some managerial, until he retired to draw his pension at 65. My mother was skilled with a needle and was a milliner by trade. She had served her apprenticeship and, like my father, worked right up to drawing her pension.

*Mum and Dad as a very good looking courting couple apparently somewhere on holiday.*

*And another of a young courting Mum and Dad
with her brother Alexander and his wife Emmy.*

My earliest photograph (overleaf, page 12), taken somewhere in Shropshire shows me looking, I must say, extremely clean, well nourished, (despite the War and rationing) and good-looking. I am prompted to mention that I appear 'clean' by a story my mother tells: She left me in the pram, unattended for some unavoidable reason. Upon her return she found me covered all over, from head to toe, in baby shit. No special technology then to steam-clean the pram, just soap, Dettol and water! I think she must have been off somewhere with my sister, who would have been five then.

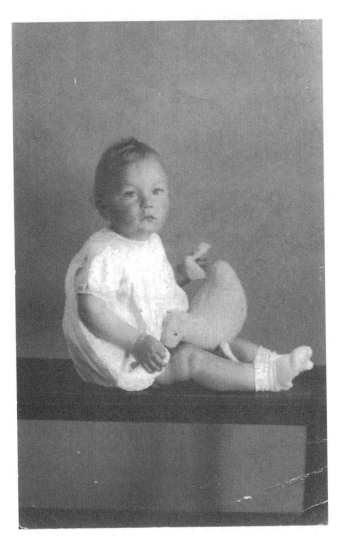

*Me at what must be 7-8 months.*

# 2. Milliners' Row

So what were we, as Londoners, doing up in that lovely county on the Welsh border: Shropshire? Father was away involved in war work, something to do with aircraft, in Oxfordshire. I never found exactly what. I understand he was involved with Dad's Army, although apart from some funny stories about coconut shells as machine guns (the sound of same thereof!) and knives on the end of wooden poles, I knew little about what he did. My mother and sister were evacuees, my maternal grandmother and great aunts were left in Stoke Newington and Hackney, London. They did fill me, as a young boy, with all sorts of stories of the blitz. The buildings in Stoke Newington behind my grandmother's home, where I used to play, were bomb-sites. Goodness what pluck they had! They would say sometimes, "Shall we go down the shelters or not bother?!"

After the war we returned to London, Stoke Newington: No.46 Barbauld Road, N16. I recall I was nearly 5 years old. I enrolled in Church Street Infants, my sister went into the Juniors. The area still had its share of bomb-sites, although prefabs (prefabricated bungalows) had been erected for the needy and those bombed out. These, I recall, were comfortable, an improvement many would say, on some of the accommodation that had been destroyed by the Boche. There were no immigrant families from the West Indies or South Asia then living in the area: mass immigration had not started and the word 'racist' not yet invented. A picture of my classmates and I on a visit to the Tower of London show all white children.

Today black folk are the dominant group at Church Street School, followed by those from the Indian sub-continent; white faces are rare.

*At the Tower Of London:*
*I am at the back to the right of the tree, wearing a dark cap.*

Before I move on from the school I would like to mention my first concerns with gender. My first love was Winifred Whittiger (probably wrong spelling). I had not been long at infant school when I decided I wanted to date her. I followed her home, probably an arrestable offence today, and then later knocked on her door. A woman answered, her mother maybe. I said, "is Winifred Whittiger in?" The answer was "No!" and the door was slammed shut. I never looked for a girlfriend again until the urgings in the loin dictated otherwise.

My next experience was my selection to play one of the key roles in the 1949 or maybe 1950 Christmas pantomime. I was to be the 'senior' ugly sister in charge in the panto Cinderella. Apparently I was a hoot at rehearsals and had the class on their knees. I was able to put on a good show because with a sister, just into her teens and sharing a bedroom, I knew all about the madness of hair rinses/colours, the wrong/right clothes. "I have nothing to wear! I look awful! Does this colour suit me?" etc. In the event, my manliness took over. The boys were laughing too much and were taking the piss in the playground, especially one little gingernut boy who was the terror of the class. So I didn't perform and they got someone else for the part. That was the end of my cross-dressing!

Perhaps I should be amiss if I don't mention our visits to the Odeon Cinema at Stamford Hill, where there was a significant Jewish population. As a boy I was always intrigued with the men in their black, long coats, hats, beards and funny curls under skull caps. My dear Mum, who worked as a milliner in a work-shop where all but one of her workmates were Jewish ladies, spoke some Yiddish and was well up on their religion and culture. Many of these lovely ladies had escaped from Nazi Europe and talked much with Mum about the ordeals they and their loved ones had faced. They were all aunties to me when for some reason or other I would have to go with Mum to the workshop while she worked or picked up work to take home. I would play amongst the hatboxes or talk to the men who did the heavier steam blocking work. I remember one Auntie Nettie, she had a Polish boyfriend who had been in England for years but could only just about utter, "Good morning, how are you?" Manuel from 'Faulty Towers' was an English linguist by comparison. So Auntie Nettie taught herself almost fluent Polish to talk to him! These ladies were something!

Football, the beautiful game! I was never very good at it, but my dear Dad, who was not a bad amateur player, and had played with his brother Uncle Harold for a team at Alexander Palace near Muswell Hill / Woodgreen, would spent a lot of time with me until my early teens kicking a ball around. I remember he took me to watch Chelsea, Tottenham and Arsenal; we would go to Arsenal to see them lose. An occasion comes to mind which still raises a smile was when his dislike at the behaviour of one of the Arsenal players was displayed in his use of language. His dislike was met by a response from the Arsenal supporters who surrounded us and one of them pulled Dad's trilby hat down over his eyes. That was all it was, there was no such thing then as football hooligans! Oh well, not in London anyway. Normally when still juniors, boys, unless they were huge, (no McDonalds then thankfully), would be passed down over the heads of the ground to sit near the Police in front. In those days the Police were there to watch the game, not the crowd!

Another memory I have of our Barbauld Road days was our special outings down to Southend on the old paddle steamers. I must have been 6-8 years old. We would catch the steamer at the pier just below Tower Bridge, beside the Tower of London. The trip would take the best part of half a day to reach Southend pier. I forget how we returned home. I can only guess it was by train, steam in those days, to South Tottenham Station. I have an image in my mind of one of my Great Aunts accompanying us. It was all the fun of the fair on Southend pier; one of the longest in the UK and complete with its own electric railway and mile long track.

My Great Aunts; there were three spinsters: Aunts Lil, Nell and Min with a fourth, Aunt Agnes who was married to Uncle George. George was my hero and I have his medals: two (MMs) for gallantry, displayed in my home today. The fifth sister was Louise, my paternal grandmother, who lived below us at No.46 Barbauld Road and was to me an austere and rather frightening figure. There being countless rows between the floors, often involving my sister. It was after Grandmother's death that we moved to Friern Barnet. All sisters shared the surname 'Bentley' and were real Londoners, ladies who had been hit hard by the slaughter of the men of their age in the Great War. Min and Lill (who despite a waterworks problem) would have been catches for any reasonable fella if he had been around. Nell, dear soul, had an eye that was not entirely focused straight and sometimes you were not sure if she was addressing you or the person behind; she was, however, my favourite. She was the Aunt in charge and ruled the flat at 2nd & 3rd floor, 33C Middleton Road, London E8. She was a good cook who always did a fine old style Sunday dinner. Her steak and kidney puddings were something with old vests/draws and the like used as pudding cloths. My dear Mum would jest about the colour of these cloths and had a name for a shade of grey: 'puddin cloth grey'. Everyone in the family could recognise the shade when referring to the colour grey.

The WC at Middleton Road was down two floors, an old style commode made by Thomas Crapper. It fascinated me as a child: all wood and blue flowers enamel. There was no hot

17

water and for baths they would have an all over wash using large china jugs and bowls. The water coming from kettles heated on the stove which had been fired by coal. I recall there was also a gas oven.

I ate with my Aunties a number of times but I was always a bit queasy about the plates and cutlery, that didn't seem to have seen liquid soap. The lavatory paper was the Radio Times, cut up and stringed together. How primitive! Lower orders? Not at all! We were still in the 50's; most things were still on ration. Lavatory paper was certainly not a priority for the Government. With President Roosevelt gone President Truman was not forthcoming with help and the country was burdened with feeding a conquered Germany as well. That marvellous display of generosity from the Americans in the Marshall Aid plan did not begin to take off until the end of the Atlee Government of 1946 : around 1949/50.

The Aunts, as we called them, were the salt of the earth. They were still around when I joined the Hong Kong Police in 1965. I remember dear Aunt Lil, who was the eldest and was particularly fond of my Dad. Poor soul, she always had trouble with her waterworks and seemed most of the time to be too far away from the loo. But she had loads of pluck and a great sense of humour. One day she carried a kitchen chair all the way from Ridley Road market, where she had bought it, down the 2+miles along Kingsland Road to Stoke Newington High street, then on down Dynevor Road to our home on Barbauld Road. She thought we needed an extra kitchen chair; as you may imagine her drawers were ringing wet on her arrival.

I recall it was at the end of Ridley road at the German hospital in or around 1951 that I had my tonsils removed. Thank God the war was six years away and I don't remember any strange uniforms.

Religion did play some part in my junior years at Stoke Newington. I recall going around to Sunday school at the Congregational church, a short walk in Albion Grove. Across the road was Clissold Road which lead up to the green and pleasant Clissold Park. A place where I recall Dad would take us some weekend evenings to watch the amateur concert parties, the very in thing for the years after the War: late 40's and 50's. Apart from introducing me to Christ and the Loving God at Sunday School there was also in the week, morning assembly at Church Street Junior School for hymns and prayers together. We were then culturally and religiously very much a Christian country, if I would be allowed to say that today.

My mother, who was confirmed in the Anglican Church, would say prayers at bedtime. Dad had not been confirmed and my impression was that the Bentleys were not Church goers, although great aunt Annie Wright, the sister of grandfather Wright, was a very devout lady who taught at Sunday school in North London for years. She was very well respected, as was shown by the hundreds who attended her London funeral. I understand she died single in the 70's, well loved in the community. I know my dear mother found her a kind, helpful and loving Christian lady. A feeling she did not extend to her mother in law, we knew as 'Big Gran.'

My connection with Christianity continued after we moved to Friern Barnet where I started to attend Sunday School and bible class run by the Crusaders Union, at a Church at Whetstone London. N.20.

Grandfather Wright died in the early 20's shortly after the First World War, weakened by gas attacks sustained in that terrible war. He was, before being called up to serve in the Royal Engineers, a craftsman working in the jewellery or fine metal work trade. I never knew much more about him. My mother could not have met him and Dad never talked about him. But then Dad would have been only 7 when he went off to War and when he came back he would have been pretty much a war-damaged man. Dad did tell me that on his father's deathbed he kept crying out: "Save the horses". His mind must have been on those terrible war sights of artillery shells blowing the poor warhorses to bits. Dad always said he was a kind and gentle man. I have mentioned much about his wife's sisters, my great aunts and can add little other than to say they were well read and educated middle class people. Aunt Min was the one who worked in accounts and was regarded as the sharpest of the three spinsters. Nell and Lill had worked more with a needle. Agnes had been a senior soldier's wife. Louise, my grandmother, sadly I knew least of all, despite living above her for 5 or so years.

My maternal grandmother ('Little Gran') Emily Tolliday (nee Bishop) was one of, I believe, 7 or 8 children, who perhaps could be described as from the rural working class. They were all Oxfordshire people working for the most part on the land. She was still living in Oxfordshire, at the village of Stonesfield, not far from the Duke of Marlborough's Blenheim Estate at Woodstock, when I was born in April 1943. My father, during the war had occasion to be involved with war work involving aircraft in Oxford and had used his mother-in-law's cottage in Stonesfield as a place to stay. She was still living there when she came to live with us in London in 1955. My mother was a faithful daughter and it was she who insisted grandmother should move to London where she could care for her. She had much earlier had cancer and was, when she came to us, around eighty years old.

As a family we had visited her a number of times in Stonesfield. It was usually just mother and my sister as my father would have been working. Her cottage was a delight, primitive and quaint. It was situated at the bottom of a hill, opposite a field below which was an old Victorian water supply tap. This was useful as the cottage had no water supply. The thunder box at the end of the garden would be emptied regularly. The contents deposited in the earth below two gorgeous golden plum trees that were situated in the small garden. There was no gas supply and cooking was on an old wood or coal fired stove. There was, however, electric light: three bulbs one over the ground floor room and two over the top floor room which was divided by a thin wooden wall. No TV, only steam radio.

*The Cottage at Stonesfield*

I mention here as an aside that at No.46 Barbauld Road we had no TV and only bought one, a 'VIDOR' in 1954, after we moved to Friern Barnet.

The cottage was a bit like the grandma's house in 'Little Red Riding Hood,' including a big bed and plenty of big daisies for the little girls to pick from the garden. In the field opposite there were cows and on one occasion I recall us infant children climbing up into the field to be chased away by a big daddy type cow.

We would always go up to Oxford from London's Victoria coach station, via Maidenhead or High Wycombe on the Midland Red Coach. No Motorway then so a more leisurely 3 hour run. As a little boy I was always keen on 'buses,' a word I would pronounce in the early days with a nice Salopian burr. Alas to lose quickly to my London voice, which I seem to have retained to this my dotage. The bus which we would take from the bus stop in the centre of the City of Oxford would be the twice weekly 'Worth's Bus'. I found it particularly pleasing, it was blue, not red like those in London, was a double decker but with very different stairs. The entrance was also in the middle, not at the back and the tickets were different, from a funny machine. The village bus stop was right outside grandma's cottage and she would always be there waiting for us.

Along the lane opposite the cottage, was the village post office and shop and across from there was Mr Devonshire's bakery and his famous lardy cakes. His name just came to me, after all these years! As Londoners lardy cakes were new and special, with their sticky outside and doughnut like base. And the fresh bread in the morning! At the end of the lane was a long drive, through grounds with lots of fruit trees which lead to a really lovely house with huge grounds, where a relative lived. I never learnt what the relationship was and who owned the house and the big orchard. The name Aunt Annie rings in my head; maybe she was Gran's sister or cousin?

Just out from the village, off the Charlbury Road, was a pig farm where we would take food to feed the sows and watch all the piglets playing around. On the other side of the village, more towards the Blenheim Estate and about 3 miles away, was an old Roman villa. There was not much left except the ornate tiled floor. Then there was St James, the Great church where Little Gran would go regularly. This was an old Norman church going back to the 13th century. I have since gone back to

Stonesfield once, long ago, when in my teens I went with my friend Barney. This friendship I describe later on, and again I visited in more recent times with the same Barney as old farts. I have a photograph of the cottage taken on the first visit, showing the cottage as it was when Grandma left it. Also one from when I last visited a few years ago, and a view of the exact location through the wonders of the electronic age and the net, shows the water supply tap still there. But the field where the cows chased us is now occupied by an estate of nice houses. Grandma's cottage is now a very impressive large country house occupying her grounds and those of some property behind.

What do I know of Little Gran's life? I remember her telling us about going to school with her younger brother Ernie. It was a small village school and must have been run by the Church of England. The discipline was strict at home and school. Children she would drum into us were, as they should be, seen but not heard! No screaming brats out of control then with their hapless parents or helpers cowering nearby. Compulsory education for 5 to13 year olds had come in the 1880 Elementary Education Act. At Christmas time for the children there were no presents only, perhaps, an orange. She was well read, ladylike and spoke elegantly, without accent and with almost a posh voice. I use to wonder if there was some inferiority complex about her humble origins and the fact she worked in service. At the age 14 she was one of what must have been scores of maids at Blenheim Palace. She told us how as a young girl she had to curtsey the equally young Winston Churchill. We learnt, however, little about her family and what they and what she had done for employment before meeting Grandfather Tolliday. I understand that it was whilst in service

24

working in the Uxbridge area that she met her husband, my grandfather. The only thing I do remember about her family was from the tale she told about her youngest brother Ernie, who went off to serve in the First World War, leaving a young wife with a lodger who had a harelip. On his return from the wars there was an addition to the family in the shape, from his wife, of a child with a harelip. Daft Uncle Ernie, as she would say!

What of Grandfather Tolliday? He died in the 1930's, I understand before my mother and father got married. I know perhaps less about him than I do about his wife. He was born in Scotland where and when I don't know. My mother told me he was born into a wealthy family who had made and then lost their fortune in the wig making business. The family had been friends of Thomas Carlyle, the Scottish philosopher, historian and writer of the Victorian age, who lived in London from 1831 until he died fifty years later and was known as the 'Sage of Chelsea'. He was cast adrift on his own at an early age and survived by working as a lather boy in barbershops in London. He had an elder sister who had married a well-to-do Swiss man. She lived with her husband in Switzerland but cared for her young brother from a distance with funds. I recall a young Swiss man called Sneider, who visited us when we lived in Stoke Newington, he was in some way related to us.

Grandfather Tolliday must have married at the start of the 20th century as my mother was born in 1909. Her parents lived near Kennington Oval, Lambeth where she was born. When a young girl, barely into school age, the family moved to the village of Cymmer, near Port Talbot, South Wales, where her father took over the local barbers shop. At the time it was a coal mining village with the mine and the shaft dominating the community. The mine provided the work for most of the town there being no other industry. It was before the National Coal Board and state ownership so would have been privately owned. My mother was full of stories of her life there. She learnt a fair amount of Welsh which was taught at school and would make us laugh how there were so many Jones and Thomas in the village that they would be identified by the jobs: Jones the post , Jones the bread, Jones with the wire, and one who they called Jones piece of cord because he always walked around with a roll of sting in his pocket; then there was Bobbie Thomas the policemen, who when seen out of uniform during the First World War, was referred to as Bobbie Thomas disguised.

The tales of what happened when the siren went at the pit head were not so light hearted. When this happened the families would rush to the pit head to see if any of the miners had been trapped underground or there had been an explosion. Coal mining was dangerous work then with the seams often very small. There were not many fat miners in the 1900's, in sharp contrast to some I met when at university in Wales in 1980. No it was a hard life. Mum would tell us how she would go around to the homes of her school friends to find the friend and her family busily scrubbing the coal dust off 'Da's' back. No pit head showers then or was it the thing to get home and enjoy the wife and kids? Another thing that interested us was the 'flics': what went for the movies. It was a penny plain or tuppence plus: hard seat or soft!

Grandfather Tolliday was ready to do his bit and volunteered for army service but was turned down on medical grounds because of his angina which was detected apparently when he was just a young teenager, as an arrhythmia of the heart.

The Tollidays returned to London. I am not sure when, but believe it was when Mum was ready for secondary school. She told us how they could not, in the new school, understand what she said with her welsh voice. She left school and took up millinery. When asked at junior school what she wanted to be when she grew up, she said a millionaire. Well in a welsh voice it must have sounded the same.

She met my Dad in the 1920's. I have seen photographs of a really good looking couple in the fashion of the 20's: bell bottom trousers and short skirts They courted for quite a long time and married in 1935 or 36 at St Mary's Church, Church Street, Stoke Newington, London .N.16. This was just a stones throw from Grandfather Tollidays barber shop, also in Church Street. Which he had opened on their return from Wales. The shop also included accommodation for the family. Almost opposite the shop was the Lion pub which served Truman's beers and where my grandfather would go every day after work for his five pints. One day my grandmother said: 'Alec I will come with you today'. He answered: 'In that case my dear I won't be going'. That would be grounds for divorce today.

I have been within the last 15 years back to where the shop and the pub was. I have found a picture on the internet recently which shows the Pub is still alive and well. My Dad also was a local and lived less than a quarter of a mile away in Broughton Road the old name for Barbauld Road. I understand it was the same house that we moved to from Shropshire.

My mother was a milliner when they married and my father worked for the Russo/British grain Trade. This must have accounted for, at times, his pro Russian stance. But to be fair to him these views changed when the full evil of Stalin's Soviet Union became clear to all. He must have been doing quite well because they could afford to live at Bushey in Hertfordshire, which is up beyond Harrow and is, and was then, a nice area. My sister was born there in December 1938.

The war caused all manner of disturbance. My father was conscripted to do war work. I never knew what it was, although as I grew older I was always a little miffed he had not been a fighter pilot, royal marine etc. The boys I played with in Stoke Newington were always boasting of what their Dads did in the war. My Dad served in the Home Guard and he would tell us of what things were like in the early days of the war when they had no weapons and would use makeshift ones from broom handles, knives and bottles of petrol. Dear Dad said that the wonderful TV series 'Dad's Army's which came out in the 1970's accurately depicted the fun, games, one-upmanship, pathos and heroic patriotism that was found in Great Britain's last line of defence against the storm troopers of the Bosche.

My mother and father were always in employment throughout my childhood. Although my Dad to the distress of my Mum was often falling out with his colleagues at work. He was always an office worker doing accounts at various levels from clerk to manager. I remember he worked for the International Tobacco Company in the City for a number of years. The firm supplied a cigarette allowance to their staff. He never smoked but he gave his supply of De Maurier tipped cigarettes to my mother and by so doing probably started a habit which hadn't really got going.

I recall that the De Maurier brand were a little up market and was unusual in that at the time, 40's to early 50's, most smokes were untipped like Players, Senior Service, and for the lower orders Weights and Woodbines.

As was not unusual Dad fell out with some 'sod' at work and moved on from the tobacco company. My memory tells me the sod was called: 'Old Turner.' I would ask my Mum as a young boy who this monster was and if it was the particularly horrible man looking at us at the bus stop. Other jobs were with the Klinger Nylon Stocking Factory at Edmonton where he was in charge of the wages department. I understand that when this company started to lose work for some of the big chain stores he lost his job. He was the London accountant of the Independent cross Channel vehicle ferry company: Townsend Ferries. This must have been his best job especially for a man without any professional qualification. There were free travel perks and I recall he took Mum across to France a few times. There were other jobs, one that I do recall which gave us a laugh, was his part of a small three man band export company. The company employed a woman called Ursula, whose name frequently came up when Dad reported the activities in the business. What made us laugh would be when Dad took home some of the orders that had been written to company by traders in West Africa clothing it supplied. The English was funny, charming, quaint, in any event what with tales of Ursula and her activities, they made us laugh. There were short periods in the early days when Dad was out of work.

For as long as I can remember there were always hat boxes in the home. These were long cardboard boxes 36 by 18 by 18 inches; inside would be room for anything from a dozen to two dozen ladies hats. They would come from Mum's work room, that of her employer 'Mitzi Lorenz Hats,' which was situated up from Googe Street tube station in Cleveland Street. My mother would go into work most days. When I was really young always arriving home early to be there when I came from school. She would take work home to do in these boxes. I was always amazed how she managed to lug the light but awkward boxes on the public transport tube and buses. At home she would finish the hats fixing with needle and thread or rubber solution the trimming needed. Once she had completed the box full of hats she would take it back to the workroom. She always seemed to be working, seated in the winter by the fire in the living room, working on her hats.

I often went with her or by myself, when at the junior school, to Mitzi Lorenzi's. Her work room would be packed with boxes, hats, a smell of solution and importantly a number of middle age ladies all busy working away with the hats but chatting as they went along. My Mum's best friend Auntie Kath would be next to her. They had been friends since young women in their twenties. Kathleen had Irish roots and was a good Catholic girl. She had three sons: Paul, Brian and Kevin who because of problems with their Dad all had at some stage stayed with us. The Dad, Joseph was a teacher who was forever kicking one of his sons out of the home. My dear Mum was always willing to help her friend and my Dad never complained and made the boys welcome whenever they had to stay with us. Brian went onto to succeed as a pop star being the drummer in the group of the 80's the Stranglers.

The other ladies in the workroom were nearly all Jewish ladies, many who had fled Nazi Europe. My Mum had some dear friends among them; I remember particularly Aunti Nettie. Mum learnt many Yiddish expressions and jokes from these lovely ladies. I learnt much from Mum and my time in the workroom of the terrible experience that was Nazi Europe but also the humour and humanity that was Jewish.

Both Mum and Dad worked until the retirement age.

I see I have used this Chapter to fill in as many gaps as I could about my family: The Tolliday-Wrights. In order to keep the Tolliday name alive I joined it in 1985 to Wright.

# 3. Long Live the Queen!

Before I move from Stoke Newington, 46 Barbauld Road N16., to fresh climes in more up-market 'bomb-site free' Friern Barnet, London. N.11., let me explain some of the events that affected my personality, my ambition, my patriotism, my character, my me! As a small boy my mother would often play with me and seated on the floor would show me a metal, not plastic in the early 50's, globe of the world and proudly point out on it all the parts that were red. Then going around the world she would say: that's ours, that's not ours, the green that's the French, the bit with two colours: red and green, pointing at the Sudan, that we share with the Egyptians and so on. She would tell me that when I grew up I would have a duty to serve and may have to go to places far and wide to help and protect the people of the Empire. OK! Today we are supposed, by many, to be ashamed of our empire and what we did to protect it. I like to think after the last two world wars, with some in the 50's still going on, she was just being a true British Mum. I had always, since then, felt that I had a duty to serve my sovereigns' subjects overseas. And many boys of my time were always waiting to be called up for National Service. The News at the Cinemas at the time were full of tommy: in Cyprus, Korea, Kenya, Aden, Malaya etc.

I never forget that winters' day in February 1952 when the headmaster of Church Street Junior School announced to the assembled school: 'Children I have grave news His Majesty King George V1 is dead.' There was an outburst of crying from the boys and girls ages 5 to 11 and some of the staff. I was 9 and know I was crying. I am still a supporter of our dear Queen and our constitutional monarchy as a superior form of democratic government. I don't know if people were more pro the monarchy in the 1950's but we had just had 6 terrible years of World War and our King and Queen had lead us through it. In regards to some of our elected politicians of late I have a jaundiced view to put it mildly and resent how many have been responsible for changing our most cherished and basic British values.

*Our class with our teacher and headmaster*
*taken about the time of King George's death.*
*I am standing at the back, directly behind the female teacher.*

My most memorable time of living at Barbauld was the Coronation of our beloved Queen Elizabeth which took place on Tuesday the 2nd June, 1953. I was just 10 at the time and my father decided that, with all the thousands of people who would be lining the route from Buckingham Palace to Westminster Abbey and back again, that I'd best be left at home. In any event just across the road from us in Harcombe Road a street party had been arranged by Dads of our street and theirs. There were union flags and red, white and blue bunting hanging from the houses and across the street. I have a picture in my mind of a policeman joining the fun. There was a line of tables with all the goodies that were available. It was only four months before that sweets had come off ration; sugar was not to come off ration until September and all other food not until a year later on the 4th July, 1954. But the Mums all got together and pooled what they could from their ration books to make cakes and other goodies.

The man who made the biggest impression on me as a young boy around this time was my Great Uncle George, the husband of Great Aunt Agnes, one of the aunts mentioned before. He had joined the army in 1897 as a boy soldier in the South Wales Borderers, fought in the Boer War, and had been a member of the 'Old Contemptibles' and was awarded the Military Medal for Bravery in the Field twice in1916 and 1918. He had been a respected RSM in the regiment which he continued serving in the TA and Home Guard right up to the Second World War. I remembered his soft blue eyes and his driving us around Monmouthshire where he lived in his Morris 8; not many had cars in the early 50's. What a thrill for a small boy!
His medals are still with me now. I have had them mounted by Spinks of Bloomsbury London and they are displayed with his photograph in my lounge.

My paternal grandmother died in 1953 and the family moved from 46 Barbauld Road, an address we shared with her, to 7 Priory Villas, Colney Hatch Lane. The famous 'Loony Bin' (not politically correct, but that is what it was called then) was down the road from us. I was excited to find I had my own bedroom. At Barbauld Road I had shared with my sister. No.7. was a Terraced house built at the beginning of the 20th century. It was the usual three up and three down with, unlike No.46, a bathroom. It was thus not necessary for us to go once a week – or was it once a fortnight? – to the public baths in Stoke Newington for our regular ablutions. However I didn't have my own room for long as by the time it came to start secondary school my maternal grandmother had moved in with us and taken the room. From then until she died about three years later I would sleep on a 'put you up' in the front room. I would not have my own room again at least for a while.

I started a new school: Holly Park Junior School. I was 10 and there for my last year before 11 plus exams i.e. secondary school determination: Secondary Modern or Grammar School. A most important examination, the former generally meant blue collar job the latter a white collar and a more sought after job. I did well at the junior school, coming always with the top 3 children. But I failed the 11 plus. I recall I was more interested in what I was doing after each exam and did not finish all the questions. So it was across the playground to Holly Park Secondary Modern School.

*Me with my mother in the front room of our home at 7 Priory Villas, Colney Hatch Lane. I note I am in long trousers and must be in the first year at Holly Park Secondary School, age 11 plus.*

The end of the first year and beginning of the second I fell foul of a group of 3rd and 4th bully/tormentors who would routinely duff me up and throw my bag and cap around. It got to the stage that my bruises were worrying my mother. I have no idea why I was picked on, other than I was new and had myself dealt physically with a boy who was picking on others in my year. It is difficult to say that any good can come from school bullying. All I can say for myself is that it made me very conscious in later life of the feelings of similar victims. I abhor people who make others live in fear and misery. But I find nothing wrong in giving a bully/thug/hooligan a short sharp shock: a clip around the ear. (OK I live in the Stone Age!!).

Thus my first two years at Holly Park were not particularly happy. My mother had complained to the headmaster Mr Grieve about me being bullied and it seemed to get better as the bullying fourth year left school to start work. You left secondary school then at 15 unless you were continuing your studies. Holly Park was very much a school for the also ran: those who would be expected to go on to work in trades, apprenticeships, offices etc. There was not much dole for youngsters then. If you wanted to learn a trade there were plenty of openings with the nationalized utilities and transport industries, and we were then very much a manufacturing country. Few, like myself would go on to further education and greater things.

My memories as a 12 to 14 year old, when I had my paper round but had not yet started work as the greengrocer's boy for Dick Saunders across the road from us at 7 Priory Villas, are vague. At school I do remember us boys in the music class going over the previous night's 'Goon Show" radio programme. Repeating the parts of Bluebottle, Eccles, Colonel Bloodnock, Count Jim Morriaty, Little Jim, Seagoon and the rest to the annoyance of our teacher Doctor Popjoy (a lovely name and a lovely man).

We would trudge up to the playing fields in Friern Barnet lane, Whetstone, a good 3 miles hike, every Friday for a game of football. The trouble was by the time we got there, especially wintertime with the bad weather and light closing in, it was time to go home. The keen ones stayed on to play. As stated I was never that good, but toward the end of my time at Holly Park I did play for the school on a couple of occasions. My advantage was my size and ability to kick the ball a long way if hit properly and not necessarily in the right direction, and my indifference to causing or receiving pain.

Out of school activities centred on my bicycle. I had first a cheap second hand one with straight handlebars, not one of your modern drop handle bar jobs. I had it before my paper round and other jobs which I will describe in the next chapter. I thus conclude my parents must have paid for it. It was on this bike whilst scooting out of the playground in the winter of 1955 that I fell off and knocked myself out. I was in the Barnet General Hospital for about a week. I remember it was in November because the boy in the bed next to me at the hospital was there with severe burns on his upper leg. The result of a prank on Guy Fawkes night when someone had put a firework in his trousers. Grandmother Tolliday, who had moved in with us to be cared for by Mum, was greatly distressed with my state. She always had a stern face for me and was old fashioned with her view of children (She was one of 7 or so) and their place, so I was secretly pleased when I heard that she was distressed.

Before I move off from my time at Holy Park Secondary Modern I should mention I was well enough thought of to be made a Prefect. I was so made at the end of my Third Year: I was 14. A Prefect at a state secondary school was not like those appointed in Public schools. For those who not aware of the contradiction in terms: a Public school in the United Kingdom is in fact a private school; parents have to pay for their brats to attend. The fees in those days depended on the amount of flogging that was administered/inflicted at the school. I am told at the schools for the rich and famous like Harrow or Eton there was flogging by masters and flogging and fagging by prefects. Fagging was a form of slavery where the junior boys had to serve the senior boys. I hate to think now what service this was! Alas at Holy Park I was not allowed to flog or fag. My only involvement in either activity would be when I saw one of the school bullies stealing a juniors' cigarettes in the lavatories. When I would give him a good talking to although giving a good thumping in the bogs was the best way of controlling the hooligans in the school. It was that or report him, but rarely, to higher authority where he could be given the cane. Our headmaster Mr Grieve was such a kindly soul that having to cane a boy caused him such anguish that sometimes he was the one nearly in tears at the end of the act of barbaric cruelty. Thus for the sake of his health, most prefects rarely sought his intervention.

I suppose the most memorable event that took place in regard to Holly Park school, apart from falling of my bike, was being selected to go on an Outward Bound Course up at Ullswater in England's Lake District. For those who have never heard of Outward Bound they were started during the last war for young men and boys to give them stamina and self discipline. The idea arose from the terrible punishment the German 'U' Boats were giving to our Merchant shipping during the Battle of the Atlantic and those awful Arctic convoys to Murmansk in Russia. There was concern that so many survivors of the sunken ships in lifeboats or lifesavers, were being lost because they were giving up too soon. Outward Bound started off, with this in mind, to be based on sea training but as time went on it was to include or be replaced by mountain training. There are Outward Bound schools now, for boys and girls, in many parts of world, including Hong Kong, my home.

It must have been the first time I was away from home, at least for any length of time: I recall for three weeks during the winter months (1957). The school was situated beside Ullswater and I have memories of the lake being frozen, hence the morning 6am dip was replaced with ice cold showers in the school. Then it was lessons, nearly all concerned with outdoors, physical training and cross the fells five-mile runs. There were lessons in rock climbing, mountain rescue and first aid; the school did provide such rescue service. There were lessons in the classrooms, but I have no memory now what they were about. I do, however, have pictures in my mind of naval scenes from the war.

We got to be familiar with the fells and mountains and the high point of the course was the 'Tod' scheme or test (based on 'On your Tod': by yourself.). You were given various map references and were expected to cover these and to be out for so many nights (3 or 4?) on the fells. You were expected to find your own place to camp, using a bivouac. I remember spending at least one night in a cave that I had found. We were not to associate with our course mates. It was cold, we cooked our own food from supplies very much like military rations: dehydrated vegetables, corn beef, tinned stew etc. We made our own way back to the school ready to report on the tasks given to each of us. I returned to Holly Park after making some good friends on the course, but they were ships who passed in the night and I lost contact. I remember our instructor well. He had these long legs which seemed to glide up the fell slopes, with us behind trying to keep up. There were often shear drops and the routes over Scafell Pike and Hellvellen could be scary.

I wrote an article for Holly Park's school magazine about the course. I recommended it to the school and the following year another boy was sent. As short a space of time it had in my existence I most certainly think it helped me in later life. This was so especially 'hanging in' when things got tough, whether being made to mark time in the African sun when a recruit in the Northern Rhodesia Police, or under fire from Chinese soldiers as a policeman on the border in Hong Kong in 1967. I hasten to say that there are also numerous other events, perhaps less physical and dramatic, which I have been able to weather far better because of that time at Ullswater over 55 years ago.

I joined the St Johns Ambulance Brigade Cadets soon after we moved. I had made friends with a John Summerwill, who lived down the road also in Priory Villas, at the Holly Park Junior School. He had passed his 11 plus and had gone on to Tollington Grammar School. I had flopped and gone to Holly Park Secondary Modern. We remained friends and went once a week to the drill hall behind the Friern Barnet Town Hall to learn how to dress wounds, treat fractures, perform heart surgery, you name it! At weekends we would perform duties always with an adult member of the Brigade at usually sporting functions. I qualified in all the first aid examinations and think I was keener than John, especially in the duties I performed. I was thus disappointed when he won the cadet cup for duties performed in our first year. I learnt then it is not the effort and time you put in, I had done far more duties than he, but how you are perceived: never be too keen, say and do as little as possible that may draw conjecture. John started to drop out during our second year by which time I had won the coveted cup. Also, I may add, the 'Cadet of the Year Award' which was history all about the Order of Saint John of Jerusalem, on which the modern ambulance and nursing service charity was based. Nearly 16 and it was time to think about joining the Adult Division of the Brigade. I had another good friend in the brigade: Barnard Humphris. We are still friends today.

It was whilst I was a cadet in the St. John's Ambulance Brigade that I had my first experience of taking part in a parade. It was summer and the whole of the Adult and Cadet Divisions were lined up, all smart and to attention on the ground in front of the Friern Barnet Town Hall. I forget what it was all for, but after standing in the sun for some time I fainted. The only one to do so! I was in the right company, all sorts of kindly ambulance men and women gave me first aide: smelling salts, loosen tight clothing and taken to a cool place. The very treatment at which I was an expert. My pulse was taken and I was told it was still there although slightly on the blink, in that it was a little irregular. I was told not to worry as such was not an infrequent thing to happen with a faint, at least that's what I thought was said; in any event I never bothered about it until nearly 30 years later. The act of fainting did play on me during future military and grander parades on the drill squares of the Northern Rhodesia Police and the Hong Kong Police. On such occasions after about 20 minutes if really hot and we were still standing there at attention I often felt the familiar feeling coming over me that meant I was going over. I would thus move my limbs and twitch often to the amusement of my squad mates. In Africa my twitching was undetectable: The Chief Inspector would have probably wacked me with his pay stick and if I had fallen to the ground he would have yelled out: "March over the weak insipid idle man." In Hong Kong there was no such Chief Inspector. Gentler beings would have inquired as to my health and comfort and provided a nice stretcher to take me out of the sun.

I also went with John Summerwill to the Crusaders Union, a Sunday school and bible class for teenagers and young men that met at a church at Oakleigh Road, Whetstone.It was run by surgeon. I still have the bible presented to me by him (looks like) Edw...Clare, when on the 4.12.1955 I was admitted to The Order of Crusader Knighthood. There were a few occasions when we would gather at his house where, after tea and cakes supplied by his wife, we would have a meeting. I remember it was here I got the first Christian explanation of 'the birds and the bees'. We had been given on Sunday a letter to take to our parents to see if they agreed to us taking part in such a meeting. Mum and Dad had never said ought to me about the subject although of course at various stages of growing up and in different playgrounds we had heard different versions of where we had come from. In the early days it sounded nonsense and the version of being delivered to your Mum at home or in the hospital by some sort of aerial conveyance powered by large bird or divine creature seemed the most plausible. As I got older it was all about orifices, and that sounded disgusting. Then it was the various ways the seed of Dad got into Mum that did not involve such unpleasantnesses as birth. Please recall we are talking about the 1940/50s. There was no device for a five year old to carry around with all the knowledge of the world contained therein, photographs and all. As we got older we learned the truth usually in a crude way.

As we learned at the special meeting it was about Mums and Dads and how they loved each other, made you and then loved you. By the time of the good Doctor Clare's talk we knew about the birds and bees but had yet to discover what must have been then the Christian as opposed to non-Christian view of sexual morality and childbirth. As you can imagine with reference to the bible we were taught the biological process: sexual intercourse, conception through to childbirth. There was the emphasis on family and love: one man for one woman, loyalty and together bringing up those wanted children. We were advised that sexual intercourse was only for those who were committed and in love and should be within marriage. In a nutshell we left (we were only just out of puberty) thinking that sexual intercourse was only for those in love and who were married. We must honour our girl friends when we had them. Sexual intercourse was a thing to be enjoyed only with commitment to each other through marriage. Promiscuity, if he used the word, was out.

Today I can hear all our young folks sniggering. I say to them and their parents' generation: please understand the accepted values and norms then and forgive our naivety. The pill was only just emerging. The lovely blond teenage girl next door to us had a lovely baby sister brought up by her Mum. My Mum said: Oh it was a late in life baby, probably a mistake! Oh well! Now the pill has freed the girls. The only thing that comes to mind now when you mention virgin is the airline. A schoolboy or girl who has not enjoyed doing what was explained to me by the doctor now is probably in need of counselling. Then there was the later total demeaning of the family with all the social legislation discouraging marriage. Also it is normal today to have children without a Mum and Dad joined together in marriage: one man and one woman to the exclusion of all others. It's two Mummy and Two Daddy families. Goodness knows what happens to the kids now, not knowing who is who:

45

Mummy one and Mummy two, Daddy one and Daddy two. 45% of the children in schools in the UK come from families where there is only one parent or there are two who are not married.

Does it matter: Yes it bloody well does!

So it was off to Tottenham College of Further Education or was it called Tottenham Technical College. There were some good teachers at Holly Park but generally it was not going to be easy to take GCE. O or A levels. Boys who were good at practical subjects and were looking to do apprenticeships later seemed to be catered for better. I, who was looking to be a policeman, drifted with girls to do shorthand and typing. At least one of my girl classmates: Evelyn, I am still in contact with 55 years later! No, I realized that I needed to go a College of Further Education to try for O and A levels. So I decided to leave Holly Park Secondary School, Friern Barnet and enrol at the Tottenham College of Further Education, more commonly known as Tottenham Tech. This was situated in Tottenham High Street and was two bus rides from my home. I was to be here for 2 years.

It must have been when I was in my second year at the Tech (1959) when my sister married George Crow at Saint James church in Friern Barnet lane. I recall that the reception was at our home at 7 Priory and the food was self catered. The Wrights: Mum, Dad, me and Dad's brother Harold and his wife Winnie, were outnumbered by the Crows. George had at least three sisters and three brothers, then there was his Mum and all the in-laws. My mother's brother: Uncle Alexander Tolliday, his wife Emmy and daughter Ellen were not there. Uncle Alec had a senior position with the chocolate giant Nestle's and was based, for most of the time with them, in the Bahamas in the West Indies. As was daughter Ellen who was married to a Bahamian. Although I recall he did return to Switzerland, the home of Emmy and the place he was educated, around the late 50's and early 60's.

It was in 1960, I had left Tech, that I took my girl friend Marilynne Kent to stay with them at their home in Vevey a town on lake Geneva to the east of the city of Lausanne. It was a lovely fortnights holiday. I remember it was my first flight in a plane: a BEA (British European Airways) Comet 4C. Auntie was a German speaking Swiss who cooked really marvellous food and looked after us a real treat. Separate bedrooms, Of course! But plenty of time together on the Lake and on outings with Uncle Alec to show our affection for each other. Alec drove an Opel car and this was something new to me. The only motorcar own by any one in my family that I had ridden in before had been that of Uncle George. George Crow had a 500cc motor bike which he had given me a spin on the North Circular road but that was it.

Sadly I had never seen much of my mother's side of the family and I was never to see Alec or Emmy again.

*Uncle Alec and I in Switzerland, alas I have none with Marilynne and only one of myself sitting by lake Geneva.*

# 4. Bikes, best friends and 'Ban the Bomb!'

At 13 I was allowed by law to work as a paper boy or delivery boy after or before school. I did both. I did over a year delivering morning papers for one of the local newsagents. I would start my round at 6.30 am and finish at around 7.15. Sundays and Fridays it would take longer with a heavy load comprising bulky Sunday papers and Friday radio times. I recall going around collecting my Christmas box for 1956. To my Dad's surprise it was nearly 5 pounds. This helped to buy a new bicycle.

The bike opened up a whole new life. We would, as a group of about 5 or 6, cycle all over the place: nearby Hertfordshire, St Albans and even to Southend and Brighton on the South Coast. One summer we took off, three of us, to cycle around Cornwall. We made London to Swanage the first day, the Lizard the second and so on right around Cornwall up to North Devon and then back through Devizes to London on our seventh day. No helmets in those days. We were 14/15. Another bicycling holiday was down to the New Forrest to the Beaulie Jazz Festival, camping in tents.

When I was 14 I got a job with the greengrocer across the road from our home. I would report to him after school to do deliveries and help serve customers in the shop. I would work all day on Saturdays and school holidays, if required. I would use a trades bicycle which carried, quite often, heavy loads of cwt potatoes; good for the thighs/calves! Dick Saunders, my boss, had been captured at Dunkirk during the War and had a particularly rough time towards its end starving and marching up and down the Polish Corridor as a POW, avoiding the Russian advance. He had a caravan at Maldon in Essex, which was another destination for our Sunday cycle trips. The money earned was enough for me to think about buying a motor cycle, which I did just before I was 16. I bought a BSA Bantam, which I painted and reconditioned in the front room of 7 Priory Villas, much to the chagrin of my poor Dad.

The summer holidays got me a break with the delivery job and a job as builder's labourer. The clerk of works to a family builder, who I knew and had delivered green groceries, employed me. I spent about 6 weeks hod carrying, cement mixing, digging drains/foundations; some real heavy work. I was helping to build a large 20-room mansion in Hampstead Garden Suburb. Because of my age, although doing a man's job, I was only paid about half the wage. Unfair! But I was still pleased to earn good money have enough to enjoy a few pints and take a girlfriend out.

This was Marilynne Kent who I saw first at the Gaumont Cinema, North Finchley. I recall the film was 'Trouble in Store' starring the fall about/slap stick comedian Norman Wisdom. She was with her younger sister Evelyn (mentioned above). She looked gorgeous, a blond, who certainly tickled my fancy. No chance I thought; I had never tried for a date with any girl before. I was self-consciously spotty and certainly no fancy dresser, the rage for my vintage was floppy jumpers and cords. We had passed the teddy-boy days with the D.A. and velvet collars. I asked Evelyn, who had been a classmate in the shorthand class, to see if her sister would go out with me. Praise the Lord she would and we went out together, off and mostly on, until I went off to Africa to serve in the Northern Rhodesia Police on the 28th February, 1962. She most certainly was my first love. Apart from my lovely Diana, my wife and mother of my two children, she was the only one. There have been a few ships that past very occasionally in the night but I have had no other relationships. Call me a one woman man, call me shy of the ladies, call me old fashioned, call me what you like; for better for worse, in sickness and in health, for richer for poorer.

Marilynne's father Ted Kent was one of these men who can do anything with machines, metal, wood: an engineer. He was the chief engineer/technical manager at a factory making adhesive tapes. He employed me, during my summer holidays from Tottenham Tech as a mate to one of his welder/pipe fitters. I have never been handy with my hands but think I did alright and never broke anything. I would travel to work in Ted's car along the North Circular Road. I was able to see Marilynne more often. My earnings got me thinking about a better motorcycle. When I resumed my studies I crossed the road from the Tech and bought at a dealer there on hire purchase a Douglas 350 cc '80 plus'. What a bike: horizontal opposed cylinder with twin carbs! I would roar up the road to near 80 in third gear then drop speed when I changed to fourth(?); great 'roadholding' and nippy. With Marilynne on the back we had great fun. Unfortunately I could not keep up the payments (8 shillings a week) with no income; I had stopped the delivery jobs. One day and man came to the house to re-possess the bike. He was a nice fellow but alas Mum and Dad would not help. In fact Dad had considered me a maniac on the bike and had so told his fellow No.43 Bus passengers as I roared past one day, up Colney Hatch Lane: 'That maniac is my son!'

I was two years at the Tech and managed to get four O levels and an A level. A further A level – British Constitution – I continued to study in my own time with evening classes.

Now seems a good place here to talk of my political activities at the Tech. Like many young people at the time I was what you could term left wing. I even bought the Daily Worker occasionally and made friends with some of those devoted old communist news vendors who would stand selling their wares outside Finsbury Park Tube Station soaking wet in the freezing cold. I got involved with banning the bomb and protesting to the South Africans about apartheid.

I organized two trips: one from the Tech in 1959 and the other in 1960, to join the thousands marching from Aldermaston (the nuclear research centre) to London, Trafalgar Square. We proudly displayed our CND (Campaign for Nuclear Disarmament) badges. I would hire a coach and insist those coming paid in advance. We always got a good response and were able to fill a 40 plus seated coach. Sometimes we were oversubscribed when some of the parents stopped the kids going.

*A bunch of us Tech students on the grass by the college a number of whom, including Budgie with his tongue out, went on the 1959 march. I was 16 and am the one in the leadership position in the front looking pensive.*

The event was over the Easter Holiday, three days marching followed by a gathering at Trafalgar Square. We would stay the nights in schools along the way and would have fun along the way with Jazz bands who played in the evenings. It was a fair old march: 50 plus miles! The friends who came would be from the Tech and some of my old cycling and motorbike friends. Marilynne came. One friend from the Tech, Michael Budge (Budgie) would amuse us with his antics and dress. He always wore a raincoat that would have had difficulty keeping him dry and was probably a vehicle for small animals. He was a very intelligent young man and like most of us was here for the cause, not just for fun.

As we marched along we would sing protest songs: 'Hok Hok Protect the Holy Loch but we do not want Polaris'. As an aside I am now a 70 year old 'conservative' (no follower of that party) to the right, some say of Genghis Khan, but I still would say get rid of that hugely expensive and useless deterrent. We marched often alongside great men like Bertrand Russell and one of my idols, that insane comic genius Spike Milligan.

One of my good friends: Barnard Humphris (Barney), although a supporter of CND and a man of my own heart was missing from the marches. He had become a Metropolitan Police cadet and understandably but cowardly was absent from the marches. Barney went on to be a successful senior police officer and married Marilynne, some more of this later.

I realize I did not mention the third CND march we did — in 1961 — to Wethersfield in Essex. I forget now why the march had changed venue. It was a similar distance but was attacking London from the East instead of the west. My memory says less about the overnights in schools with jazz bands. We must have been getting older and less likely to be refused a drink in the pubs along the way. I recall Marilynne was with me and some of the experienced marcher friends from previous adventures.

I have also omitted telling of our sit-down protest outside the South African Embassy or was it the High Commission? This was against Apartheid. The only thing that sticks in my mind about this protest was the fact that we were moved on by the police with some rumour of being inconvenienced with the use of water. Today I know that in the 1960's and ever since the police in England had no crowd 'control' water cannon. Such 'weapons' so loved by the more vigorous and efficient European Police Forces. The police then would have had to rely on water from the London Fire Brigade. Its members belonged to the FBU a union whose Chairman Frank Horner was or had been a prominent member of the British Communist Party. Thus such threats would have been empty.

After leaving the Tech what was I to do? I had my heart set on being a policeman helping lost boys or girls with pop, jokes and sweets. That is beginning to sound politically incorrect. We couldn't then, as now, have men dealing with little children. Scout masters, Jimmy Saville and all that! No I would become a Scotland Yard Detective or join the Colonial Police Service. There was at the time a series on TV: African Patrol with Richard Bentley playing the part of a Kenyan Police Officer. But I still needed to get my GCE results and finish my last A level. This I was doing with evening classes.

I needed a job. I went to Truman's Brewery in Brick Lane E.1. I liked their beer and wanted a heavy labouring job: Macho and all that! I was put on beer delivery. A drayman, but, not of course, with the dray horses, those dray men proper had been with Truman's since the founding of the Company in 1666. Truman's was then the oldest brewery in the country. I was put on the lorries. A crew of three: driver, and two draymen, one with the paper work. The Lorries, heavy goods vehicles, were for the most part were Dennis Pax., 5 or 6 tonners. The drivers kept them in good condition and their green livery matched the green in the uniform/clothes worn by the crew: trousers, jacket, great winter coat with leather inside sleeves and a green peak cap with its Truman's eagle badge.

Labouring men we may have been but I look back on the nearly a year I worked there with some fondness and pride. One man to unload the 5 to 6 tons of beer from the vehicle and throw it down a ramp into a deep pub cellar, to another man who caught each full grate and then stacked each with its 24 bottles to be taken by the third man away on a barrow to be placed in the required part of the cellar. The loaded crates would come speeding down the ramp. Then there were the same empty bottle crates, which would have to be thrown out of the cellar, sometimes 8 to 10 feet up to the driver on the pavement above for him to put them onto the lorry. Your arms, wrists and backs took a pounding and you certainly burnt the calories. The late breakfast fry-up with a pint of tea would go down like a treat! Even when it was snowing you worked up a sweat. My arthritis today: hands, back, knees! With all the health and safety laws now would such deliveries be permitted? Then there were the unhealthy drinks from the publican! Also not permitted?

Each day was different: one or two returns to the brewery for fresh loads. We would do one pub in the morning, two in the afternoon. Start was always at 7.00am finish around 4 to 5pm. Different pubs each day; sometimes trips were way out to a number of different pubs, clubs, off-licences in the countryside to Hertfordshire and other home counties. Always, new routes, new pubs, new landlords. I have often joked to friends and colleagues in the Police and the Legal Profession that this was the only proper job I ever had.

My leaving the Tech and the extra cash I had from working allowed me to buy another motorcycle. This was a BSA 500 twin with a plunger rear suspension. It was more powerful than my Douglas, but not so nimble and fast on the acceleration. It was heavier and better for two. Marilynne would often ride on the back. I remember taking her down to Brighton along with a group of mates who rode motorcycles. None were as powerful as my BSA. I recall there was a two-stroke James and a Fanny Barnet (Francis Barnet) amongst them. I was stopped by the Brighton police for speeding. I unlawfully had Marilynne on the back and was still, without a full licence, should have been displaying 'L' plates. I later received a traffic summons in the post charging me with speeding and no 'L' plates. The police were kind! I paid the fine through the post. We slept the night under the Brighton pier and rode back to London the next day.

I saw Barnard around this time a fair bit when he was free from his police cadet activities. He had the use of what today would be a vintage car: a Morris or Austin 10(?). We both were beer aficionados and would travel the home countries sampling as many of the local beers as possible. It was the beginning of the real beer drinkers revolt. The big five: Watneys, Whitbread, Courage, Carlsberg/Tetley and Scottish & Newcastle, perhaps I should add a sixth: Bass/Charrington. These giants had swallowed up numerous smaller famous breweries many with their antecedents going back to the early 18th and 19th centuries. Names like Benskins, Friary Meux, Taylor Walker, Wethereds, Fremlins and Hancocks come to mind. What a lovely example of a special mild was Taylor Walkers 'Main Line' and Benskins Bitter!

My own Truman, Hanbury and Buxton was eaten up by Grand Metropolitan and I noticed during a visit to Brick lane this year (2012) it is represented now only with a wall plaque. Truebrown, Ben Truman, their Alton and Burton Bitter beers are, alas no more. The big National brewers had then largely stopped brewing real English beer and had pushed the easier to produce, store and sell larger: Cold fizz! The country owes a lot to CAMRA, the Campaign for Real Ale, for arresting the downward slide to bad beer. The big Nationals have been forced to keep traditional breweries open, even though they themselves have stop making real ale. Today there has never been a better choice: Nationals; Big Independents like Banks's (Wolverhampton) and Greene King (Bury St Edmunds) and Fuller, Smith and Turner (London W.4); Independents of different sizes ranging from those with less than twenty tied houses to those with hundreds, gems like Adnams of Southwold. Then we have the hundred plus micro and pub breweries, which have really expanded with CAMRA. Yes a pub holiday of the British Isles can offer much: Bitter Ale, Mild Ale, Strong Ale, Brown Ale, Light Ale, Sweet Stout, Dry Stout, Porter, Barley Wine, Old Ale, and Winter Ale. Plus three types of Irish Stout: Guinness, Beamish and Murphy's. We even have some of our smaller breweries offering brews in the continental tradition e.g. Wheat beers.

# 5. Colonial Directions

Mum and Dad were not too keen on me making a career as a drayman, as happy as I was. I did have a few GCE's and had always been set on being a Policeman. So off I went in the winter of 1961 for an interview at Northern Rhodesia House in the Haymarket to join the Northern Rhodesia Police (NRP). And the 27th February 1962 saw me in the back of Barnard's car with Marilynne, driven by his good self to Gatwick Airport. 'Take care of her', I said, as I walked away rather sadly to board the plane. The plane was a British United Airlines, Bristol Britannia turbo prop. You could actually see if the engines stopped, without jet engines its speed was a mere 300 knots per hour. I recall we stopped for petrol thrice: Rome(?), Entebbe, Uganda(yes) Ndola, Rhodesia(yes). I recall there were other police recruits on the plane, including one Ted Stevenson. Ted is a friend to this very day. He had been training for the priesthood until H.M took him into the Intelligence Corp. for his National Service. He went on after service in the NRP to join the Royal Hong Kong Police where he served until his retirement as a Chief Superintendent in the 1990's. I mention in the course of his service in the RHKP he lost a leg below the knee. I hasten to add that he had not lost it, in the manner of forgetting where he put it, but had lost it whilst bravely carrying out a colleague from a mine field which had been established as a defensive measure around one of the police posts on the Sino/ British border in 1967.

The journey to Lusaka, the capital of Northern Rhodesia, our destination was uneventful. It seemed to take ages but time passed with the help of beer drinking. The plane ran out! We were met at the airport by a large European Instructor and shoved, nay, pushed up the steep tailboard of 3 ton Bedford troop carrier. Then it was out along dirt roads to Police Training School at Lilayi.

My Colonial Adventure Begins.
We drove over a railway line through the gates of the training school. A huge parade ground loomed large, a flag pole flying the union flag and that of the Northern Rhodesia Police the NRP, with its crest a fish eagle with a fish in its claws, by the reviewing stand.  Behind this, the admin block housing the offices of the Commandant and his staff. The classrooms are behind and the recruit Inspectors, three storey barracks, adjacent to these.  The quarters for the officer staff and the African lines for the recruit constables and the other ranks staff are a distance away from the 'training area'. There was a guardroom, always a threat to the recruits, inspectors and constables, inside the camp near the armoury and motor pool. It was all a bit of a shock, at least for those of us who had not done National Service or served in the British Police Service. We were in the minority.

I was the youngest in the group, barely 19. You were not able to be a proper policeman, with all the powers, until you were 20. So as soon as I was taught: to stand to attention, which hand was right and which was left, how to salute, bang your foot in so it would cause arthritis in later life, call the appropriate people sir, polish boots, eat with cutlery silver and get my kit, it was off as a police cadet to my posting. I was to go north to Ndola on the Copperbelt, a provincial capital and an administrative town, railhead and location of a copper smelter. I was to go in uniform with my peak cap with its derogatory blue band, showing that I was a Cadet an inferior being to be ignored by the African policeman. To demerit me further I was to go second-class on the railway. First-class was for officers, second-class was for African NCOs, third-class was for Africans or white folk destitute and nearly starving. The train was a steam train. The driver and fireman were European. I learnt later when drinking at Ndola with some of the Rhodesian railwaymen that they could only use Europeans as firemen because... wait for it: The Africans did not have the strength or stamina!

The journey was about 200 miles. It took over 8 hours overnight and was slow because in front of the train was sometimes a mechanised trolley with a police inspector and constable clearing the track: ensuring there was no explosives or line derailment. Although Northern Rhodesia had none of the problems of Kenya in the late 50s and early 60s of the Mau Mau: the most ghastly of rebellions with its bestial oaths and its cult of torture and murder, it did have some trouble with one of the African nationalist organisations the United National Independence Party (UNIP) lead by Kenneth Kaunda. He was to be the country's first president when it became Zambia and was in office from 1964 to 1991. Later he was challenged by his opponents, after his one party rule was abolished in 1991, that he was not a citizen of Zambia but of neighbouring Malawi! There had been some attempts at derailing trains.

On the train I was able to talk about the NRP in conversation with an African police Head Constable (a rank above sergeant).

61

I was met at Ndola Railway Station and taken to the Inspectors quarters next to the Ndola Main Station where I was to live and work until I returned to training school about four months before my 20th birthday in 1963.

*Ndola Main Police Station, the Inspector's quarters are behind it to the left of the photograph.*

I have no record but I guess now I was about 11 months at Ndola, leaving to go back to training school between just after Christmas 1962 and the end of January 1963. My first impressions were of my fellow policemen with whom I shared the Officer's (Inspector's) Mess. A real cross-section: The PMC (for the ignorant the president of the mess and usually the senior living in member of the mess), Mike Wright was a very large Rhodesian, his father had been in the NRP, a real gentleman who would suffer occasionally from malaria; when his body gave off so much heat that his bedroom was like a furnace (I met Mike recently at a reunion lunch near Cape Town in April, 2011, as large as ever). Then there was Paddy Dixon one of a number of Celts. He was a real, popular character, full of the old blarney and like most of the mess members, kind to this young ex drayman from London. Then Ken, a Scotsman, an ex-miner and still a member of the mine worker's union. Dan, a hard, rather glum English speaking South African. Ted who I have mentioned already, although then he had the benefit of both legs and had not acquired the nickname he did in the RHKP: Ted the Leg. Then there was a religious Protestant who had seen the faith and become a Catholic. Bert Roeder, an Afrikaans speaking South African, a man I really liked, who took me on rural patrol; more of this later. There were other characters, English from public and grammar schools. For those of you who don't know, when I say public it means a private fee paying school for the sons of gentle folk. My school had been where the public went: a state secondary modern school! And you couldn't get more public than that! There were no African officers in the mess, at least not in 1962. Of the English lads I recall Roy Tailor another member of the NRP, who went off to Hong Kong. Dave Crowley, a London Irishman who was a Court Prosecutor. Hugh Careless, despite the name he was not in the traffic branch. Gavin Williams 6ft 4inches with his crash traffic helmet and Roger Madge. It is 50 years on so forgive me if other names have gone or may be inaccurately recorded. There were 20 or so living in mess members. Also other officers, who would live outside and worked at other stations in the Division or at its headquarters, would use the mess for recreation. This was centred on the bar, tended by a nice, shy, young, polite, well-spoken African: Stephen.   I recall his surprise and sometimes apprehension when at mess nights things got out of hand and mess games were played. Goodness what children we were! British bulldog or Bok Bok as it was called there. Two teams: one providing a line of bent backs anchored by a standing man at a wall and the other, a similar number of men running and jumping on one by one on the line of backs until it collapsed.  It was a game later we brought to Hong Kong to play at the police training school; I don't think it pleased all there.

Not every night in the mess was a mess night in that mess was caused.  Every night the bar was used, weekends more often; senior officers, who as Divisional officers would be members, sometimes came in to share a chat and a drink. There were some non-police who were honorary members. I remember Don Mac....: a Scottish surgeon: Mac the Knife. A great man, the good he did was really something. His devotion to his African and European patients, the operations he performed were an example of the dedicated colonial surgeon at his best. Alas no more!  But like all such men he needed 'bottle' that came from the bottle. Thus he was a man who enjoyed his dram, while he shared his wealth of stories.

So what was a mess night?   It was a formal dinner held whenever there was a need for one. We would all dress up in mess kit, bow ties, white starched jackets, cummerbunds, polished shoes, hair combed, medals, whatever. The dress was smart but not expensive, uniform blue trousers were OK. Those of that persuasion were permitted to wear skirts (ok! kilts) although I think if worn outside the mess the wearer may have risked arrest from one of the more inexperienced African constables. There was always a guest of honour who would sit at the top table; a senior police officer, usually with lots of things on the peak of his cap, with gorget lapel patches even.

I recall one really special dinner. The guest of honour was Sir Ivor Stourton (any friends, relatives, colonial historians please forgive the wrong spelling). He was the Inspector General of Colonial Police and must have been one of the last. He was a great old gent, full of fun and a wealth of interesting and funny stories. We were all concerned that Northern Rhodesia, like most of Africa, would soon be independent and not want the filthy British and their policemen to remain. We thus were interested if there was anything left for us colonial policemen; Hong Kong came to mind. For reasons I am still not sure of, Sir Ivor did not encourage us to go there.

There was mess life outside the mess in the form of outings. Once, twice or thrice  foolishness raised its head and we went off to steal mess trophies from police messes in other divisions; Luanshya, 120 miles away comes to mind. These could be useless things picked up in the course of police duty or even a mess pet. Ndola had 'Fagan' a huge tortoise with the NRP badge painted on his shell. He had been named Fagan by Paddy Dixon and lived in our garden eating all the flowers. We stole theirs and the swines, weeks/months later, came in the dead of night and stole Fagan, only to be reclaimed during another operation.

*Fagan with me and my friend Jock MacRoberts in behind the mess.*

I have already said I was not really a star at football, although I did play for Holly Park Secondary during my last year. I think I was in the team because of my size and at right back I was able to deter the smaller forwards from approaching the goal. I could run fast, swim well and had lifted weights at Rube Martins Gym at Bruce Grove, Tottenham when at the Tech. I had also then had two months discovering that I was not much good at the noble art of boxing. The little 'uns always seemed to knock the hell out of me. At Ndola I went rugby training with Roger Madge. I had never played before but was told I had a good turn of speed, was able to swerve and manoeuvre and handle a ball. I didn't take it up; instead I got involved in playing for a short season of Gaelic or Irish football. A round ball with long kicks and throws, forward if you like, no running with the ball but bouncing it along so many paces. I only played a few games and was not asked to become a professional. Most of the team were not police, although it was some of the older policemen who had got me involved. I mention now how well some of these looked after me. I remember Ormond Power and his wife who had me at their home for Christmas. Ormond was a really tough nut. He had been in the Royal Ulster Rifles and had served in Korea.

No I was not very sporting. I spent most of my off-duty time in the mess. There was a TV although such modern media was new to Northern Rhodesia; I recall it was cable. Although often I was boozing, either in the mess bar or in one of the bars in town, e.g. The Elephant and Castle, where Londoner Jack Catchpole – the publican and man sometimes behind the bar – would tell us his stories. Jack was also the public hangman for the Federation of Rhodesia and Nyasaland. A nice man but he certainly could eye you up. Then there were: the Edinburgh Hotel and nearby a 'chinese' restaurant, I don't think they were Chinese; the road house run by a Greek; the Bioscopes (local name for the cinema); a weight lifting gym; a swimming pool. Then there were visits to another divisional station: Kensenje, policing mainly a European township. Here was another police mess, smaller than Ndola but with a bar and it's own skiffle group. Because of my ear for music I was chosen to play the tea chest bass: broom handle, a piece of cord and a tea chest. Was I good!

From life in the mess I learnt much and matured. I realised to be careful what I said and that not everyone had my Londoner's sense of humour. I was attacked once in the mess for a remark I made about a member's injured leg. He was a South African, with obviously no sense of humour and a hard nut. He joined the Hong Kong police later in 1965 and stayed retiring in the rank of Senior Superintendent, by then of course all was forgotten. I was thrown on the ground and knocked senseless before Mike the big PMC pulled the assailant off me. With rough games like Bok Bok and some pretty tough, hard men, you needed to be robust/smart.

A cadet's job in the Force was not really defined. He was to listen and learn and generally help without exercising any police powers: arrest and charging. He was often in a difficult position with the African constables. He would be given particular tasks to do with them and then be forced to use his 'personality' if they were slow in obeying him. He could not give them direct orders.

I was assigned to most of the branches and duties in the Division. It must have been in the summer months of 1962 when I was attached to the criminal investigation department under Superintendent Peter Setterfield. There had been a series of murders; African politics were involved. Mr Setterfield was a meticulous detective and leader of a major investigation. I recall him on his hands and knees looking for clues. There were no specialist scene-of-crime officers then and limited forensic evidence collection. A case much depended on finding witnesses and protecting them from harm. There could be powerful and sinister people involved. Thus a secure accommodation was set up for the witnesses in one of the police camps. My task for Mr Setterfield was as camp manager; I was to ensure the witnesses living in the secure camp were properly fed and had what they wanted: beer, cigarettes and washing material. I would pass any complaints or requests to Mr Setterfield. It was not on the terrible Mau Mau scale, but clearly witnesses were in fear for their lives. Keneth Kaunda had said in 1961 that if majority rule was not granted there would be disorder which by contrast would make Mau Mau look like a children's picnic. That year had seen the worst political violence and disorder on the Copperbelt in its history. There were murders, arson and intimidation against Africans who refused to buy party cards or contribute to the Nationalist party. Many were just ordinary workers who did not want to get involved. Others were members of the older ANC: the African National Congress, led by a colourful character, Harry Nkumbula, whose support was stronger in the south of NR. His supporters would retaliate and were not beyond initiating violence themselves. In 1962 when I arrived in Ndola things were not so dramatic, at least in regard to public order. But political intimidation and violence was still at a serious and high level.

A number of men were committed for trial for murders but I had left Ndola by then. Mr. Setterfield would have shone as a top Criminal Investigator anywhere. I can say that after nearly 20 years as a policeman.

I also for a short spell went out with Gavin in one of the traffic patrol cars. These were lovely vehicles: Rover 100's, black four door sedans, capable of going down the main roads to Kitwe, Mufulira and Broken Hill at 90 to 100MPH. There was the police ambulance that carried riot equipment. It was not unusual for there to be a real disturbance after a traffic accident. The injured had to be taken away and an angry mob kept back. It was not after all the North Circular Road, London. N.11... You must recall the British had been in NR for perhaps only two generations: 70 years!

What I really enjoyed was going out with Bert Roeder, the Officer In Charge of Rural Patrols. We would go out early in the morning with an African policeman, if he was a sergeant I would sit in the back of the Landrover. We would visit the outlying European farms and settlements, including one owned by Len Catchpole the brother of Jack. Len was a prominent member of NR society and rumour was he had some connection with Moise Tsombe the secessionist leader of Katanga up across the border in the Congo. We would also visit African villages and some times would camp out for the night. One of our duties was to inspect firearms and I was always impressed with the way Bert handled the shotgun licence checks. Those held by the African leaders or chiefs. He would salute them, then with much dignity ask to inspect the weapon and its secure store. This would be a strong wooden or metal container often chained with a padlock. An inspection record would be signed.

The British in Africa were as paranoid about civilians with guns as they were in the UK. These chiefs, I like to think, regarded their shotguns as a badge of office helping them to maintain authority over their people. So sad how later Africa, including once British administered territories, became awash with guns: AK 47 Kalashnikov rifles. In Uganda the Lords Army's satanized child soldiers with such weapons, are today, after 20 odd years, still terrorising and killing their own communities. I ponder often: with all the lunacy involving gun ownership in the USA, what mayhem, what anarchy can come from weak and corrupt governments.

I recall on one two-day patrol we shot a duiker (a small deer). We ate some and gave the rest to a village.

*Me in my cadet's uniform on rural patrol carrying a 'Greener' shotgun.*

I have mentioned 1961 and have said how I was attached to Ndola CID in the summer months of 1962. Almost exactly a year before, in September, there was to be an important meeting at Ndola between the United Nations Secretary General Dag Hammarskjöld and Moise Tsombe. Katanga was a mineral rich province of the old Belgian Congo whose border was only a few miles away from Ndola. The meeting was on neutral ground with a senior member of the British Government to serve as an intermediary. Hammarskjöld flew from the Congo's capital in a UN chartered DC-6, on board was a Swedish crew and a number of UN officials and security men.

The plane crashed on the 17th September just after midnight. The location was just 9 miles outside Ndola in a wood near a charcoal burners' compound which was just off the road to Mufulira (my future posting as an Assistant Inspector). All aboard were killed, one survivor dying in hospital five days later. The crash and the investigation by Ndola CID was still on everyone's mind. As can be imagined all manner of conspiracy theories were floating around: sabotage to the plane, its engines; shot down from the ground with gunfire or missiles; bombs on the plane; shot down by another aircraft, etc. Nefariously done by whatever means and whatever national agents working for people in high places in: Rhodesia, the Congo and places further afield. I had visited with Bert Roeder the charcoal compound where the plane had gone down and had talked to police officers involved in finding the aircraft and being part of the investigation team. The UN's enquiry agreed with the Commission of Enquiry set up by the Governor General of Rhodesia which was that pilot error was the most likely cause but kept open the possibility of; a time-bomb on the plane, an attack by hostile aircraft and incomplete landing instructions, which the Rhodesian Commission had rejected.

It must have been January or February when I said goodbye to Ndola. I recall I travelled down to Lusaka then on to Lilayi by car driven by one of my mess-mates who was going on local leave. I was not the apprehensive youth I had been a year or so before when I had been driven over the level crossing into the training school. I had heard 'Chiefy' (The Chief Inspector)

Oliver, the man who WAS the Northern Rhodesia Police Training School. I knew of the hard time that was coming.

# 6. The Recruit Inspector's Course

Chief Inspector David Oliver (Chiefy Oliver) was **the** Northern Rhodesia Police Training School. He was the epitome of the Regimental Sergeant Major. Perhaps not the very model of a modern Sergeant Major. No! His strict discipline and manner of enforcing it would be looked at today with disapproval, to put it mildly. He would probably be regarded as cruel and deserving of punishment, even criminal sanctions! But he was marvellous at his job: to turn rural Africans, some who didn't know their right from their left and whose education was only up to primary six school level into smart confident policemen. He also had to teach and instil self-discipline, especially to the recruit Inspectors like us. We would leave PTS after 16 weeks, expected to be able to command platoons, shifts, units, even small police stations: commands of 40 men, within our first tour of duty. Which in normal times was three years. He was feared, respected, admired; revered even, by many recruits, African and European. His photograph could be found hanging in the quarters of the African Sergeant and Head Constable members of training staff. I add that later I would learn that his picture could also be found in the quarters in the African Lines serving Police Stations and units outside. We, old men now, who were fortunate to be at PTS when the man was there and not on leave, still talk about him at reunions and the like. The way he changed us from a bolshie rabble (perhaps that is only me speaking, Oh well!) into smart, well turned out, self-disciplined  young colonial police officers. A legend in his own lifetime. A man impossible to imagine that he started life as any thing less than 45 years of age. Who dressed in any but an immaculate uniform, whose Sam Browne belt and boots shone like the morning sun. In my later life I learned from an old magistrate in Hong Kong that he had been knocked into shape by the same David Oliver. This time as First British Sergeant at the Palestine Police Training School in Jenin, Palestine. He must have been then in his early 20's, but still apparently with his moustache looking twice his age. And what a place to be a policeman then: 1947/48!

Our quarters were on the first and second floor of the Inspectors mess. This can be better described as a barracks. We were two to a room occupying two floors. At the end of each corridor were the showers and lavatories. Every inch of these had to be kept immaculate. Woe betide the offender who left a 'jobby' floating in the toilet bowl or an offensive stain anywhere. We would slide along the floors on squares of blankets polishing the floor in our rooms and the common areas. Inside our rooms the bedding had to be laid out hospital fashion and our rifles and revolvers handcuffed to the steel frames of our beds. No photos of girlfriends or mum and dad. A bad inspection meant confinement to camp for the whole squad. In fact we were not allowed out of camp for the first 6 weeks. Inspector Storey, our drill, weapons and squad instructor, was not above putting his boot across your highly bulled toecap. This to enrage the composure of Chiefy Oliver or the Commandant and so bring down punishment on you. If he wanted to be really nasty he would find things in the Toilets/Washrooms deserving of banishment of privileges and confinement to barracks for the whole squad. Even the church parade argument didn't work: 'But Sir I never miss church'. So much of our time at PTS was spent inside the camp. We can't have been allowed out in those 16 weeks for more than about 6 times. When we would go to Lusaka have a few jars and a decent meal. What to do at PTS when we were not 'on duty'? There was a bar, with strict opening times. Then there was reading and preparing for exams and tests. We were expected to learn by heart and word perfect 30 to 40 definitions: what is Robbery, Theft, Burglary, Housebreaking, Child stealing, Murder, Manslaughter, and Witchcraft etc. We could play Karamoja, a cross between rugby, football and wrestling which we played against other recruit squads, African constables, inspectors and the staff.

Our lives off duty were then the mess. On duty, it seems now that most of our time, was on the square: Morning Parade, Commandants Weekly Parade, foot drill, arms drill, anti-riot training, weapon training and drilling, by way of teaching the African recruit squads. We had a classroom which we shared with no one. It was here we had our lectures and tests and exams on law, police procedure, powers of arrest, leadership, anti-riot tactics, Chinyanja language (The language of Nyasaland, don't ask me why were not taught one of the main N. Rhodesian tongues) general duties and first aid. Then there were the ranges, a march away, but within the camp. Where we fired off and qualified on the Bren light machine gun, the sterling sub -machine gun, our rifles and revolvers, the greener shotgun and anti-riot weapons. We had only two instructors: Eric Storey for the Square and all things painful and Brian Suttill our law, criminal procedure, evidence and general duties instructor. We had an African to teach us first aid and a European to teach us Chinyanja!?

There were periodical exams throughout the course with important finals which you had to pass or be back-squadded. A thing which was real! If I could mention recruit Rumble. It was said this sallow, skinny youth, with an 11 inch neck had been at the school for over a year without passing out. And despite cries to home to his dear old Mum Chiefy would not let him pass out until he was qualified to do so. You could not try it on; he was wise to that: suffer or pass out properly.

If you could imagine 300 men on Saturday morning parade for the Commandants Inspection. All with their rifles clean and at slope arms. The sun is baking down, they are in their best full dress uniforms: the Inspectors in their pith helmets and the other ranks in their fezzes. The parade is lined up with a row of 5 squads in three rank formation to the rear and another 5 squads similarly lined up to the front. The railway line is behind the parade, to its front is Chiefy, looking resplendent in starched shorts that could stand up without him in them and leather work that is gleaming in the sun. Behind him is the Reviewing Stand awaiting the Inspecting Officer. Each of the squads has its drill instructor standing in front. There are two recruit inspector squads each with perhaps two or three locally recruited Africans. There are three such fellows in my squad; good lads doing their best to fit in. Our drill pig: ex-Coldstream Guardsman, Eric Storey stands in front of us with his drill cane under his arm. Suddenly a Rhodesian Railway engine sounds its whistle, drowning out the commands. Chiefy roars like a lion: 'Engine cease your Noise'! As if by magic there is immediate silence. A murmur comes from the lines of African recruits: 'Wah! Bwana Oliver is so powerful he can command the engine' He further demonstrates his power and screams: 'Sergeant Tempo' addressing the second squad in the rear: 'that man number 4, centre rank is moving'. Then by magic vision again he finds the only man on parade whose puttee had come lose.

78

He would go around the parade rank by rank scrutinizing the turnout of one and all. There were occasions where a really 'idle' man on parade would be sacked on the spot. His uniform would be removed down to his underwear and he would then be marched out of the school down the road into the distance. He was as severe to those in the Inspector squads and European men who were idle on parade could find themselves reporting to an African drill sergeant who would be given the order: 'Sergeant see what you can do with this idle man' This was much to the delight of the recruit constables who enjoyed showing the idle European what they could do on the square. He was however fair. The African marched out of camp would be brought back by Land-rover cowed but eager to resume his life with his mates.

Although a fierce disciplinarian who believed in field punishment, the lash was no longer used, running around the square, rifles over the head and push-ups were regarded as good for you and character building. But there were limits. Inspector Storey got a 'bollocking' one day from Chiefy for having us mark time for 45 minutes, a complete lesson, in the burning sun with temperatures in their top 30's. Some us were not far off flaking out. Eric sat on a chair the whole 45 minutes, before he called a 'Squad halt'. I recall he sat there drinking tea.

My roommate was Bruce Hudson, who was also a fellow cadet. I recall he had huge rugby playing thighs. He was more familiar with the military type training than I, having been a keen member of his school's army cadet force. His father had been a professional musician with the Grenadier Guards. Another cadet was Jock McRoberts a friend for many years. Jock was always his own worst enemy. He did not know the word humble or humility. He had grey hair at PTS despite being only 19. He certainly looked 40 and was taken by the recruits for, at least, a superintendent. This, at first he wallowed in, and took his bullshitting to extremes. He became unpopular with only myself befriending him. It was decided he was to be tried by his squad mates and fellow mess members. If found guilty his balls were to be polished with black boot polish and he was then to be hoisted up the flagpole near the reviewing stand. I was appointed his defence counsel and decided that with the case so strong against him that I had no alternative but to throw him at the mercy of the court. This I did. There was little to say in mitigation (I now recall similar places of justice in China in Mao's time). Dear Jock is alas no more. He passed away a few years ago.

I don't recall any passing out dinner but presume there must have been one. A nice chap from the Rotherham Borough Police Force won the baton of honour. I just passed out with a first aid certificate and went off with Bruce Hudson again north to the Copperbelt. But this time to the mining town of Mufulira. A place where the population was evenly split: half UNIP (United National Independence party, lead by Kenneth Kaunda) and half ANC (African National Congress, lead by a jovial beer drinker Harry Ngkumbula). I would say that it depended much on job, tribe and location whether the population was or was not overtly political. I like to think a significant part of the population were happy to avoid both groups and enjoy just their chibuku beer (an African brew made from maize and sold in half gallon pots). Jock went off to another Copperbelt town: Kitwe.

*Me and Jock MacRoberts in what looks like our pass out do.*
*The haircuts indicate the training school and the suites and glasses a 'formal' do.*

Before I leave life Lilayi and Chiefy Oliver, I mention our squad's chance to see the future leader of Zambia and to serve him. Towards the end of our 16 week training course we were all assembled and told by our instructor on all things not painful: Inspector Brian Suttill that we were required to go to Government House at Lusaka and serve the Governor as waiters and barmen at a reception for the leader of the United Independence Party and President in waiting, Dr. Kenneth Kaunda. The designation Dr. was not, as was delivered to his followers, one based on his medical learning, but was an Honorary Doctorate bestowed by some centre of learning outside of Africa.

We were taken to Government House in a Police bus and were briefed there by the Governor's ADC, who was a NRP Inspector. He told us our duties and how we were to be on our best behaviour. We were to be especially polite to the African politicians and to meet their needs, and to refer any requests to him. We were not to be seen to drink or eat anything at the Reception. Although after everyone had gone and we were packing up he said it was alright to take a drink. And this is what we did. Our bar at Lilayi was healthily restocked with a number of opened but unused bottles of spirits, including whisky, a tot of which was always available for Chiefy Oliver when he came into our Mess. It was a sort of cocktail party without the cocktails. His Excellency the Governor had laid on plenty of booze, for which us recruit police officers had charge. But Dr. Kaunda was a non-drinker as were some of his party. We were dressed in our white mess bum freezer jackets, black bow ties and our uniform blue long trousers and would go around, some of us, with fruit juice, soft drinks, beer and wine on trays. Others in our squad would look after the bar and serve as waiters from there the guests, making special drinks as requested. I recall there were few calls for tots from the gin or the whisky bottles.

*It helps to set the scene of life in the NRP if I display some photographs of the uniforms we were required to parade in, as you can imagine we were expected to be immaculate. The uniforms are: In full dress, winter working dress and summer working dress with riot kit. The three uniforms were just three of the six that we were issued. We mostly wore shorts but long Khaki trousers were issued for Court dress. I also display a photograph showing some of the school buildings used as staff quarters and classrooms.*


*Previous page; clockwise from top left, full dress, winter blues working dress, anti-riot dress and kit.*
*This page; Jock and I outside.*

# 7. A Half-Pound of Steak

Mufulira, a Copperbelt town with a huge copper mine run and owned in those days: 1963 by Anglo American Mines. There were two police stations: Mufulira Central and Main Location. The former also shared its location with District Headquarters and its associated Traffic and CID units. I recall the boss of the District Police was Superintendent Bill Townley (Uncle Bill), who was later to help me with a complaint made against me by one of the UNIP youth brigade gang leaders. I was posted to the Central Station, my boss was a lovey man: Superintendent John Eade who had a wealth of Police service in the Metropolitan Police, the Bermuda Police and the Palestine Police before joining the NRP.

I was assigned to a shift comprised of one other European Inspector and 50 other ranks who performed three 8 hour shift duties, using the 24 hour clock: a week of A shift 07.40 to 16.00, then a week of C shift 23.40 to 08. 00 and finally a week of B shift 15.40 to 00.01.There would be one leave day a week. Which would in effect run Sunday off first week, Monday off second week and through to Saturday off on the seventh week. The following week the leave day would be a Sunday, thus a long weekend came every 7 weeks. We were working then, a 56 hour week. I can see eyebrows rising. If such was the policeman's lot today, with a 40 hour week and the like! No overtime then!

The shift would start 20 minutes early with an inspection of appointments by its senior officer, checking all were present and properly dressed: shorts starched, leatherwork polished and short batons in their place. The NRP, although in many respects run like the old RIC (the Royal Irish Constabulary), was not routinely armed. Officers and other ranks, like the UK police, patrolled their beats armed only with a short baton which was kept concealed in a pocket in their uniforms. The shift would be briefed as to wanted persons, vehicles, recently reported crime, crime trends and whatever John Eade and the shift commander thought was necessary. Men that had come on duty too drunk to stand were sent home to be dealt with later. Those who refused to leave the parade and go home were 'offered' temporary accommodation in the station cells. I recall one of the new African Inspectors in such a state that he had to be physically helped home and when he violently refused had to be manhandled into the cells. Drunkenness was not uncommon with members of the NRP and the Inspector concerned got little more when he sobered up than a fierce bollocking from the Station Commander, John Eade.

The beat area covered European style housing, a high street shopping centre, and African housing locations, some within the urban area and some outside in villages. The other station, Main Location, covered the huge underground mine and its Processing Plant, plus the quarters and support centres for the African miners, single and married men. Both police stations had in their areas: beer halls, large open and covered places enclosed with a wall with an entrance and exit. These beer halls provided predominantly African beer.

This was nothing like beer you would get in your local. It was made from maize and looked and had the texture of thin porridge; certainly not for the uninitiated western palate. It would be served in quart or gallon size cups and was probably 2 to 3% alcohol. African beer was a tradition and in the native areas far away from the new townships it was largely made by the woman folk. It was a meal in itself and very much part of an Africans' diet. The Government with its licensing laws ensured, at least in the townships, that there was some control over its production and supply. The dangers of 'moon-shining' and local home brewing were controlled in that only African beer made by approved commercial brewers could be sold. Chibuku was the product sold and drunk by the gallon in most of the territories beer halls. It would be delivered in tankers and must have helped significantly the fiscal running of the various townships. As can be imagined pay nights at the mine was a busy time for the police.

Mufulira Central also had its African bars selling more familiar drinks: Lion, Castle larger and Sable Stout being the most common. These bars were often owned by Africans. They also provided companionship for the miners with the likes of Susan Matwetwe or Helen Banda; ladies more at home on B or early C shift duty, and always nicely turned out. The nicer ones seem to be Ndebele girls from Southern Rhodesia.

As mentioned already Mufulira was at the sharp end in that UNIP and ANC were roughly evenly matched in supporters, both real and those who could not sit on the fence. It would be an unusual week if there was not some sort of 'political' violence. Weekend Chibuku would aggravate the situation. Individuals or small groups would be stopped by gangs, usually from the UNIP youth brigade, and asked to produce their party cards. Failure to comply would result in an assault. The seriousness of the assault would depend very much on the victim's ability to purchase a card. And perhaps more on the state of intoxication of the assailants. Serious assaults with the use of knives, machetes and the like were common. A particular area in an African township known to be a stronghold of one party may be attacked, houses surrounded and some set on fire.

An incident I will always remember was one in which I and about four constables on foot patrol got involved in chasing a mob in one of our townships after a house had been set on fire. There had been trouble there before and always the gang would vanish soon after the crime. This time we saw where they went. We surrounded the house and I banged on the door shouting: 'Police'. A man came to the door, who I later learned was a UNIP official, he protested about being disturbed, telling us to go away. After a tense standoff the gang emerged from the house armed and determined to resist arrest and obstruct our enquiries. They brandished their weapons and there was a violent disturbance.

Later the UNIP official made complaint against me for using my baton to strike him and denied he was sheltering any of the Youth Brigade. His complaint was investigated according to police regulations at the time by a very senior officer: Superintendent Townley. There was an investigation but fortunately for me there were independent civilian witnesses who were able to say what had actually happened. And the UNIP official's involvement with the Youth Brigade and its township thuggery further revealed.

Most of our police work was centred on violence in the townships, not all with a political overtone. There were groups

88

involved in robbing the miners of their pay; drunkenness, European and African (I arrested and charged my first drunken driver, a European from the mine), burglary and theft in the European housing estates and of course the occasional shop theft. I was very much an operational policeman, out on foot or in the Land-rover/Jeep (we had both) on patrol along the road 10 miles to the Congo border, where there was at Mokambo another police unit.

I liked the African men under my command. They were loyal and I remember one incident when I was struck down in a disturbance in one of the townships. I was on the ground being kicked and hit to near unconsciousness with sticks. I was told later it were two of my men who drove the assailants away from me and got me to secure ground.

The use of tear gas was routine in Mufulira, especially pay night when there was often serious disorder in the beer halls. Also there were the frequent political gatherings/meetings. Usually one or more of the politicians would get authority to hold such a meeting. On a piece of large open ground a dais would be set up by the organizers from where the speakers would harangue the crowd assembled before it. They would use, to the loudest and greatest effect, a public address system which they had brought with them. They would have their own transport. Some good folk from Sweden had purchased and provided a van for the UNIP youth brigade which they found useful during their operations.

At each of these 'licensed' meetings there would be in attendance seated, just off the Dais, a police inspector. His duty was to ensure that the licence conditions for the meeting were followed. A key condition would be that nothing would be said to encourage violence and disorder. This included breaking the law: Riot, Unlawful Assembly, Affray and a key one at the time, Criminal Sedition. Which in a nut shell is uttering words which bring hatred or contempt towards the person of the Queen, her government, or to promote feelings of ill will or hostility between different classes or groups of her subjects. A good example of such crime today is best found in the sermons of the learned clerics in the Finsbury Park Mosque and their successors.

I recall a day when it was my duty to be on the dais. Mr? (his name now escapes me) would be directing how his party would drive the filthy British from this land.: "The Europeans will be banished and their homes given to Africans". Depending on the volume of the cheers and the state of agitation of the crowd in response to each of these perfectly reasonable promises I would have to decide whether and how to intervene. I therefore stood up. There was cry from hundreds/thousands WOOOOOOOOOOOO!!

I said: 'Please Mr.. .Don't say those things, temper your exuberance'. Whereupon it was time for off. My constable, who was working the car battery driven recording machine, and I packed up and returned to our vehicle parked behind the Dais. He had a shot gun and I had my Webley revolver that day, but discretion was the better part of valour. Our vehicle was rocked up and down as we left. The mob seemed satisfied in putting some wind up us. The rocking of one's vehicle at the height of a disturbance was not such an unusual occurrence. I remember one incident when I was driving but had Constable Siyowe on the roof with a riot gun (a long barrel gun that fires tear gas shells). He had been firing at the feet of a mob with his own feet anchored to the front of the vehicle by another constable holding his lower legs through the front window, Tear gas was very much a useful weapon of the least force for dealing with riotous mobs, so much so that I always managed to keep a couple of spare grenades in a safe locker in my quarters. It was the use of these one late evening that brings me on to another topic and life in Mufulira Inspectors Mess.

Mess life at Mufulira was similar to mess life at Ndola. It was quarters for about 8 or so single men housed in a single ground floor block with some accommodation shared by two other single men in a married quarter in the camp. There was a bar used by mess residents and other officers from the District, and a dining room. The former was run by an African bar man, a 'rollypolly' man in his 30's with a great sense of humor, OK. he had to have! The later, the provision of food and cleanliness of the common areas, was the responsibility of a house keeper a Mrs. Rutter who would report to the PMC.. She had come to NR during the war as a refugee from Eastern Europe and had married an Englishman working there. A lovely motherly figure who ensured we had the best of fare.

Our off duty life was again similar to life at Ndola, although Mufulira had a smaller population both African and European. Life centred at the mess and its bar. Although there was no Fagan eating the plants in the garden. There were places to drink outside the mess. I recall the Mine club; the Memorable Order of Tin Hats (MOTHs) club, Rhodesia and South Africa's equivalent to British Legion or Australia's RSL clubs; then there were a couple of drinking places in hotels in the town. There was a cinema at the Mine. And Kitwe, a large mining town with much more going on, was up the road about 70 miles away.

Three of us: me, Dick Younge (Dick would go on to serve in the HKP and retire as a senior Superintendent) and Spud Murphy were all keen on modern jazz. I had bought a Decca Black box player and had built up a substantial collection of records during my year or so in the country. We would have gin and jazz sessions, sometimes combining these with formal or fancy dress mess nights. I recall a Poet or Peasant party once.

I had bought a Ford Zephyr for 50 pounds which was thirsty but able to move at incredible speed and helped take me and mates to Kitwe and Ndola for work and adventure.

Our African policemen were often under pressure from the political violence. Which sometimes raised its really ugly head and lone officers were murdered by the gangs. I and another English man who had got to like the porridge like Chibuku beer would, in order to help with morale, go across to the African lines, and share a few gallons in the African Sergeants mess. It was a sour tasting brew but certainly grew on you. Well I was a Brewers' Drayman!

To get back to my tear gas grenades! I came home to the mess one Saturday night after finishing B shift. I was surprised the single block quarters were in darkness and there were no lights coming from the bar or lounge. I went in through the doors to the mess block only to be overcome by tear smoke. Inside sitting at the bar were three or four mess members all with drinks in front of them wearing their gas masks? Goodness! Where did the gas come from? I rushed to my room and saw that my two grenades had been taken from the 'secure' cabinet above my wardrobe. I was furious and ran out to see Bruce

Hudson grinning. I asked him: 'what have you done?' The reply was a smile and a F...Off. 'You need a lesson' says I followed by me hurling him to the ground and giving him a good belting. Not, usually a thug, I said: 'that's enough we will speak again tomorrow'. 'No we won't' says he and as if with almighty power erupts up and at the same time wallops me with his right fist in my right eye. Wow! What a whack. OK says I, 'I've had enough now.' I slink away and he goes off growling I can expect worse to come. In the morning the eye is a champion black one and I am greeted by Bruce with a half-pound of steak from Mrs. Rutter's fridge. It's a man's life in the NRP!

What of the purloining of the grenades? It seems we might both be in the shit, but no, not both, only he, had committed an offence. Not me because the grenades were taken for use against a potential enemy. We had to be able to turn out ready for action on the bugle call alarm. But him! That is a different story. As it turned out nothing happened to either of us. Either it didn't get back to our superiors. There were no squealers and there was nothing for which was unaccounted; or, they didn't want to know. We were in troubled times at a troubled place on the Copperbelt.

As an aside I mention here that 45 years later in Hong Kong I defended in the District Court an off duty Police Sergeant for having three .38 rounds of ammunition that was not authorized. He risked up to 18 months imprisonment. I managed to get him acquitted on the grounds that the rounds had been slipped into his bag by one of his men. This was not London and the Met where the mere thought of using tear gas and harming rioters would bring dismissal of the Commissioner and if used compensation and apologies to one and all.

93

My 15 or so months at Mufulira were spent for the most part on normal general uniform duties. I had taken statements, visited crime scenes, been involved in riots, fired tear gas on a number of occasions and been duffed up a few times. I had one out of District duty. This was when I was required to escort a "political" prisoner or witness from the Copperbelt to Luapula Division for delivery to a Special Branch Officer at Fort Rosebury. I was to have a driver and one escort constable. I would wear my revolver. I never got to know who my prisoner was or why I was taking him up to Fort Rosebury. I was to guard him and ensure he came to no harm. I recall I took him the long way around down to Kapipri Mposhi the up again into Luapula Province. I recall we stayed one night on the trip there, (or was it coming back?), at a White Fathers mission. They had been there long before Rhodesia was British territory. There were three fathers, Irish, Canadian and I believe French or Belgium. I will always recall how impressed I was with the lovely church, school, and turnout of the children and their beautiful voices singing in the church. The harmonies: the deep basses of the staff, the trebles of the young boys singing hymns in the rhythmic and melodic African way. You hear negative things today about such missions. But from what I saw and heard, these fathers had devoted their lives to their charges. They were good, holy men healing, educating and doing God's work.

The other thing about the mission was the WC. A thunder box with a difference. It was a comfortable seat over a deep drop leading to a flowing stream below. You could estimate the depth by counting the seconds from bombs away until to splash impact!!

It was back to Mufulira after about 5 days away and not long after that that I booked my ticket back to London. It was to be a month's journey visiting some very interesting parts of Africa some of which would be no-go areas today. Earlier in 1964 I had gone off south with Bruce Hudson for a trip to Southern Rhodesia. We hitch-hiked down the Great North Road all the way down to the Wanke Game Reserve stopping at Broken Hill, Lusaka, Choma, Livingstone (NR) and Wanke and Bulawayo (SR). We had an assortment of lifts and nothing in particular happened. We stayed at Police messes along the way and when we got into Southern Rhodesia the BSAP (the British South Africa Police) allowed us to sleep in their quarters, or on couches if beds were not available. They were a completely different police force to the NRP. We came under the then Colonial Office. SR had its elected parliament and as a self-governing was not a colony. The ranks were dissimilar. The European officers would be ranked as constables, later to be called patrol officers, the Africans were also constables, but African constables. Their uniform leatherwork was brown, ours black, their shirts Khaki as ours were grey. Their history went back to Cecil Rhodes and the British South African Company. The law there was different, based on the Roman/Dutch system. The roads there were dirt grade roads, ours from Livingstone right up to the Copperbelt were all surfaced all weather roads. We looked at the men and the police stations and thought ourselves better off. Bulawayo, however was a city and bigger than anything in NR. It could almost have passed for a mid-size southern counties UK market town, more black faces of course.

# 8. To Nairobi then the Nile

I recall it was about September 1964 that I flew off from Ndola airport to begin my journey back to Blighty. It was by East African Airways Viscount to Nairobi. I had joined the International Police Association (IPA), perhaps best described as an international brotherhood of policemen and women from countries all around the world. Its aim was to promote fellowship and friendship and to assist officers traveling away from home. It was recognized as a world fraternal body by the United Nations. I contacted the IPA member in Nairobi and he kindly showed me around and entertained me for dinner. He was an English man, a chief Inspector in the Kenya Police who was nearing early retirement. I was in Nairobi for 5 days before I started my overland trip up through Africa north to Alexandria. The first leg was by road in utility vehicle through Kenya, west into Uganda.

We drove via Nakuru over the Great Rift Valley into Uganda crossing the border at Tororo then on to Gulu the last major town in Uganda before we made for the border with the Sudan at Nimule. The road journey was uneventful. The towns we went through were neat and well ordered, the African people cheerful, polite and colourfully dressed. There was certainly no look of malnourishment or fear in the faces of the people. Looks I have unfortunately found too many times in faces in South Asia. We stayed one night at a government run guesthouse; I was familiar with these in NR. They were for travellers, usually senior civil servants, who needed clean and well run accommodation in places where there were none such suitable. I don't now recall where we stayed the night, in any event I was impressed with how Colonial British it was: the servants in their white sarongs, the dinner and English breakfast, the furniture, pictures on the wall, all under the supervision of a lovely large black Ugandan lady house-keeper. You closed your eyes when talking her and she could have been from the Home Counties.

Next day we motored on passing through Gulu the last town until we got about 100 miles north to Nimule on the border. I don't recall if I needed a visa for Sudan then, it was 1964 and the area had not yet descended into chaos. My memory is there was a long drive from one border checkpoint to the next.

I left Uganda with a good impression. What I had seen in my short time there was apparent good governance: well maintained all be it dirt roads, tidy small towns and villages, no fear in the people, properly turned out police and well-spoken and educated were the few Ugandans I spoke to. Yes! Uganda with its new Independence had a lot going for it. Idi Amin dada was in the not too distant future. And here I was going across the border to his birthplace: Kokobo the area between Uganda, Sudan and the Congo.

From Nimale it was another 100 odd miles to Juba, then the capital of Sudan's Equatoria Province, now capital of the new state of South Sudan. Here I left the vehicle and the two African drivers who had so ably and cheerfully drove me from Nairobi. I boarded the vessel that would carry me up the Nile to Kosti where I would board a train to continue my journey north. I have used the word vessel, but that doesn't tell the reader how strange, unusual, fascinating it was. In the centre was a paddle steamer with three decks, the first two had accommodation, first class on the top deck with about four of five cabins with WC and shower. There was a viewing platform/lounge for all at the stern. The bridge with the coxswain was also on the top deck. In the front, back and sides of the steamer were barges. Imagine a rectangle: the steamer in the middle, with a barge directly in front of it, with two others of similar size and dimension tied to it, then to the rear of the steamer the same construction, one barge attached to it with two others tied each side. Then tied port and starboard to the steamer are two other barges. Thus in total nine floating vessels: the steamer and eight barges. On these barge were being loaded all manner of livestock, and people: dark skinned Nubians, Arab types from the north, descendants of the Mahdi's Fuzzies who broke the English square, all manner of Sudanese folk; there was also other cargo bales and boxes etc. The whole thing to me was more like a group of African villages with their men, women and children and livestock afloat and ready to move. The numbers must have been well over 500 people. There was a unit of Sudanese Railway Police to police the floating township; twenty or so men. There was an opposition/insurrection against the Government in Khartoum on-going in various degrees since the mid 50's.

There were three other first class passengers: a European magistrate on leave from Tanganyika and his lovely Goanese wife and a Superintendent from the Sudanese Police. As a fellow policeman I talked to him and expressed my admiration and respect for the police I had seen so far. They were smart, disciplined with their bush hat uniforms. And handled well the hordes of natives (can I use that word) who tried to get on the floating township as it stopped at the various places along the way. Reasonable force was always used with whips being the least amount! He spoke excellent English and we shared common police talk. He mentioned the problems of discontent in the south, the animist/Christian culture being so different from Islamic north. He inferred things were in control in the south.

It was a long journey to Kosti and I would spend my time, often sitting with the magistrate and his wife, looking at the White Nile, its banks and the people and animals living and working there. The first days we were going through the Sudd Wetlands, home to the tall Dinka people, naked for the most part who would be seen standing in the river with their spears to catch the huge Nile perch. One day really amused us, the Goanese lady in particular: there was a Dinka man 6 feet, 6 inches tall and up to his knees in the river holding his spear with his penis still touching the water: Crotch to knee!! We stopped at a number of small settlements, unloaded and loaded people and things. Each stop was an event with our police dissuading non-payers and the like from forcing their way onto the barges. Malakal was a major river port by which time we were out of the Sudd Wetlands with its lush vegetation and river life: Hippos, crocodiles, giant perch, and bird life. Malakal was perhaps half way to Kosti which was approximately 900 miles from our starting point at Juba. At about 8 to10 miles an hour the ferry must have taken the best part of 4 days. Sadly I have no impression now of life on board. The entertainments provided were cards and the occasional Nile Lager. Swimming even with water all around was not recommended. At Kosti, a really bustling town with Arabs and the dark skinned Africans hawking their wares, we left the Sudanese Railway Steamer and boarded one of their stream drive locomotive trains which was waiting for us. There was no time to look around and enjoy the nightspots!! The train would take us the 240 miles to Khartoum and the ride was uneventful. First class was comfortable: soft seats and a table in front.

We were on the platform at Khartoum Railway Station for just a short while. The northbound train to Wadi Haifa was waiting for us. It was a shame that I did not have time to explore the capital of the Sudan, situated with its sister city across the junction of the White (up from the Sudan) and the Blue Nile from the South East and Ethiopia. There was so much to see. Sudan you may recall was run by the British as the Anglo Egyptian Sudan until the mid-50s. Its British civil servants in the political service were regarded as the cream of the Overseas Civil Service. It was a vast country: one million square miles, the biggest country in Africa; culturally so diverse and materially backward. It certainly was an asset to Great Britain and came to our control in the 1890's after General Kitchener had invaded the Sudan, in the course of which he built the railway I was to use.

The train going North to Wadi Haifa and the border with Egypt was steam driven. The five or six carriages were painted white. This to reflect some of the heat that came from the burning sun that blazed down on the Nubian Dessert that we were to cross on our 450 mile journey. It was a hot trip and I remember the sand blowing across the desert and somehow into the dining car where I was eating. The sand got into the food and into the tea I was drinking. It must have been hell for the engine driver and his fireman. We got to Wadi Haifa in one piece. I recall it was morning so presume now we must have slept on the train, although apart from sharing a compartment with an American man, who was on his way home from a number of years serving in the Peace Corps in the Far East, I have little recollection of that leg of my trip.

At Wadi Haifa we left the train and made our way over the border into Egypt where we boarded another Nile steamer. I have been using the pronoun 'we' in the sense that there were other fellow travellers. Apart from the American gentleman I was alone and knew no one. This Nile steamer was very different from the one run by the Sudanese Railway. There were no barges, no flocks of sheep, chickens, hundreds of people etc. It was not a floating village. It was still a paddle steamer, larger than the other with bigger and better accommodation and service. I was to be on the vessel only couple of days. The journey to Aswan up Lake Nasser, for that is what the Nile had become, took a day. This included a night on board. It was a comfortable trip, not Thomas Cook Nile Cruises, with Hercule Poirot type shipmates, but alright for a regular passenger service ferry.

We steamed North with the famous Temples of Abu Simbel on our left (East). They were to be seen not far after we had steamed off from Wadi Haifa. The images of those amazing huge statues dedicated to King Ramises and his beloved Queen Nefertari who reigned in Egypt more than 1200 years before Christ are still very much in my mind. But I am puzzled. I have learnt because of the rising water level caused by damning of the Nile and the creation of Lake Nasser the Temples would have been flooded. Thus with the assistance of UNESCO a huge engineering work involving a number of skilled people from different countries began to break the entire temples into pieces and then to reassemble them 200 metres from the Lake and 55 metres higher up. This reconstruction started in June of 1964. I was on the ferry about three months after this. What I saw then was the Temples in their original positions before or as they were being dismantled. The water level was being controlled by the Dam.

We sailed past the temples on up the lake to Aswan the major town in the Southern Egypt. Here I stayed one night at a hotel before journeying on to Luxor home to the temple of Karnak and the Valley of Kings. Aswan was not without its share of Egyptology and I spent the day sightseeing. This was marred, as was visiting the tourist sights anywhere I visited in Egypt, by hawkers pushing 'genuine' relics stolen from the tombs and other centres of antiquities. These men could often get abusive and I found that the best play was to say: I'm Russki. You may recall that after the US and the UK had refused to build the Lake Nasser Dam, President Nasser had turned to the Russians. They then were 'popular'; the filthy British were made even filthier with their invasion with the French in 1956 to retake the Suez Canal.

One day at Aswan, the next it was the train the 'short' 110 mile Journey up to Luxor . It must have been at least 2 days at Luxor sightseeing. Ancient Thebes, as it was known and there since 3000BC is a feast of Egyptology: six great temples, colonnades, sphinx, statues, wall inscriptions, chapels and museums. The three places I visited were Karnak Temple Complex, 2 kilometres to the north of Luxor with its vast mix of decayed temples, pylons and statues. Connected to it by an avenue lined with statues and sphinx was the Luxor Temple. This was the largest of the six temples, two like it on the east of the Nile and four on the other side. Also on the other side of the river and requiring another day to visit was the Valley of the Kings and the lesser Valley of the Queen. Both were tiring days walking around in high temperatures. One thing sticks in my mind is being surreptitiously asked by a 'guide' whether I wanted to see something special! For a payment up front, fool that I was, he took me into a closed area of a temple. I forget exactly where but all along the walls was 4000-year-old pornography. Goodness I didn't realize they were doing those things then which were still illegal where I had just been a policeman. It was display of man and his various and questionable sexual appetites. Shocking perhaps then 1964 but today available for all to view on the internet, or so I am told.

I knew I was to catch ship at Alexandria to take me across the Mediterranean to Venice and time was running out, also I didn't fancy the 320-mile train ride to Cairo, my next stop. I therefore took a plane for the under two-hour journey. It was another Vickers Viscount aircraft.

At Cairo I stayed at the Shephard's Hotel, which had been there since the mid-19th Century and had seen all manner of historical giants stay there, including General Kitchener, King Feisal of Iraq and Sir Winston Churchill. The original hotel had been burnt down in an anti-British riot in the 1950's thus the one I was staying at was relatively new. It was four stars and the most luxurious accommodation I had stayed at so far. I was in Cairo for two days whilst I visited the Pyramids and the Sphinx at Giza. There were three pyramids with the Great Pyramid of Giza being the oldest and biggest. It is so impressive; built 4,500 years ago (Yes! Four thousand five hundred years ago). At 480 feet tall it was the tallest man made structure until

Lincoln Cathedral, 3,800 years later in the 14$^{th}$ Century. Some of its stones: huge granite stones weighing from 25 to 80 tonnes were quarried from hundreds of miles away at Aswan, others, limestone were from nearby and some of these from across the river. Inside the vast structure were ascending and descending passages leading to chambers which were the resting places for the Pharaoh, his Queen and followers before they went off to immortality somewhere above. I went inside the Pyramid and was amazed as to the size of the chambers and the way access to them was denied by a series of sand and gravity driven heavy stone slabs that could come crashing down to entomb intruders and seal the deceased and the yet deceased servants who awaited their astral journey.

I understand that so well built was the Pyramid that there was a gap between the huge stone blocks of only 1/50th of an inch. The engineers, who were they? How did they get the huge stones into position then up to the heights needed for installation? What equipment did they have? How did the cut the stone? Measuring the heights and levels? Determining how many blocks and their sizes? We must recall that we are still in the Early Bronze age, no steel cutting tools. The spoked wheel and chariot are new. Experts say as many as 40,000 workers were involved, some evidence shows they were not slaves but skilled workers. Most of the world was still in the Neolithic time in the Stone Age or coming out of it there was nothing then, before or for a thousand years after to compare or compete with the Pyramids. The way it was positioned in relation to the earth and the cosmos is also remarkable. Similar observations have been raised concerning Stonehenge in Wiltshire, England. There have been suggestions that visitors from another world may have been involved. Where did this technology, the mathematics, the engineering skill come from to build this extraordinary structure, when there is nothing to show us historically and archaeologically where the skills came from. There was nothing before.

A ride on a camel, a visit to the museum then back to the Hotel. Next day was the train to Alexandria to catch the Italian Ship to Venice.

The 225-kilometre train journey to Alexandra was comfortable and uneventful. It was a nearly 3-hour ride. At Alexandra I boarded an Italian ship to take me to Venice. Which I recall required a night in a small cabin. I understand now that it was the regular Alexandra to Venice ferry that takes three days. Alas my memory fails me now and I cannot recollect the crossing of the Mediterranean at all. It was one night in Venice, enough to explore that fantastic City before I boarded the train that would take me through Switzerland and on to Paris where again I had one night and had time to go most of the way up the Eiffel Tower. Then train to Calais and over on the cross channel ferry in a two hour trip to Dover. Here a train to London Victoria Station, then the underground and finally the 134 bus and home to 7 Priory Villas.

My adventure was ended. A journey that took at least 16 days and was over 4,500 miles.

It was nice to knock on the door and have it opened by my lovely Mum. Oh the joy! Into the corridor and there was dear Dad. Later it was my sister Jill upstairs and my niece Belinda, a toddler of 3. They had moved in with Jill's husband George, a salt of the earth Londoner who was still working at Smithfield meat market as a porter. My old bedroom upstairs was now Belinda's. I now had a fold up bed in our old front room. Once the gaiety was over I handed out the few presents I had brought. All that I can remember was the bottle of spirits and the cigarettes. My sister smoked much and my mother some. Dad, who had worked for the International Tobacco Company had never smoked, nor did George. I at the time did, having been spoilt in Northern Rhodesia, a place where they grew tobacco, and where they were so cheap. We would use in the police the rear white packet of a 50 'Matinee' as a notebook. The packets fitted comfortable in our uniform shirts. I recall the 50 smokes cost 2 shillings and 6 pence. In England at the time they would have cost double. So keen was I to bring in enough for us all, that I stuffed my pockets with extra packets. But so obvious was my concealment that one of the Dover customs officers took me on one side. He asked me to turn out pockets and there were 120 cigarettes over my entitlement. I said sorry and explained I was on my way home from serving Her Majesty in the Northern Rhodesia Police. He told me I was a silly sod and to go, or words to that effect!

I was home only two days before there was another knock on the door. I opened it and there stood before me on the step was my old friend Barney; fellow beer critic, ban the bomber, co-member of the St Johns Ambulance Brigade: who accompanied me to West End theatres to treat, on occasions, ladies from the audience or cast who may have been overcome by the vapours and needed smelling salts. And also there was Marilynne, the love of my life, my first, my only love and my compatriot in attempting to ban the bomb. 'Welcome home David, we are married' said Barney. I can't say it was a shock. My mother had told me almost the first day I got back. They were married just two or three days before that. I was angry when I saw them. She looked so gorgeous. I hoped she would be waiting and engagement whatever. (But now I realize I was away for almost 3 years. I had told Barney when he drove us to the airport on the 28th February, 1962, to look after her.) I have been telling myself ever since that I floored him on the step and slammed the door. But that is a lie, and Barney has since told me so. It was then a 'Go away' or words to that affect and I was not to see either of them for many years. It was not until I returned to the UK (Wales) in 1980 with my family to study law that we became good, No, dear friends again.

It was a week or so at home before I was getting bored and fed up with our usual family rows. I needed a job. I bought an old Ford Consul with some of the money that remained from my small gratuity from the NR Police. I went in search of work, obviously my vast experience gained in my 2 and a ½ years in the NRP would make me very employable in the security industry; not the securities industry, I was too honest for that!

# 9. Undercover Observations

I started to look around. I realized that private security companies seem to be everywhere now. I had not really noticed them back in 1962: Securicor (in the traditional blue of the police), Security Express (in green uniforms), The Armoured Car Company (with its guards in US type uniforms) and others. I checked the phone book for Securicor and saw they had a Detective Division with their office in Chelsea. I found them at Swan House, No.4. Cheyne Row, Chelsea. The building was historic, it looked at least mid-Victorian. I have since learned that the famous writer George Elliot (Mrs. J. W. Cross) had died there in 1870. I entered the building gingerly and told the doorman I had come about the job, at least that's what he thought I said. Because he said 'Oh you must mean Mr......" and was shown into this man's office. He was surprised when I introduced myself and said I was just back from the police in Africa and was looking for job. He said that they were not recruiting but said he was interested in me as I had come at the right time. There had been an increase in the Division's workload and I could be of service. He outlined what the work would entail. I would be on the staff payroll, not on that of uniform guards. My work would for the most part be that of an undercover operator. In addition it would involve surveillance on foot and vehicle, statement taking and report writing. I would be required to advise on security weaknesses in the places I operated and my recommendations for improvements. As a member of staff I also may be required to crew the armoured cash carrying vans belonging to the Armoured Car

Company based at West Drayton, London. This company had recently been taken over by Securicor and we were required to assess that company's security both in its vans and at its Vaults. That was what we were told, however I learnt later it was because of trouble with adequate personnel. Securicor did not wish to take on extra staff for its new subsidiary and could not use its own guards because of union problems.

I started work at Swan House within days. They seemed happy with my NRP discharge certificate but said it may be necessary to further check my background. My first assignment was to work undercover as a labourer, overhead crane driver and slinger at a large steel stockholder in the West Midlands. I lived in digs and worked about a month at the yard. It was an old established company that dealt with all types of steel ranging from rolled bright steel to reinforced steel joists and steel bars of every thickness and length. The company's instructions required that lorries would come in for loading every morning at around 7 to 8 am. They would be loaded by people like me, usually working in threes: the overhead crane driver, the slinger and the labourer. Once loaded the load would be checked against the work sheet/invoices by the checker, who was also the yard foreman and senior man. I have always liked the midlands folk. I was born in Wellington, not far up the road from Wolverhampton. And in particular Midland's wide selection of real ale has always raised my spirits. I got on well with the workers at the yard and would drink with some of them in one of the nearby pubs. I emphasized my not insignificant cockney accent and did my best to find out what fiddles were going on. My time at the brewery Truman Hanbury and Buxton had shown me that the 60's was a time for fiddles in the delivery business. It was before electronic monitoring, surveillance cameras and all. I also did evening and night surveillance on the yard. After my month at the yard I observed no steel being taken illegally. My conclusions were that the checker/foreman and his workers appeared honest. The confidences I had won with the workers, including one I got very friendly with, disclosed no organized thievery. I prepared a lengthy report on my findings with a conclusion that any losses experienced could have been the result of poor stock taking and monitoring of deliveries in and out of the yard. I gave a number of recommendations concerning the exit weighbridge, stock taking, and the employment of security personnel and security at night. I checked out of my digs and told my mates I was off to join the Rhodesian Army.

I reported back to Swan House and my manager there. I completed my report which as I have mentioned did include recommendations which meant further business for Securicor in the form of a static guard at the Yard in the daytime and coverage a night by one of our mobile patrols.

I was assigned a number of other undercover jobs: a timber merchant/stockholder at Islington, London. This involved similar work to that in the steel stockholders in the Midlands except I was portering wooden products. It entailed slinging for an overhead crane, which ran along on rollers above the warehouse, and sometimes driving it. The job was memorable because it reminds me of the strength I had then. I was able to the amazement (or perhaps amusement: 'look at the silly sod!') of some of the co-workers to carry five wooden fire doors at a time. These must have weighed 50 pounds each. I got the knack, like meat porters at Smithfield market of carrying them across my back. OK, stupid Macho man, no wonder I have severe back problems today! I also had other easier labouring jobs like at a factory making cleaning products, including lavatory cleaner at Leyton, London; a large car parts stockholders in Leeds, Yorkshire; and another steel stockholder at West London. By this time, to help with my job and my cover stories, plus because things were getting crowded at 7 Priory I had moved out to digs.

My job in the Detective Division also involved me in tailing a suspect lorry from East London right up to Norfolk. There were two of us in the tail, each driving one of the company's minis. We lost track of the lorry after a tail lasting about 3 hours. We were not entirely useless as we were able to report its route and some stops along the way.

Another Division job was as spot check inspectors at Top Rank Bingo. We would arrive unannounced before the assembled punters, usually hundreds of middle aged and elderly ladies, sat in a huge ex-cinema. The caller would address the assembled throng: 'Ladies and Gentlemen these men are senior officers from Securicor here to ensure the games are conducted in fair manner. Please be patient whilst they conduct their security checks.' We would then examine the winning card or cards and the magic machine that blew the numbered balls into the air. A few hellos to the winners to show that these ladies were genuine punters: they were known and were with their mates. Then we were off. I, at the time, knew absolutely nothing about Bingo and it was just an exercise in 'Bull Shit.' Apparently it pleases the Punters and was good for Top Rank's business.

I was also detailed as a bodyguard on a couple of occasions. These jobs involved covertly accompanying diamond merchants from Hatton Garden about their business. These included for the Detective Division escorts out of London and the UK. Although I never got further than London.

My pay with the Detective Division was very good. I had a reasonable salary as a member of their staff. I also got my pay from my employers when working undercover. Then there was the overtime and expenses I could claim. These included those after work hours when I considered it necessary to keep surveillance on the various premises. Expenses included entertaining with my workmates: doing things I hated: drinking beer in unfamiliar pubs! Thus I had plenty to give to my dear Mum with whom I returned to live after it was no longer necessary to live in digs.

I was with Securicor Detective Division for about 9 months before I went off to join the Hong Kong Police: Another adventure.

# 10. The Lure of the East

I was interviewed for the Hong Kong Police at the Crown Agents Offices not far around the corner from Swan House, in Millbank (a stone's throw from the Houses of Parliament). My interviewer was Superintendent of Police Mr. P. T. Moor, a real gentleman who went on to become Deputy Commissioner of the Royal Hong Police (the successor to the HKP). I was asked about my time in Africa and why I didn't want to join London's finest, the Metropolitan Police. Who wants to check doorknobs and walk around in the dead of night freezing cold! Then it was the medical officer. A quick cupping of my not too significant tackle, presumably to make sure they were there. There were no foreign female recruits for Hong Kong's finest yet! And I was in. My vetting had been done already or so it seemed.

About a fortnight later, on the 10th April I was on a BOAC flight, Boeing 707 to Hong Kong. Believe it or not sharing my aircraft, also on their way to join the Hong Kong Police were Paddy Wickerson, from South London and Greg Bell a Scotsman. Both had been in my recruit training squad at the NRP Training School in Lilayi. I recall an event at Lilayi now when Paddy was made as a punishment by our squad instructor to stand on one leg on the drill square and yell 'Chitimakuloo, Chitimakuloo" until he could no more. The name concerned was the paramount chief of the dominant tribe in the north of Northern Rhodesia and our instructor thought it was important he and us knew such important facts. It was no punishment for Paddy who was a super fit footballer who relished physical punishment. At both training schools he would often on his own initiative run around the parade ground more times than the usual 10 ordered as punishment by the instructor. In contrast yours truly was knackered by round 6 especially when the temperatures were 30 plus Celsius. Two other ex NRP men were on the flight: the tough South African I knew from my time at Ndola, Dan Robinson and Bob Brooks a Scotsman who I had met at Kitwe in NR. He was to become my closest friend. If it is not an arrestable offence I loved the fella. He was one for the hard stuff, didn't make old bones and died before he was 60. I am still in contact with his dear wife Marilyn. The flight was uneventful. There was one stop in India, Calcutta. The iron curtain was still down so there were no short cuts over the Soviet Union. It was not then your 12-hour flight of today.

We were met and welcomed to Hong Kong at Kai Tak Airport by the man who was to be our class instructor: Senior Inspector Ken Clark. Hong Kong was very different then. There was no Cross Harbour tunnel and to get to the Police Training School at Aberdeen, on the south side of the Hong Kong Island we had to cross by vehicular ferry. We were driven there in a closed van that in time we got to call: the bread van. Police Training School (PTS), Aberdeen was similar to Lilayi in that there was the familiar parade ground with classrooms nearby. But behind the complex was a hill with a service road up to the top. Ah! I thought here is where they get to torture us. Our quarters and our mess were improvements on Lilayi. We had a room each and there was a room boy each floor to do room, boots, belts and uniforms! It was a bit different to the NRP where we spent the best part of an hour each day bullying up our boots and belts. They were expected to gleam, although there were occasions when Inspector Storey would use his boot to scratch the toecaps just before commandant's parade. There was nothing so uncouth at Aberdeen. We were briefed by Ken Clarke about the rules and behaviour at PTS. There was no problem going out at weekends as long as we were there for Monday's morning parade. Our squad would not be formed until our local colleagues joined and in the meantime we would attend a Cantonese course at the Government Language School situated then in low-rise buildings at Queensway, at today's Admiralty MTR station complex.

We would leave PTS every weekday morning at 8 am. Some mornings we were worse for wear having destroyed all powers of concentration through drink the night or weekend before. The journey down to Queensway in the bread van also didn't help our readiness for instruction; especially Cantonese. After over 45 years with the Cantonese I am familiar with the 'music' of its tonal speak: a grunt rendered in one tonal pitch can mean something different said in another. One that comes to mind is the word for shoe said in another tone it can mean the unmentionable part of the female. A foreigner using the wrong tones can thus cause great hilarity or real offence with Hong Kong people. Our teachers at the school: a lovely Chinese lady married to a British policeman and two learned Chinese gentlemen in their late 50's were so kind and patient. They would get us to sing out the tones. I recall there were 5 or so and two 'clipped' tones. The lunchtime we would spend nearby in the China Fleet Club where it would be a pint of San Mig' $1.10 and a pasty 70 cents; less than $2.00 for lunch. For those with private means it could be two pints for lunch and a real sandwich. Back at the language school in the unconditioned summer air of the classroom it was difficult to keep awake. Not infrequently a head would crash down onto a desk with a

'Terribly sorry Miss Ng'. The end of the day it was back to PTS in the bread van. At the end of the 12-week course we were examined on our verbal dexterity by strangely, a European Cantonese speaker. At least I think he was European. We all passed our exams which would qualify us for promotion to Inspector. Then it was back to PTS in the bread van.

The part of our language training out of the way it was time to get our uniforms and start our police training. These uniforms were not much different to those we wore in the NRP: starched khaki shorts and shirts, black belts, boots and gaiters, webbing belts for training and blue winter uniforms with peak cap. We had no special full dress uniforms, Bombay helmets and the like! There was emphasis on foot drill but no arms drill. We had no rifles and would not get our service revolvers until we passed out. PTS was used to train recruit officers like us and recruit constables. Those of us from the NRP were surprised that there was no rifle drill at all at PTS. This was to come some years later I believe as a result of pressure from us Africans. Although an hour on the square in 30 plus degrees is not a particularly pleasant task for anyone such training at Aberdeen certainly lacked the real pain, punishment, discipline and precision of Lilayi. Our drill Chinese drill instructors knew their stuff but they lacked the presence and nastiness of those we felt were found in other colonial police and army training depots. Punishment was only a few times around the square which Paddy Wickerson always seemed to relish. No marking time for one hour, no rifles held over your head until you dropped. Civilised! However we noted that the recruit constable squads were getting a far harder time from their drill instructors; cuffs around the body being not an unusual practice. Commandant's and Pass Out Parades when we had to stand in the heat at attention for long periods I did not find easy. I would often be twitching, convinced I was going to join some of the recruit constables who had flaked out. In Africa this had not been a problem for me; so powerful was Chiefy Oliver at such parades, with his 'Leave those weak insipid men on the ground', that you dare not faint or show signs of doing so.

Classroom work was centred on law and police procedure, much of it was familiar with us ex policemen. There were outside lecturers from other government departments; one that comes to mind was a European gentleman from the Public Health Department. He talked for an hour about rats in Hong Kong and how many there were, their sizes, homes, and way of killing them. He had a great sense of humour and was a gifted lecturer. There was some weapon training and range courses. Leadership, riot drill and anti-riot, crowd control, and more weapon training would come later in our careers at the military style Police Training Contingent (PTC) later to become the Police Tactical Unit (PTU). There were exams throughout the course and final at the end. We then looking as smart as we could, marched out onto the Passing Out Parade and finally marched past the reviewing officer, who was I believe the Governor Sir. David Trench. Danny Robinson was awarded the best recruit baton of honour. We also learned after that he had been appointed at the start of the course by the directing staff to be the squad spy. So was it a reward, we were in Hong Kong!

It had been too long and tedious at Aberdeen. We had spent much time drinking in the mess and we Africans had tried to liven things up with the occasional game of 'Bok Bok'; apparently with disapproval and disbelief from the PTS staff. We had also encouraged new squads arriving from the UK to

119

take part in initiations, one of which involved riding the fans (large overhead electric fans). We were not sorry to leave PTS for our postings and it is likely the staff were more than pleased we were going.

Paddy Wickerson and I were posted to Yuen Long Division in the New Territories (the NT), that part of Hong Kong that under the treaty of Nanking had to be given back to China in 1997. Don't we know! It was in 1965 very rural with, apart from Tsuen Wan in the Southern part of the NT, no large centres of population or commerce. Yuen Long was one of about five market towns: Tai Po, Shatin, Fanling, Castle Peak and Sai Kung. Ok! I realise some will take issue with my giving them such appellation. In these towns there were no high-rise buildings then, none of the huge housing estates and shopping malls of today. The tallest buildings in Yuen Long were the HSBC Bank and the Police Station both of which rose to the dizzy heights of four floors, including the ground floor. Yuen Long had one main street and a few side streets going off it. The market occupying most of one of these: the Tai Tong Road appeared to be the centre of the town's 'commerce' and was to occupy much of our time clearing hawkers and their obstructions. There were none of the major highways in the NT then. The road system went back to the early days of British takeover and many roads were based on earlier roads and tracks going back to the days of Chings (The Manchu rulers of China from the late 17th to early 20th centuries). The system was a double sometimes three lane irregular ring road going around the coast west from Tsuen Wan to Castle Peak (Now called Tuen Muen) the north east to Yuen Long then further east to Fanling and Tai Po then South again via Shatin to Kowloon and the Colony (proper) of Hong Kong. There were smaller roads in between some like the road over our biggest mountain Tai Mo Shan linking Yuen Long (Sek Kong) to Tsuen Wan was a modified 'jeep' track that had been built by the British army.

Our quarters at Yuen Long were across the small parade ground from the police station, a mere 40 yards walk. They were comfortable, at least for the likes of us at the time. Today even as young rookies we would expect more. We had our own room and shared a bathroom and W.C. with the flat adjoining it. Downstairs was a lounge, in which we set up a Mess bar, and a dining room. The Mess was used by officers from the main Divisional Police Station and from our other sub-divisional stations: Lau Fau Shan and Pat Heung and employed a cook amah to prepare our meals. This good lady would excel herself when we later had formal mess diners. The Mess with its bar was to be the centre of our off duty life. We were over an hour and half to town and apart from a few bars used by the British Army in Sek Kong there was not much to do.

Our work involved shifts, similar to those we had performed in NR. We would start the shift by inspecting and briefing the men, usually 30 to 40 men; unlike the NRP, each constable would be issued with a 38 Colt revolver with 6 rounds (this was not the USA and the need for multiple fire power!), which would be loaded under the supervision of a corporal or sergeant. I mention here that the corporal rank was abolished before the 70's. The men would then march off to their duties: beat posts, patrol car or station.

I recall that because of the size of urban Yuen Long there was not the need for many beats. There were, however, plans for town expansion and beats had already been allocated and numbered for areas next to it that were now paddy fields, used for rice or vegetable growing. Our duties would be to patrol the town, check the beats and any places where there had been reports of illegal activities. All gambling was illegal in those days outside that of the Royal HK Jockey Club Race Course; there were then no Jockey Club betting centres all over the place. Previously the Kai Fong (Community leaders) had indicated their vigorous opposition to such 'licensed' gambling as it was against Chinese tradition and culture and would encourage crime. Ha Ha! Next to the British they are probably the biggest lovers of the game of chance in the world. It was said in police circles that the reason they opposed it was because they ran most that existed illegally. Illegal drugs were a problem; opium pipes were still popular amongst the older men although drugs like heroin were taking over as the most used. Opium with its strong, not unpleasant smell and need to be smoked with others in a divan was much easier to detect than heroin, which could be taken solitary by injection, smoked in tin foil or simple tube or pipe. Thus the more harmful, in my view, heroin was causing a decline in opium taking. As rookie Inspectors would not be encouraged to raid places but to report what we had found so that gambling authorizations could be obtained for senior officers and raids conducted. As Inspectors we had a general authorization to raid premises for drugs but again we were encouraged to report our suspicions for onward information and action to the Divisional vice squad. This did not prevent us acting when we came across drug takers in staircases, alleys or anywhere in our view and the same went for gambling we observed in the street.

Other work involved the divisional patrol car/s; unlike Hong Kong Island and Kowloon there was no NT District Emergency Unit (EU) providing a 999 response. Yuen Long Division provided its own cover for its western part. Tai Po and Shatin its two other sub-divisions provided their own. Things have very much changed today with an efficient 999 co-ordinated cover through out Hong Kong. On mobile patrols we would perform road blocks checking for illegal immigrants from China and for contraband (fireworks were not yet illegal as the 1967 Disturbances were to come). There was not much action at Yuen Long and I was envious of my colleagues like Bob Brooks who was full of stories of life at Yaumati Division. I was not long at Yuen Long and was transferred to the Frontier Division.

Ta Kwu Ling (TKL) Police Station was situated a stone's throw from the Sum Chun River which marked the border between British Territory (BT) and Chinese Territory (CT). If you sat on the verandah of the officers' quarters you could see the villagers from Law Fong Rural Production Team (CT) coming through the gate in our border fence to come to work the fields (BT) just below the station. They were not supposed to go beyond these fields and come into Hong Kong.

TKL Sub Divisional Police Station was one of three Border Police Stations that faced China: Lok Ma Chou (LMC) in the west TKL in the centre and Sha Tau Kok (STK) in the east. Only TKL was right on the Frontier. Apart from the three police stations there were police posts strung along the border usually within view of their neighbours. These were situated on high grounds for security and observation purposes. Each was manned by a corporal and 7 men who stay at the post only leaving it on their leave days. The post was armed with a Bren Light machine gun (the workhorse of the British army for World War Two and generations after) and enough firearms for each man at the post) On top of the Post was a high powered search light that could be directed forward 360 degrees. The function of the post was to display sovereignty and to re-enforce the security of the barbed wire double fence that went along the border all the way to its western land end. It stopped where the Sum Chun River widened and became a natural barrier. Thousands of people had fled China since 1948. There had been a huge influx in 1962 and numbers varied from a flood to individuals who climbed the fence or cut through it, others came hidden under the goods wagons that crossed at the Lo Wu Railway Bridge. At Sha Tau Kok there was illegal immigration by swimming across Mir Bay to our Mainland or its Islands like Kat O and Ap Chau. The attitude and efficiency of the authorities the other side of the border controlled the volume of those fleeing China. In 1962 thousands came, pushing the border fence down, other times their border closed area was tight and people arrested by the PLA could get heavy punishment.

Two of the border posts: Kong Shan under (TKL) and Pak Kung Au under (STK) were 500 feet and 900 feet respectively above ground level and were a hell of a climb up the hundreds of steps and path to them. And for the village female coolies who were hired to carry up supplies and fuel for the post's generator even worse. The duties in the post were to monitor the other side of the border and register sightings of vehicles military or otherwise, movements of military personnel and anything unusual. They were to report movement of persons crossing the border and where possible arrest illegal immigrants. It was a boring job but was usually filled by volunteers who received a hard lying allowance for being there for the month, plus they could save money. They spent their time cleaning the Post, cooking, cleaning the weapons and some of them, I recall, would cut and carve wood for walking sticks. I had one black thorn stick for years.

There were three of us at TKL: Mike Harris the boss the SDI (Sub Divisional Inspector), Eric Crowter the OC Posts West and me the OC Posts East. My post were Pak Fa Shan and Kong Shan the later overlooking the gate for our BT villagers at Li Ma Hang, they had fields the other side in CT. Eric's Posts were the hill posts Nga Yiu and Nam Hang. Although on Eric's side, we both visited and supervised the men at the Lo Wu Rail Crossing, where in those days there was limited passenger traffic walking across the bridge from our KCR Train (Kowloon Canton Railway) to theirs on the other side of the bridge; and the road crossing at Man Kam To. This was where goods from China would be pushed across a bridge by coolies to be loaded onto Lorries parked in a large loading area. The goods included livestock. Our duties as OC's Post would be to consolidate sightings reports for submission, if necessary through Mike to Divisional HQ at Fanling. Again if necessary these would be forwarded to the Military. At the time the British army was not allowed in the border closed area. This was an area about a mile wide the entry to which required an entry permit. These were given to the villagers who lived within the area and to those needing access. The military were not generally allowed in to the closed area and when accompanied by police for special visits would wear plain cloths. The army did have two observation posts on the very tops of the mountains but access to these was not controlled by the police.

I was enjoying my stay at TKL. Mike and Eric were good mates and the food was good. Cookie and his wife, a couple in their 70's who had escaped from China under some duress and would growl when you asked them what they thought of Chairman Mao. He was a marvellous cook and I can now picture him rolling out the pastry to make minced pies and the like. The stories that must have been in his head about China! I never discovered the circumstances of him and his wife coming to TKL He didn't seem to venture much into town although I have some recollection there was a son.

The Cultural Revolution in China was going strong. The inspired thoughts of Chairman Mao were to be seen and heard everywhere in Hong Kong and across the border. Communist China Banks and Department stores, left wing schools, union premises, companies were all displaying his thoughts and picture. There were his thoughts in books, large ones, pocket size, even in English, badges with his face always in the same pose but in different sizes and colours. There were banners all over the place, getting more and more against those who opposed the revolution. At the beginning it was 'Down with American Imperialism, Down with English Imperialism' (Scottish and Welsh Imperialism was OK) and one to warm your heart: 'Down with Soviet Revisionism'! Later as events progressed the venom turned more towards the Hong Kong British and particularly the Hong Kong Police. One morning I noted that the Law Fong villagers from the production brigade had put up banners in their British Territory side fields and were having a bit of a Chairman Mao worship knees up. I ignored them and went off to check my posts at Pak Fa Shan and Kong Shan. Because the border seemed to be heating up a bit I took a carbine with me. Walking back to the station I noticed that the Law Fong Banners were still there and were sufficiently inflammatory to excite a beach of thee peace. Thus I took them down and brought them the 150 or yards backs to he Station. Mike Harris came down from our quarters upstairs. 'What have you done? Take them back!' Alas it was too late the mob had arrived with banners and howling for my blood. 'Get upstairs quick and hide' says Mike.

I was transferred the next day to Lok Ma Chau. I never learnt how Mike had got everyone to leave the station without setting it on fire; although I understand there were apologies and promises I would be reprimanded and transferred. Perhaps the Mao madness was still relatively benign: no deaths, injuries or officers abducted into China. I think I even slept the night in my bed at TKL. The SDI/LMC was a 6 feet 5 inches giant from Herefordshire, Larry Abel. His main love was a Staffordshire bull terrier, who liked to scrap with other dogs, called Teddy. LMC was one of the early NT Police Stations built on a hill overlooking a wide expanse of rice paddy extending to the Sam Chun River and the border fence about a mile away. It had one hill post Ma Co Lung (MCL) and a post on the Mai Po Marshes called Pak Ok Chou (forgive me if I have got the spelling wrong). The station area included the entire border and the closed area west of the Lo Wu railway line up to the boundary with the Yuen Long division. To the west of LMC Police Station again there was a wide expanse of land including a number of fish farms and the large Mai Po Nature Reserve. The Reserve was treasured by naturists, particularly bird lovers. It was used by migratory birds from Northern China and Russia and all manner of water fowl and waders could be found there. The closed area dissipated in the Sum

Chum River estuary at the southern end of which was a Tsim Bei Tsui Marine Police Post which was the base of launch 15 an armour plated paddle patrol boat whose maximum speed was that of anemic duck.

There was only two of us at the time living and working at LMC Police Station, three with Teddy. The quarters were nice with a view from the lounge verandah of the Sum Chun River and the few buildings beyond in China. I mention now that the biggest building across the border from TKL was a two-story customs building at Lo Wu. The only buildings viewed anywhere along the border from TKL or LMC were village houses. None could have been described as town. At the east of the border was STK which was a market town split in two by Chung Ying Street (Chung is Chinese for China and Ying for England). STK was always a district headquarter town, although again there were no buildings of any significant size in 1965/66. Today 2013 if you look across the border at TKL, LMC and STK you see a large city which together with its suburbs probably has a population nearing HK's 7 plus million. Sheng Zhen (Shum Chun in Cantonese) has an underground rail system, its own university, hotels, parks, factories everything a modern city should have. Today HK people flock there for cheap clothes, CD's, all sorts of things and to dine and visit theme parks. **Who would have thought it?**

LMC covered a larger outside the closed area than TKL and had few people living within its closed area. Its population outside was much greater and included large villages like San Tin and others. The main highway from to Yuen Long ran through it along which were a number of villages and houses standing alone. The area had a number of ponds which provided business for a number of restaurants along the road, some of which also had boating and fishing. All in all much more was going on in LMC. It was my view that we were not doing enough to hunt down illegal gambling and drugs and that started Larry and I to distance ourselves. By this time I had begun to realize that Hong Kong had a real corruption problem. There was talk amongst my PTS classmates that some in the police force were on the take in regard to vice and even illegal hawking. Apparently Chinese Staff Sergeants had a big hand in what was a system. There were only a few of these: a Staff Sergeant Class One to each District. Hong Kong and Kowloon, one for the uniform branch (UB) and one for the CID; the NT had only the one for the UB. In addition each Division had one UB and CID Staff Sergeant Class Two to each division. My suspicion in regard to Larry was totally wrong but understandably with just two people living together it was better if I moved. I was transferred to Sha Tau Kok.

Sha Tau Kok sub division was the best of the Frontier Stations. It had Pak Kung Au (PKU) the highest of the border hill posts and Sha Tau Kok village and post. The village, as mentioned above, was more a small town divided down the middle into BT and CT by Chung Ying Street, along which were old boundary stones. Chung Ying Street was patrolled when secure and it was considered necessary to maintain sovereignty. There was a small Restaurant right on the barrier on our side of the street which had a rear window look that opened onto CT. You could sit there having your morning tea with the People's Liberation Army soldier scowling at you through the window.

To the west and east of the barrier were businesses, likewise, with windows opening onto CT. On the east side of these businesses was an open drain which marked the border. And running parallel to this on our side was San Lau Street with a row of two storey building housing residences and shops. San Lau extended to a pier, about 100 yards long used by the irregular ferry to Kat O Island and Ap Chau and Police Launches which patrolled Mirs Bay, the whole of which was claimed and used as BT. We would use these Launches, which really were small gun boats to take us to the Islands and others as well at the villages along the coast of the STK peninsular to the East. There were a number of villages that were quite large; Lai Chi Wo with a population at its height of 600 (my estimate). The journey by launch to these saved the four to five hour hike over the hills from the main station. I did this patrol over the hills a number of times. And because of the distance would try to stay overnight in one of the villages or return by launch. There were the occasional reports of pigs destroying the crops. We would answer this with a team of our older, experienced NT born and raised local men going out for 3 to 4 days hunting these. And what fine creatures these boars were. Great roasted!

I never forget on one patrol to Lai Chi Wo I spoke to a little boy who was playing, he looked Eurasian and I said in English: 'How are you, where are you from'? He replied in broad 'scouse': 'I's ul rite I's from LIVERPOOL' (sorry if I got the accent wrong). The dear little chap was the offspring of hundreds of NT people who had left the villages to work in the UK restaurant business as cooks and the like; many did very well and rarely returned. They would, however, send the younger preschool children back to stay with grandma and granddad. In later life I would become very good friends with the Chung family from the Lam Tsuen valley in the NT who worked at their Restaurant in Aberystwyth Wales.

Life at STK was good; three fold 'policing': 1. The trek up the hundred steps of PKA post where sometimes I would stay and enjoy a 'post chow' with the men and then remain there to watch the sun rise in the morning over Mirs Bay. 2. The STK village with its sensitivity, uncertainty and not infrequent excitement, what with stone throwing, inflammatory broadcasts, and troop movements and changes the other side. 3. And lastly delightful hiking on the STK peninsular and Islands, and through the villages that stretched along the STK to Fanling Road. I was being paid for this! My boss at STK was a pleasant fellow who I accompanied on a short leave to the Philippines, where he had a friend in the Pasay City Police. (The Philippines in the 1960's!!! Guns galore like the US and the cops! Say no more!) My boss, later on in my career, when I was in charge of the CID at Yuen Long, would try to have me disciplined for an operation I launched to tame an area in the division. But that is another story. He was no a close friend after that. I believe he is still alive. After a period which I thought was too short I was posted to the Police Training Contingent (PTC).

PTC was divided into a cadre course where we learned about the paramilitary side of our constabulary duties. These involved the control of crowds in all their forms ranging from peaceful demonstrations to riotous mobs. There were lectures from the training staff on Platoon (40 men) and Company (three to four platoons) orders and riot drills and the weapons to be carried and used by each officer. These included in 1966 rattan shields, greener shotguns, a carbine for a marksman/sharpshooter, gas pistols, gas shell firing federal gas guns and gas grenades. Each cadre course would include the officers and NCOs of the

131

company in training: the Company Commander a Superintendent, a second in command a senior inspector (later to be regraded a chief inspector) the platoon commanders and their second in command, a total of 6 to 8 Inspectors and the four section corporals and one platoon sergeant in each platoon making a total of 12 to 16 corporals and 3 to 4 sergeants. There were also lectures on leadership and field craft. Unlike PTS the training and discipline was much tougher. At the completion of the cadre course the company would form after the constables had reported in. The company would then be trained by its officers and NCOs.

The training staff would organise exercises involving house searching; riot control with or without our gas masks; the use and live firing of all our weapons; map reading and field craft. There was emphasis on our smartness, turnout and drill movements. Our drivers were expected to keep their vehicles in first class conditions and spotless. At the commandant's inspection Superintendent Peter Godber would climb under the vehicles just wearing his white shirt. If he was to emerge with oil on it the poor driver was in trouble. So keen were the drivers to have their vehicles gleaming and bulled up that when they started their engines to drive off the parade ground the paint on the leaf springs burnt off clouds of smoke. It was certainly tough at PTC. It had its' Chiefy Oliver (recall him of PTS Lilayi?). This was Chief Inspector Les Guyatt who had served with the Indian army during the last war. He didn't have the aura and power of Chiefy but he certainly was a fine example of a British army training RSM. He was always immaculate and with his square body and waxed moustache looked the part. My company commander Charlie Johnson a Scotsman who had spent most of his time in Special Branch and did not inspire in uniform was nickname by the men what translated to be the: 'hunchback chicken'. I got on well with him. He recommended me for the best platoon award at pass out but I had fallen foul of Peter Godber in regard to my strong views about corruption. I had been hounded at PTC and it was clear he was not going to let me leave with the best platoon on my record. I was annoyed as my platoon: all marine police officers, who in those days still wore a uniform based on the Royal Navy, clearly deserved it. But I am sure the recipient of that honour, my friend Dave Allen an ex matelot, would not agree. After passing out a company then became one the Force's reserve riot companies to be used to support Districts in the event of disturbance. It was 1966 and the Maoists were at work in neighbouring Macau. There had been riots where the Portuguese had been overwhelmed. I was convinced it was our turn soon and when there was a practice alarm call out at PTC I was convinced it was for real and made sure I had everything: map case and was fully kitted out. I was reprimanded for my tardiness in forming up with my Platoon.

We were only at PTC for the routine period about 6 months. Colleagues who came later in the year got involved with Cultural Revolution when it was HK's turn and spent almost a year as Force Reserve. It was back to Frontier Division, if only for a few weeks, to Sheung Shui police station which was not on the border. It looked after the two market towns and surrounding villages of Sheung Shui and Fanling. Policing Sheung Shui was like Yuen Long, busier perhaps as there were only two of us at the station: The boss, Chinese officer Peter Chik, a Shantung man from North China, and me. It had the two KCR Railway Stations at those towns and two lively markets. There were shops in each town and as nearly always in the NT a gambling place or opium divan somewhere to be found.

I was needed elsewhere; The Emergency Unit New Territories (EU.NT). This was largely a Pakistani unit base at Fanling Headquarters also known as NT (New Territories) Depot. It was also the HQ of the Frontier Division and housed the Fanling Mess, a bar well used by all the officers from the border stations. Officers serving in the Frontier division were not allowed to leave the division except on their weekly leave day. Thus with little to do, the trip to the mess for an evening drink was almost routine. The only other alternative was to visit the Betta 'Ole Bar at the Fanling Railway Station. The 'Ho Di Lung' as we called it in our bad Cantonese had been there since the Korean War. When thousands of soldiers had used it before going off to Korea to fight the Chinese; their neighbours a mile and a half up the road! On the walls behind the bar was a collector of military badges dream. Perhaps two hundred or more, regiments long gone, some from the Indian Army. They stayed with the family who ran the bar, even when it moved premise, well into the 90's. But alas where it is now is a question mark. It was to be exciting and historic times at EU.NT

EU.NT stood for Emergency Unit New Territories and as the name implied was there to deal with all emergencies where the NT divisional police stations needed help. The unit was fully equipped and trained as riot unit; like those at PTC. It was divided into three platoons and a head quarter section. All but Number 3 platoon were composed of men from Pakistan most of them from the Punjab and the North West Provinces, the later in particular famous for its fighting men. I was given No.2

134

platoon which included a few men who had joined before the War. My platoon Sergeant Munamar Gul had been serving when the British surrendered to the Japanese in December 1941. He had been told by his senior officers that as the police were part of the civil power, not military, they should endeavour to continue to serve as police officers under the Japanese. The similar situation of the 'bobbies' on the German occupied Channel Islands comes to mind. Sergeant Gul was an impressive man with his waxed moustache and smart turnout. He would tell me stories of how he went on patrol with Japanese soldiers; although perhaps understandably not much information came out. He and other police officers like him were only doing what they had been told to do by their British officers. All the Pakistani police were welcomed back into the British police force after the war. The same was not true of a number of Indian/Sikh police officers who had been particularly nasty to the populace. There were a number of people who served the Japanese, some understandably of necessity, some willingly, some eagerly and for gain. Some of the Chinese secret societies (the Triads) co-existed with the Japanese and even helped to guard and control the slave workers, foreign prisoners of war and Chinese who extended the Kai Tak Run Way (Successor to the Airport). The last Pakistani men to be recruited from Pakistan was in 1962, some had joined at 18 or less; so there was a wide range of ages in the unit.

I liked the men in my platoon. The Pakistanis were at the NT Depot a self-serving community. They had their own married quarters, where presumably wives lived as you often saw children emerge and go to their school. It seemed Muslim wives never came out of their homes! There was a canteen which kept us supplied with splendid curries/dahl and chapatis, the later made by a deaf Chinese cook who used his armpit as a rolling pin to shape the unleavened bread into shape. The meat for the curries came from animals slaughtered in the Muslim way in the depot. There were always a few cows or goats around on the patches of grass under the supervision of Bill an old Pakistani constable who seemed to be in charge of all things non-police in the depot. Whether it was illegal to slaughter our own beasts I never found out, presumably the animals didn't mind, it was at least being done by people they knew.

Another character at the Depot was '48' a Pakistani corporal who was really in charge of the depot, at least in regard to the armoury, stores, and all things worth anything. The man was always there and when things got hot on the border and we were really under pressure he was indispensable and worth a gong (medal). Our direct boss: the Officer in Charge (OC/EU.NT) was Frank Knight from Dagenham East London.

Frank deserves a paragraph on its own. He was in many respects larger than life. He must have been of Royal blood or at least a 'knight of the realm'. His father, who I recall he said worked at Ford's, must have fallen on hard times. Frank only ate and drank the best. He spent much of his time at the Hilton Hotel, then, with 12 floors, the tallest building in Hong Kong. It was here he belonged to a lunch group which included senior members of Hong Kong society, including a senior Chinese judge. Talk was that once when given a final demand for his Hilton bills he indignantly replied: 'If you keep sending me these bills I will take my not insignificant business elsewhere.' He had the proper voice, no London/home counties accent and dressed the part without ostentation. He was a Chief

Inspector, one of quite a few hundred; there were at last two superintendent ranks and four commissioner ranks above him. Yet, the story was he was known by his friends in Hollywood, Shirley Maclain was one, as THE Chief Inspector of the Hong Kong Police. When things started to hot up and the control room was manned at Frontier HQ Frank would arrive for duty with 'pandora's box' which was an elegant lunch container in which were all the goodies you can imagine from either the Mandarin or the Hilton Hotels. No cheese roll and a bag of crisps for Frank! There was smoked-salmon, dainty puffs, parma ham and perhaps a flask of the best soup. He also appears to have been 'close terms' with Sir David Trench, our Governor at the time. This was demonstrated when my platoon and I were swimming one day in the pool at the Governors Lodge just outside Fanling. We had been told by the boss above Frank, Duncan McNeil, that Mrs. Governor, Lady Trench, a charming lady from the USA had said that we could use the pool. So off we would go. Most of my men had always regarded water was for washing and drinking, thus apart from me, my men's swimmers seemed to have been borrowed! Please recall the girl's gym knickers of your school days: blue with elastic around the thighs. To the lodge we drove, we were met by Lady Trench with a tray of lemonade. Enjoy yourselves she said and into the water we plunged. Ten minutes later a dispatch arrived from the Depot from Frank: 'You must get out of the pool immediately; you have no right to be there'. I noted the message and ignored it. Another ten minutes another dispatch: 'Get out or you will be defaulted '(on a discipline charge). I rang Frank from the Lodge: Piss off say I, we have lady Governor's permission, get out or be charged says he; so got out we did! Back at the Depot red faces! I know she didn't mean for you to be in the pool. Did, Didn't, Did, Didn't, Did.

137

Off to see Duncan McNeil. Cool it Dave, we all know Frank. That was it, Frank as a member of the higher orders, knew that Lady Trench couldn't really have understood that it was us lot in her pool, a decision had to be made for her. But despite his surfeit of bull-shit, I liked Frank. A real character who, as later events on the border would show, had plenty of guts.

# 11. Holding the Line, just...

I have explained how the Emergency Unit New Territories was the unit to deal with serious disturbances in the NT. There were similar EU' s in Kowloon and Hong Kong Island. These had already been called into action because of the incidents stemming from a Industrial dispute at a plastic flower factory in San Po Kong, Kowloon in May 1967. A few days later a Hong Kong Island mob had attacked Government buildings 'looting' and setting fires. The infamous Peter Godber, then to command very bravely and ably the Police Tactical Unit, lead his men as they were violently attacked in Garden Road by a mob intent on damaging Government House. Alas he was later to fall from grace when in 1974 he was arrested by the new ICAC. Hong Kong's Communists, in order to show solidarity with their Maoist brothers across the border, who were into their second year of Mao's cultural Revolution, thought it necessary to side with the workers and confront the (filthy) Hong Kong British Colonialist. It seemed to many of us the dispute was just an excuse to take the British on and let them know their days were numbered and in view of Chairman Mao's thoughts those days were soon. In fact the trouble was to escalate especially after some serious incidents at Sha Tau Kok, which I as a EU.NT Platoon Commander was engaged to deal with.

The 1967/68 disturbances would run from May 1967 to January 1968. During that time 10 policemen would be killed and 212 injured, 5 killed and 11 injured during an incident at

Sha Tau Kok on the 8th July, 1967.There would be a total of 51 people killed, 15 from bombs that were planted in public areas. These including a seven year old girl and her two year old brother killed by a bomb wrapped as a gift outside their residence. And over 1100 were injured, 340 by bombs.

The incidents at Sha Tau Kok were spread over two months, June to July although there were signs of protests earlier in the village after China had made protests in May to the Charge' d Affairs for the Hong Kong British to stop their fascist oppression. These were in the form of banners and loud denouncements screamed out accompanied with revolutionary music from loudspeakers positioned on buildings in Chung Ying Street. The area, always tense was even more so and the PLA soldiers at their posts the other side loomed larger. Our Police boss of Frontier Division, a truly lovely man from the South of Ireland Mathew O'Sullivan, affectionately know by all as "O" Suk (in Chinese uncle "O") had worked in special branch and had a good feel of things just the other side of the border. EU.NT were to be on alert, with one of the three platoons on immediate call: tooled up and ready to go.

In the event my platoon was not involved with the border and STK until Saturday the 10th June. We had been sent to other places before then and had performed road blocks in the south in Tai Po and Tsuen Wan. But things were hotting up and there was intelligence that demonstrations in support of the Hong Kong Patriots involving people from our side of the border and the other side would take place in the STK village. The protesters would be from those in the area covered by the STK Rural Committee joined by their brothers and sisters from the other side of the border.

The STK Rural Committee included all those villages within the closed area and those to the east across Starling Inlet. I knew the area as the STK Peninsular. An area remote and accessed then only by walking paths or by sea on a police launch. Most of these villages looked north onto Mirs Bay and the inhabited Islands of Kat O and Ap Chau, the former at one time with its own secondary school. There were also a number of villages included which ran along the STK Road down to the boundary with Fanling. All these villages were predominantly occupied by Hakka people. Traditionally they came down from Northern China to settle here around the 16th century. They were forced to occupy land that was not used by the more indigenous Cantonese speaking people. Thus the villages were often in the hills or along the less fertile or inaccessible parts. They wore distinctive dress, the women in particular and spoke their own language. Their woman were fiercely independent and had refused, unlike most of their Chinese sisters to have their feet bound. They were tough, hard working, patriotic people. From the late 1930's these Hakka men from the British side and the Chinese side had formed an anti-Japanese Communist guerrilla group known in English as the East River Column. The name, of course, is taken from the river the runs east to west into the Pearl River about 50 miles north of the border. These tough men fought long and hard against the Japanese. Included in their number was a Eurasian boy called Alexander Lew.

He had joined them as a young teenager in around 1938. And still had the scars on his shoulder from carrying a bren gun when I worked for him as second in charge of Tai Po Police Station in 1968. His history would make a marvellous movie. A boy guerrilla who joined because he thought he was joining a

141

bandit gang to make money; later came to HK joined the HK Defence Force in time to fight the Japanese again and be made a prisoner of war; escaped from the Sham Shui Po Prison camp; made his way across the NT to be helped by the East River Column; ended up in Chung King with the British Army Aid Group; was sent to join General Bill Slim's army and the Chindits fighting in Burma; after the war he was clearing mines in Vietnam; and eventually ended up in the HK Police as Sub Divisional Inspector (SDI) with me at the largely Hakka market town of Tai Po. I mention here his dad was a local Hakka seaman who had married a cockney lady from London. I regarded him as the salt of the earth. I learnt much from him especially why there had been so many from the Hakka villages who were supporting the communists.

The men of the East River Column had assisted Alec to escape and had lead him to guides who would eventually get him to Chung King. They had done so with a number of British soldiers and the occasional US Airmen who had been shot down over the Kowloon hills. From what I have learnt from Alec and my own readings of the memoirs of soldiers who had escaped, you were not safe from capture by the Japanese until you were clear of the punti (Cantonese) villagers north of the Kowloon Hills. These folk were likely to inform on you or turn you in. You must then to hide and seek help from the Hakka villages further North.

Alas, after the war despite some recognition in its immediate aftermath, the bamboo curtain and the Korean War made any body associated with the Chinese Communists taboo, but understand that did not prevent some of the younger members of the column and in particular their sons from the NT villagers joining the Hong Kong Police. Many of these were very fine officers who stood loyal throughout the disturbances. There must have been divided loyalties amongst the local Hakka community. It must be appreciated why there was support for the Hong Kong patriots. The protesters were patriotically supporting China against the British, or at least they thought they were. The New Territories had only been part of Hong Kong for at the time only 69 years!

As a post script to my reference to the East Column above I would recommend to those interested in the history of Hong Kong during World War Two to look at "East River Column" by Chan Sui-jeung published by the Hong Kong Univerity Press 2009. It certainly touched my heart and saddened me that later and for so long its members didn't receive the recognition and honour that was due to them.

To return to my involvement with the really nasty incidents at the STK village and the EU.NT. I have mentioned two dates: 10th June and the 8th July. There was another date: the 24th June.

The 24th and 8th dates I have confirmed from records and reports. The 10th date I do from memory. All dates I recall were on Saturday and were two weeks apart. On each day we were at the village fully tooled up, armed and in full riot kit. That meant that the platoon was divided into four sections of 8 men each and a head quarter section comprised of drivers, vehicle guards, a banner carrier and orderly, the platoon Sergeant and the Commander an Inspector. The front rank or section would carry riot shields and long batons (the baton section) the next section would have tear gas firing weapons either in the form of long federal gas guns or in the form of shorter gas pistols (the gas section), the third section would be armed with Greener shotguns and carbines (the arms section) and lastly the fourth section would be armed with standard police revolvers plus riot shields, these shields were made of rattan. Unlike those we carried in Africa which were made of arrow stopping fireproof steel... The banners carried by the Orderly were of three types. In English and Chinese: 1st warning Disperse or we use force, 2nd Disperse or we use gas and 3rd Disperse or we open fire. The warning was given over a loud hailer with an attachment to your gas mask. Which hopefully you could deliver even with your gas mask on.

As I have indicated I have no record as to whether the above 10th of June date is correct. I do know my Platoon together with the second Pakistani platoon under my colleague and fellow ex NRP officer Gordon Baker was involved on three occasions with violent confrontation at the village. On the first occasion, the 10th June, the Unit were positioned in the village one platoon lined up just in front of the Police Post facing the Chung Ying St barrier, with the other two inside the police post. It was there to keep the mob, which had earlier been pushed back into the Chinese side from emerging back again. The platoons were to take it in turns each to line up at the ready. There were rocks thrown from the other side as well as bottles and rocks launched from slings. Things were tense and on one occasion my boss in the Post told me to get my men out of the police post to relieve the Chinese platoon who were under pressure. I recall that apart from some cuts to our legs from missiles the day finished without major incident. I have no recollection if we did have cause to use gas on that occasion. The Unit returned to its base at the Fanling Depot, where we withdrew to the Depot Officers Mess for a few beers and talk with brother officers as to events on the Frontier that day.

I recall that the 24th June was the day, the leftists as we called them, called a general strike. There were only a few buses still running and those had wire screens on the front windows to protect the drivers who were for the most part from the Taiwan (Republic of China) supported non-communist unions. Many in the civil service were on strike, including the PWD mechanics who serviced our own police vehicles. There was even a problem in regards to staff in Police canteens. Hong Kong ever resilient started to see hundreds of privately owned vans (the 'parents' of the modern Public Light Buses) take to the streets to augment the few buses of KMB and CMB. The Police Force started a whole new branch in the form of Police Officer cooks. It was not as sophisticated as the Royal Army Catering Corp, but was a start in keeping the troops fed.

On the 24th June, we were in the STK village again. As before villagers from the closed areas on both sides of the border and some further away came to show their anger at the Hong Kong British and their running yellow dogs. Missiles were hurled at the Police Post. A large mob armed with home made weapons of various types assembled just across the border and then tried to push their way over Chung Ying Street into the open area at the junction of the Border Road and the STK Main Road. My Platoon were formed up in our riot formation just in front of the Post. We displayed the warning banners that force and gas would be used. The missiles in the form of rocks were coming so fast and heavy that I ordered up No 4 rank so we had two rows of shields to cover behind. From behind these No 2 section would fire tear gas. Gas masks would be fitted as some

145

of the tear gas wafted back to us. I recall the mob made several attempts to surge through the barrier to attack us and the Police Post. I say barrier; there was a mills barrier just at the end of Chung Ying Street as in ran into the end of the STK Main. The Platoon were steady and the platoon orderly with the banners and his carbine did an especially good job protecting me and watching the roofs the other side for signs of any armed men. Fish bombs (dynamite used by fisherman for the lazy way of fishing) were being thrown although they had caused no real casualties apart from the odd numb foot or two if one went off too near. The stone throwing had, however caused injuries to predominantly the lower legs. Our two ranks of shields saved us serious harm to the upper body.

The Peoples Liberation Soldiers were not visible although our tear gas did go over onto their side. We stood there for quite a while until relieved by our other platoon although I recall our efforts had dampened the ardour of the mob.

We were back at the Fanling Depot by night sweaty, tired and smelling of tear gas. A few jars in the mess and then dinner. Various publications concerning events at STK that Saturday mention there was an armed attack on the Police Post. Weapons and fish bombs there were, but the really deadly armed assault on the Police and Post took place a fortnight later on **Saturday the 8th July, 1967.** When 5 policemen were killed and 11 wounded.

The company fell in early that morning the 8th July, 1967. We were in hard order, helmets, weapons and gas grenades shells and rounds for our pistols and guns. Our Company

146

commander was Duncan McNeil a sensible, steady man who had done military service, who we all liked. In normal times he had a senior administration job at the Depot. We were briefed to expect trouble; and some days before, it may have been the previous Saturday a PLA officer had been seen just the other side looking at our positions and seemingly to give directions. At that time in Maoist China the PLA all wore the same Khaki uniform, made from rough but sturdy cloth with no badges of rank. The only way we knew he was a senior officer was because he wore a much nicer tailor made 'baggy" uniform made from anything but rough cloth and was sheltered from the sun by a younger soldier more humbly dressed holding an umbrella.

The Company took up positions: 1 and 2 Platoon, all Pakistani men, in the police post itself, and 3 Platoon, all Chinese fellas, at the Rural Committee office 600 yards back along the STK Road. In the post the men were distributed around, some on the first floor and the rest on the ground floor around the different rooms. It helps to describe the layout of the police post. It had been built in the 50's and was a stone structure, square with two storeys. The first floor was built as an observation post to watch activities at the barrier and the area behind in Chung Ying Street. It also gave a view of the Border road going off to the west and with buildings on ours' and theirs' side. It was generally like all the police posts along the border although the hill posts were smaller. These would have Corporal and 7 PCs. The STK post being also the reporting centre for the village and nearby villages was larger. In normal times there would be a sergeant OC village, a corporal in the post with other officers both in and outside on patrol. It thus had more police officers and had more space for sleeping and

147

feeding. On top of the post there was a searchlight, like all the posts. The first floor and some places on the ground floor had gun or viewing ports, these were usually closed with a thick steel shutters. All around the post there would be 'attack on post' positions marked with a number and a weapon which was to be handled by the officer at that post. An attack was to be sounded by the banging of a gong and an electric bell.

Well it happened! There was a really nasty mob. Loud speakers from the other side shouted abuse: taunting the police and telling the policemen there were the running dogs of the Imperialists and would soon meet their deserts; not ice cream sundaes! Rocks like swarms of locusts were hurled across at the post. A screaming mob approached the post. Duncan ordered the Attack on Station alarm to be sounded: the gong was struck and the Frontier Control was notified by radio. A man carrying a satchel placed it at the gate of the perimeter fence; about 20 feet from the door of the post. It was obviously a bomb. Duncan McNeil, fortunate in being left handed, was able to aim his carbine at the man through one of the gun ports. As daft as this may seem, a right handed man would have had great difficulty in trying to get a shot off. The man was hit and was dragged away. There was a lull. Duncan's round and some tear gas rounds caused the mob to keep their distance. The Corporal at the Pak Kung Au police post up on the mountain above the Border road reported from his radio troop movements moving up to the border below his post and further towards the STK village. He ordered his men into the attack on post positions. We were in for something. Duncan ordered that the post Bren gun be readied. It and a box of magazines were positioned on the first floor behind one of the gun ports. I lay on the floor looking along the barrel, one of the

PCs, he was the Force Hockey goal keeper was next to me ready to help with the rounds. We waited for a long time, the mob was still there, the hate messages still screaming through the loud speakers and there were still missiles or fish bombs being thrown in our direction. Duncan called me down to the ground floor for a situation report with Gordon Baker. I forget how long we were there or if we had a cup of tea or not, in any event suddenly there was a rattle of machine gun fire. It was in a number of short bursts. There were rounds ricocheting around the walls inside the first floor of the posts. We certainly were in for it. I rushed up the steel ladder to the first floor, The men were trying to dodge the bullets by lying low and against the wall. The Hockey goal keeper had been shot right in the head. He was dead. Another had been hit but was still alive but bleeding profusely. He was cared for on the ground floor and every effort made to stop the bleeding. Our radio and telephone communication had been shot out by the machine gun fire.

I recall that our only contact then with outside was by landline. We waited, I remember the platoon sergeant, it was not my Munama Gul, one of the hockey players, saying to me when I was on the Bren gun: 'Sahib we must not open fire until their military men come.' There was more shooting. Later we learnt that a machine gun, it must have been the one aimed at us and down the STK Road, had open fire on a PTU Company that had advanced along down the STK Road to push back the mob attacking the Post and everything else Government. (There was a clinic and a Post Office). Three of the Chinese policemen in the Company had been killed and 11 wounded, some seriously.

We also learnt later that soldiers from the other side had brought a machine gun into HK. They had come well in to HK through our villages to just below the STK Main Police Station, which I would estimate to be over a mile and a half from the border fence. This machine gun also opened fire. I understand there were casualties from this gun as well as the one pointing directly south along the STK Road.

We were waiting for a Military assault on the Post. The noise of gunfire went on for some time. I recall I fired my pistol at a group of the mob who were crouching in a drain just a few yards from the Post who seemed ready to rush.

Clearly we needed help from the British Army. Duncan McNeil got onto Frontier Control on the remaining landline, to where a joint Military/ Police Command Post had been set up. He said we needed the help of the Army.

It is important to know that the British Army had never been permitted, at least in uniform, to come into the closed area. Visiting army officers would have to wear their civilian clothes before coming on tours of the border. There were two military Ops (Observation Posts) high in the hills one overlooking China to the North East and the other to the North West, but outside the closed area. They were thus able to see much of what was going on.

We were told to hang on, authorization would be sought to bring the army into the closed area and help defend the post. Assistant Commissioner J.B. Lees, a gentleman, the New Territories Police Commander was in the Command Post, I understand together with the Brigadier commanding the 48th

Brigade of Gurkhas. He told us things were moving and to remain 'calm'. He told us to ensure that we take down the union jack, which flew in front of the Post, when we had to leave. Oh yes in front of the Post! Echoes of the US marines at Iwo Jima!

The Governor Sir David Trench, another good man, was not in Hong Kong and Police Commissioner E. Tyrer had apparently lost his bottle and was either relieved of his command or sent to the UK for urgent talks, his deputy Ted Eates took over command. Ted was an old colonial policeman who had seen service in Africa. Apparently the decision to move troops in needed the OK of The Prime Minister, no less than Harold Wilson. He must have been in the Pub or somewhere, because it was most of the day before we were told they were on their way.

Things were quieter by the afternoon apart from the sounds of single shots, some of which hit the post and some fish bombs being hurled at us. Later in the afternoon things seemed to hot up with the sound of gunfire: short bursts.

We realised that if we were going to be relieved we had to go out by way of the rear of the Post. Here we would be shielded from the machine and any other guns that were positioned just north of us on the buildings opposite. There was no suitable and safe gate at the rear of the Post, we therefore started, with kicks and shovels, from the post emergency equipment, to make a hole in the rear wall. This we did, then settled down and waited.

Eventually a head popped in through the hole. A very posh army officer voice said:    'Police, Gurkhas!'. It was the

Commander Officer of the 1/10th Gurkha's. He emerged carrying no weapon but carrying a map case. A brown face then emerged, that of his Orderly carrying his SLR. (self-loading rifle) I recall he was grinning. Army were now in charge and what a professional lot they were. We got our injured and two murdered colleagues ready. As ordered we collected all the post arms and ammunition and proceeded to leave the Post in groups in an orderly 'retreat'.

I later learnt that the OC EU.NT Frank Knight had tried to get down to the village in a police armoured car. I mention these were nothing like those in the military. They appeared to belong to the 1930's. They had no fixed weapon but had firing ports. He did not get as far as the post, but I understand did stalwart work. Dear old Frank may have been full of a lot of bull shit, but he had plenty of guts.

There was another armoured car from the Life Guards. This came in later and came under machine fire as it provided cover for the Gurkha's who were digging in just behind the village. The young officer in command got a medal for his action!

Back to the Depot. No. 48., the Pakistani Barrack Corporal; who ran the stores (maybe much else as well) was there to see every thing secured. A marvellous chap; I don't know if he was ever properly recognised. The men went off to mourn the deaths of their two brothers. We returned to the mess to wash and changed. I was covered in blood it was all over my helmet, shirt and shorts. It had come from the injured men although later in the shower I saw I had a few cuts. Our mess amah, a sweet lady looked quite terrified, but the Army had things under control. I understand the whole border had been covered with arcs of fire from machine guns. The Royal Artillery had their guns placed in positions to counter – if necessary – an armed attack on the Border.

After a night where I got little sleep – I kept hearing the noise of gunfire – we were debriefed by Army Intelligence. We described how we had heard and experienced the gunfire. In particular the gunfire that came from China which came down the STK Road or from the gun that was taken into our side through the villages.

We told the Finko (Field Intelligence) officers that the firing at us had been in short bursts, clearly well aimed. They had aimed at the post gun ports, knocking the steel covers away and injuring the officers laying behind them. They must have seen the barrels of our guns showing through the openings. Their view was the men behind these weapons were not part time village militia ('Man Bing') but regular soldiers from the PLA. This was evidenced by their short and well directed fire. The 'Man Bing' did not get much training with machine guns and their firing would have been more erratic.

As events proceeded the official explanation for the incident was that it was militia acting on their own initiative with no involvement of the PLA. Also throughout the incident the Gurkhas had kept their cool and despite being what must have been at times heavy and regular fire did not open fire in response at all. Oh yes! Pull the other one!

The two EU Platoons were given 3 days leave and off I went to Tsim Sha Tsui to see my mate Bob Brooks for a few jars in Joe's Bar in Cameron Road and then a decent kip at the Park

Hotel at the end of that road. Joe and his Bar and his customers could be the subject of a book in its self, but perhaps for later pages.

Back to work and stand by duties at the Fanling Depot ready to be called out. It was more securely guarded now and the Platoons would practice 'attack on depot'. All Stations and Units in the Force had positions around their perimeters where officers were to take post with the assigned weapon. An alarm would ring; I suppose not unlike the turnout call at a fire station.

I was further involved with an incident at the Sheung Shui when we raided a rich dealers shop which was to be searched and arrests made. The occupants had barricaded themselves in with rice bags and missiles were thrown at us. Tear gas was used and I went in with my gas mask on to remove the barrier. I was hit by glass and sustained an injury to the right knee. I was treated by a really overworked doctor at the local Government clinic who used 8 to 10 stitches to close the wound. I must have been another man then, as eager to get back to my men, the good doctor sewed me up without anaesthetic.

I forget what happened to those in the shop. Although in my memory there is something which said that those inside were not really bad people and there was young lady inside who must have been terrified. Mao and his Cultural Revolution sure did test and divide loyalties of our people. Getting them to show feelings, which were not really theirs; the faces of the mobs screaming with hatred and the vitriol from their mouths, many sweet girls and nice boys who not long before had been going to school, villagers who before had been on good terms with the local police. There was a Sergeant at STK Main Station who was from a village not more than 2 miles down the Road to Fanling. He could not return to his village. There were other Hakka policemen who likewise were under threats if they dared come home.

Things were hotting up. I lose track of dates but July through to October were dangerous times on the border. There was a serious incident at Man Kam To. Which is the place on the border where goods: vegetables, meat etc. is pushed across a wide pedestrian bridge into HK by coolies (probably politically incorrect to use that word now) on wooden carts. The goods were then loaded onto lorries belonging to the Man Luen Company, a company perhaps obviously with communist connections. They were then driven away down the road and out of the closed area towards Sheung Shui. The area where the loading took place was called the lairage area. Overlooking this, but not on really elevated ground, was the police post. It was bigger than the hill posts and about the same size as the STK village post. In this incident the coolies and others from China threatened the post and those inside: the Assistant Divisional Superintendent (ADS) Frontier Bill Paton, Trevour Bedford from the District Office and Jim Main a border policeman and friend from PTS, with demands. I have always believed it was during this occasion that Frank Knight again got involved, this time whilst remonstrating with the mob there he was pushed across the bridge into China. I may be corrected if I am wrong. I have checked records and found that Frank was abducted on the 14th October. He escaped later from detention some miles from the Frontier and made his way to the border fence which he climbed back over on the 26th November, thus he was

155

nearly 6 weeks away. A big trencher man was Frank who had lost significant pounds in China. He was certainly a man with a lot of guts not all from his life style. When certain wags joked in the Frontier mess that Frank had so pissed off his captors that they let him go Matthew O'Sullivan quite angrily said that is not the truth: 'Frank was a brave man'!

I was not involved with the Man Kam To incident apart from providing back up with my platoon south down the Man Kam To road. I was however in the incident when tens of thousands of Red Guards (Mao's young storm troopers full of love and compassion!) came to the border. They assembled at Sam Chung (Shenzhen), then a small town/ large village, the biggest building a three-storey customs post. They were screaming their abuse and demands as they faced the Lo Wu Bridge they then marched along their Border Road. They had poles, sticks and banners describing the atrocities of the Hong Kong British. Their apparent intent was to cross over the Lo Wu Bridge and join their compatriots suffering under the heals of the fascist British. We had been forewarned what was coming. EU/NT were deployed about a mile back on the road leading to Lo Wu. Which is situated in the Lo Wu Gap, between two hills. We were to confront the mob, using minimum force(!) if it got across the bridge and was on the road bent on advancing further into Hong Kong. I understood the Gurkhas were in position each side of the gap to use appropriate force if necessary. The screaming mob did not cross the bridge. The soldiers of the PLA with fixed bayonets prevented them crossing. They thus were forced to turn and marched along the Border road, their number created a procession 2 miles long, I understand as far as Law Fong, which is opposite Ta Kwu Ling Police Station and way beyond. There must have been 50,000 plus. Work it out yourself: a procession 2 miles long with 6 to 8 persons abreast, they were a frightening force. What would have happened if the PLA had allowed them to cross?

There was a British fellow in charge of Immigration Department there at Lo Wu a Bob Adair, who would sometimes drink with us at the Fanling Mess and sometimes the Better 'Ole. Wah he said it was touch and go! But it seemed there were still saner minds in China and that Premier Zhou En Lai still had control of the army in the south here. Again there were stories that troops from the North, non-Cantonese speakers had come down to bring some order the other side.

The disturbances continued in HK with violence directed at the police and the citizens of Hong Kong. Largely in the form of placing bombs fake or genuine in public places and killing or planning to kill policemen. These were apparently orchestrated by the All Circles Anti-Persecution Struggle Committee lead by Mr Yeung Kwong. But to be fair their involvement in anything violent has been denied and was the work of elements working without direction. Mr Yeung Kwong was awarded the Grand Bahemia medal by the Chief Executive Mr Tung Chi Wah. A Knighthood in UK reckoning. Now 46 years later I look back at Mr Yeung and some of his followers, like the Brothers Yeung. The Yeungs were young men who were, perhaps like me in my youth in the CND (Campaign for Nuclear Disarmament), caught up with patriot fervour. They were doing what they thought Chairman Mao and the leftists wanted: to bring down the Hong Kong British. The Yeung brothers went on to be prominent members of Government, now serving either in the Legislative or Executive Councils: no higher honours.

But forgive me if I feel a little resentment touched with a modicum of anger when I wonder how their actions, together with thousands of others here and just across the border nearly finished the Hong Kong that we love. It was touch and go at one stage. We could have ended up like Maoist China at the time: in chaos, violence and disorder. The thousands of red guards on that day described above; the bombing campaign and terror that lasted most of 1967 and beyond; the fleeing of investment and people from Hong Kong. It was clear much depended on the nerve of the Governor and the loyalty and determination of the Hong Kong Police. Am I wrong to think that the Yeungs and the others in the "struggle" should be grateful that we all stood firm? That is until Premier Zhou tried, at some risk to himself from the gang of four, to call a halt to what was killing, finishing this Pearl in the Orient.

With deference to those who lead the "struggle" rather than be disgruntled about our present Government not rewarding you as Yeung Kwong was so rewarded, you should be grateful to the old Hong Kong British Government for ensuring you have the life you have in Hong Kong today.

I was posted out of EU/NT back to my old division: Yuen Long. This time I went to Tai Po, as described before, a mainly Hakka market down on the railway line. I was to be the ASDI (Assistant Sub Divisional Inspector) under Alec Lew. Duties here were relatively normal. There were demonstrations, bombs fake and real but none of the tension of the Border. One day a mob came up the hill to the Station. It was one of the first built in the NT and went back to the time of the take over of the New Territories in 1897. I was not there but it was reported that Alec chased them down the hill himself waving a sterling sub machine gun over his head. He knew a lot of the mob and they knew him. No need for a lot of riot police, tear gas etcetera. I patrolled the town routinely moving obstructions, arresting hawkers and doing the occasional gambling or DD raid. Alec left me to myself. Only two incidents come to mind: a bomb was found a few feet outside the communist products shop in the town, which was festooned with pictures and cartoons of the fascist actions against the Hong Kong patriots. 'Keep away compatriots, welcome white skin pigs and yellow skinned running dogs.' I called the bomb disposal, the army, usually Royal Engineers (RE) would respond. They were not usually trained bomb disposal officers so would put a charge on the bomb real or fake and blow it up. The Force had only two experts themselves. They were really ballistics officers. Fred Ewins and Bomber Hill as he became known. They did a marvellous job but were really stretched. Fred was getting on well over 60. He had been in the Shanghai Police. Mr Hill lost his hand handling a device. It seemed to be a tactic of the strugglers (the enemy) to place many fake bombs, so many in the early days that some police men who responded would look at it and then pull it away. A European senior Inspector in the Traffic Branch so acted to clear a bomb, which looked like a fake, from the tramlines on Hong Kong Island. The road traffic was building up and horns were sounding. He was blown to bits.

To get back to the Communist Store. The RE decided it would be 'safer' for the public to blow the 'bomb' up just inside the store. It seems that's where it came from! We made sure no one was near the bomb and it was so exploded. Most of the bang

159

came from the RE charge. The damage to the store was fortunately 'moderate'.

Another incident was a report of a device real or fake on the railway line just near Tai Po Kau Railway Station. I responded and saw a package wrapped in white paper with the usual Chinese characters: Keep away compatriots etc. It looked like others we had seen: a home made device either a fake or one made for a number of fireworks. Then you could still buy them in HK. They were prohibited after 1967, to the joy of the Hospital and Ambulance services.

I lay on the railway line and hurled rocks at the device yards away. I with my rocks, one by one, knocked the package way off the line. Once off the line I pounded it with rocks. It didn't go off. So sod it! I threw it away; it contained newspapers. There was a cheer from all those on the trains: hero or silly boy! That was before the Traffic Inspector was killed.

I now recall I cleared a similar obstruction on the road to Plover Cove (Tai Mei Duk) in the same way, this was outside a village which clearly evidenced which side it was on by the profusion of 5 star red flags.

I was with Alec for about four or five months and was then promoted to be SDI/Plover Cove. A small Station that was built to police the building of the new Plover Cove Dam. We got much of our water from China but as events showed someone over there could show their displeasure at Hong Kong and its authorities by turning off the supply. This they did during the disturbances. Thus we needed a better home supply. I forget when they started to build the Dam. It must have been started around 1962-63 and some work was still going on when I went there at the end of 67 beginning of 68. I had one Sergeant two or three Corporals and about 25 men; maybe less. We were more in the way of watchman to keep an eye on the dam, especially because of the disturbances. We did patrols around the dam and its walls and also amongst the villages along the Tai Me Duk Road. The Pak Sin Mountain range loomed above us which still had a few thinly populated villages. If a strenuous walk was required it was a good excuse to walk the range and show the flag. I was only at the Station a few months when it was decided to close it. It soon after became a base for the Village Patrol Unit; a body of very fine, largely Hakka men who would patrol the outlying villages. In those days the roads were fewer and patrols over the hills often required 2 to 3 days out.

My command at Plover Cove was short. The bosses decided to mothball the sub-divisional station and transfer responsibility to Tai Po. I was transferred still within the Yuen Long Division but right to its western end: to Lau Fau Shan. I was the SDI, a real command with plenty of responsibility.

But before I go to the next Chapter may I mention that my 6 or so months at Tai Po and Plover Cover I spent in single men's quarters just of the Tai Po Road. It was a two storey house, four men sharing, one of whom was a force character called Charley Fisher. The living room of the quarters was totally occupied by a model train set; engines and rolling stock galore. I hope to mention much about Dear Charley as I go along.

# 12. Rising Through the Ranks

Things were still tense in 1968 in the Northern New Territories. At Kam Tin a PC on patrol from Pat Heung Police Station, also in Yuen Long Division, had been shot dead by a hired assassin from China. A young officer barely in his 20's who was taking a non-regulation break at a well liked won-ton noodle shop in the village. Our Intelligence was the same assassin had orders to kill Alastair McNiven, the Divisional Superintendent, as he drove to work over the Lam Chuen Valley. The assassin was arrested by a team under a really great CID man Brian Gravener, like many, an indispensable officer who they couldn't promote. He had been accompanied by my dear friend and best man at my later wedding Steve Stephenson, another old comrade from the NRP.

A transfer as the Sub Divisional Inspector/Lau Fau Shan (SDI/LFS) meant I was the Officer Commanding a rural border station high on a hill overlooking Deep Bay on the very west of the New Territories. Across the Bay was the then small Chinese town of She Kou. Today it is a suburb of the City of Shen Zheng with a population approaching Hong Kong. Around most of the Bay were oyster beds. These were farmed by people from both sides of the border and had been cultivated long before the British took the New Territories. The ownership was complicated, something I never understood, which needed a degree in the customs, history and culture of the western New Territories to fathom. Apparently ownership was cross border and rested with 'Tongs'? Since the communist take over in China and the proscribing of private ownership, complications and disputes had arose. The oysters were big business both for eating and the making of sauce. There were a number of Restaurants in the Lau Fau Shan village, just below the Station where I would frequent to partake of the delicious molluscs. I would only eat them fried, done in batter. To eat otherwise risked mercury, cadmium and other delights, from the pristine waters of the Bay, weighing the digestion down.

*Me as the SDI/LFS, my dog Jomo, the station detective constable, a patrol corporal and two police constables. Behind are the oyster beds*

*Me at the front gate.*

My sub-division stretch northeast along the coast to Tsim Bei Tsu (TBT) police post, which guarded the entrance to the Sum Chun river. The river marks the border, and then southwest to just beyond Nim Wan (NW) police post. The distance between the posts was about 12 kilometres. Going inland it ran 3 kilometres parallel to the coast as far down as Nim Wan where it turned to the coast. It thus was approximately a diagonal rectangle.

There were a number of villages along the coast. South were Ha Pak Nai and Sheung Pak Nai and North was Sha Kiu. These villages and Lau Fau Shan were used by the oyster workers who would scoot across the mud flats housing the beds on wooden boards. Goodness! Their feet must have been like leather what with the sharp shells beneath them. Further inland were the prominent villages of Mong Tseng and Ha Tsuen with their rice paddies. There was also Tin Shui Wai and its fish ponds, and just salt marsh. There were some oyster beds just to the east of the Tsim Bei Tsui police post. Today Tin Shi Wai is a city of over 250 thousand people!

*Me in the station motorcycle side-car with Jomo.*

There was also part of a British Army Firing range.

Then the use of the land for container parking had not yet started and the area had not become environmentally unfriendly. It was still rural green. Oyster shells were all over the place and there was a business turning them into lime. Ducks were everywhere as my dog Jomo was to find out.

I forget now from whom I took over the Station. If he reads this I am sure he will remind me. It was a nice Station; two storeys with my quarters adjacent to it. I was the only officer, although there was another Inspector's sleeping quarter. The report room, my office, the cells and the armoury were on the ground floor and the other ranks barrack room was up stairs. There was a search light on a tower outside. A perimeter chain link fence with barbed wire enclosed everything, including a nice sitting out area for me and any guests. A glass of beer to look over the bay.

I must have had about 8 NCOs and 80 PCs plus 4 driver PCs. There was also a CID section with one Detective Constable. These were to cover the main LFS Station, the Nim Wan Post and the beats and patrols. The Post at Tsim Bei Tsui was manned by marine police complete with their, then naval type, uniforms and a special unusual launch. This was launch 18 which was armour plated and powered by a paddle wheel. It must have belonged to the 20"s or before. The armour plating was so thick it could take heavy calibre fire but was so slow it would take the best part of the day getting to Hong Kong. I understand maximum speed was less than 4 knots. It was to patrol the Shum Chung river, so perhaps the armour plating was not a bad idea, especially as things had been on the border for the most of the last year.

So not a bad command! I was very pleased. Also I had within the last few months been advanced in rank to full inspector. Then there was the Yuen Long Officers Mess to visit, about 6 kilometres down the road. There was Shek Kong Camp with the 48 Brigade and the army cinema. In the Sek Kong village next door were a few tatty bars. I was going to enjoy the next 9 or so months before I went on my first leave at the end of Autumn 1968.

Our duties at LFS were to watch the Chinese side and guard the coast from the main station and the NW Post. We were also to maintain a presence in the LFS village and to patrol the villages and the Coast road. Launch 18 when it was operating stayed at the Shum Chun River by the TBT Post. There was rarely a regular Marine launch in the Bay so it was important our duties were particularly alert to landings by illegal immigrants or visitors.

I would regularly hike down the Coast road to Nim Wan Post at different times of the 24 hour clock. The duties at the Post had to be tested on their weapon handling and map reading ability and their observation log checked regularly. Sometimes I would join the men for their meal. There were plenty of good walks: over the hills via Nim Wan to Lung Kwu Tan in Castle Peak's Sub Division or the other way via Mong Tseng ,Tin Shui Wai and Wang Chau to Yuen Long. A stiff hike deserved a cold beer at the Yuen Long Mess and a chat with the boss: Superintendent Alastair MacNiven and officers from around the Division. Alastair was one of the most popular bosses I ever worked for. A Scot who certainly liked his San Miguel beer. Alas he is no more!

Two dramatic events happened on my watch at LFS...

I was woken early one morning by the Duty Officer to watch what was happening in Deep Bay. I was amazed to see a Chinese naval type vessel towing a number of 'our' oyster sampans back across the bay towards Shekou. It is over 45 years ago now, but I recall there were at least 8 sampans. I reported immediately to NT Pol/Mil control and got the Bren gun ready. The NT Police Commander Eric Rose (nickname 'Spadeface') not an unpleasant man, soon got on to me and asked if I could stop the Chinese vessel using the Bren gun. I advised him it would not be a good idea. The vessel was armed, 2 plus kilometres off and our sampans were occupied. It was too risky. Looking back it would have been foolhardy not fainthearted to have opened up with the Bren.

Months later we learnt that some of the abducted oystermen had been executed, including the father of one of my police constables. It concerned oysters and the cultural revolution.
There was still chaos going on in China as flashes in the sky evidenced: Artillery from fighting between various factions of the military.

The other event occurred one evening when I was called back from the Yuen Long Mess. It had been a late dinner. The NCO on duty advised me that there had been reports of Man Bing (Chinese Militia) in side our Sha Kiu Village. As mentioned above this was primarily an oyster workers village. I was not now a rookie border cop and knew what the militia could do. I took a carbine from the armoury and took a station reserve PC, also so armed, in the station Landrover up to the village. We parked some way away and entered surreptitiously. We hid and listen. It was total silence. No sound, no movement, no lights. I then decided to make a racket and banged the door of a wooden building I knew the oystermen used for meetings. I kicked it open; no one inside. We patrolled around the village. There was no sign of any one awake and about. If any Man Bing (Militia) had come they had gone and despite our noise and shouts of 'Police'! No one responded to make a complaint or report. We returned to the LFS Station.

Only a few weeks ago (today is the 2nd May, 2013) I was in contact with John Hazleden who took over from when I went on leave. He remembers intelligence reports which spoke of the intention of the Man Bing opposite to abduct the SDI/LFS. If it was me they would have had a job. I would have sunk their boat: 220 pounds of me!

It was a good posting and I was reluctant go – at the end of my tour – on leave to the UK. I had an interesting trip planned but before I move on I feel I should mention dog Jomo again. He was like many Dobermans: mad. A good guard dog who I would let lose at night to run between the two perimeter fences, clearly alerting any sleepy station to any intruder. He would often accompany me on patrol and was known by the population. But sadly he would get bored with his guard duties and get out from under the fence and go down the LFS village to chase ducks and munch a few. Their 'owners' would come up the station the next morning and demand – rightly – compensation, which I was to hand out. It was amazing how valuable some of these ducks were, thoroughbreds! Oh well it was important to keep every one happy. Jomo had to have his freedom restricted with a stronger chain. When I left I handed him over to the Police Dog Unit at Ping Shan, just down the road from. I was to retrieve him on my return from leave. Which I did. The OC one Senior Inspector Orsler advised me: 'Sorry Blob he ran away!' 'Blob' was one of my nicknames, it must have been down to my attractive but round figure!

I proceeded on my long vacation leave to England via way of the Philippines, Papua New Guinea, Australia and Canada. Time marches on and I will leave details of that journey to another place. Although I feel it appropriate to understand my career as a Policeman if I explain briefly why I went to Papua New Guinea.

There was much talk of corruption in the Hong Kong Government when I was at the Police Training School. As my service continued out on the Divisions this became centred on the Police Force. At first the stories seemed far fetched and seemed to concern senior Staff Sergeants, of which there were very few, considering the size of the Force; then probably 18,000 men. No one had ever approached me with offers of money or favours, although I had enjoyed Station and unit parties at Christmas and Chinese festivals. As my service progressed I began to realise how little in the way of official equipment and expenses was provided 'officially' by the Police Force. Believe it or believe it not, even items like 'STOP POLICE ROAD BLOCK' with the accompanying flashing lights etc. were provided by the Barack Sgt, an individual who was expected to provide all the necessary things to run the Station or unit. Police stores budget must have been small as even the stationary supplied had to be augmented with that

171

purchased outside. During the hard times of the Disturbances 67/8 when the police was in 'Form Company' mode (Riot Companies/Station Units were on almost continual 24 standby call out) police comforts were provided. In this regard, apart from the Police Band doing the rounds to entertain and help with morale, the Government were not doing much. Tired and thirsty men were given refreshments and assistance that kept them happy, together and motivated by, what I understood was, an unofficial system.

My old friend from the NRP Ormond Power with another NRP Officer had joined the Royal Papua and New Guinea Constabulary. The country and the type of policing seem to me more like the NRP so I decided to go there and see what were the prospects.

# 13. Hong Kong gets hold

After an interesting time in Papua New Guinea where I visited the Police Training School and explored Port Moresby, the capital. I flew up to Lai in the North and then hitched a lift on a truck, driven by a very young Aussie up on the dirt Mountain Road to Goroka in the Highlands.

I spent some time with Ormond Power and the other ex NRP man. If I recall correct he was Mike Grant. He was a pilot for one of the small airlines that served as transport in this vast wilderness of forests and mountains. A country of myriad tribes, peoples, languages and cultures but hardly any roads. His plane would have carried maybe a maximum of 12 people and be able to land on tiny air strips sometimes on the sides of the mountains. You sure had to know how to fly. Ormond advised me against joining the force there. He had been recruited to form a riot unit on the style of the Mobile Unit of the NRP. This you remember was a hard disciplined, effective armed paramilitary police unit. He told me how he had been called to turn out to deal with a mob running riot in Port Moresby. He had dispersed the mob using tear gas. The paternal like Australian run administration did not like the use of such force. Ormond and his unit were deprived of their tear gas. The locals took advantage of the weakness in the authority of the Police. Ormond said things were going to get worse as a firm hand could not be used as it was in similar situations in Africa.

I decided I would go back to the Hong Kong Police. A place, a people and a job I liked.

I arrived after back – after visiting Australia and Canada – in England on Christmas Day 1968. My dear lovely Mum opened the door.

I forget how much longer I had of my leave. I must have taken 6 weeks to get back. That would mean I had another 4 months or so to go. In the event I returned to Hong Kong in The spring of 1969.

To my disappointment I was posted to Colony Pol/Mil. This was the control room which in the event of a real emergency, like that experienced in 1967 with the riots and trouble on the border, would become fully operational. It would be manned by senior officers from the Police and the Military. Things were still not really back to normal, although there had been no disturbances requiring the Force to mobilise into Form Company status since early 68. A skeleton-staff in the form of an experienced police Inspector and an army officer usually of captain rank was maintained to pass on reports from the Frontier and District Controls Rooms. The Governor and his top Police and Military staff needed duty officers in Pol/Mil to pass on matters that affected the security of the Colony. In particular what was happening on the border.

In the past during the disturbances China had stopped vital foodstuffs crossing the frontier by way of rail at Lo Wu and road at Man Kam To. They had also turned the water supply off on a few occasions. Thus it was important to monitor what goods were coming in. Hong Kong got most of its meat and vegetables from China as well as all manner of other groceries and manufactured products. If this was not coming or the traffic was lessened in any way there were contingency plans to obtain vital supplies from elsewhere. I recall in 1967 in the early days a huge oil tanker was hired to bring drinking water, just in case we were to be blackmailed into submission. As it turned out the supply was only discontinued for a very short time. I performed 8 hour duty: day, evening and night shifts. It was boring; little happened and the times I had to alert my bosses rarely. Routinely there would be reports from the Frontier telling me how many goods wagons had crossed the border that day and what they contained. If I could give a few examples: 15 wagons of pigs, 5 of cattle, 8 vegetables, 6 builders materials, etc. Sometimes to liven things up I would test the honesty and utility of this reporting system i.e. did any one read these reports! I would include on my own initiative things like 2 wagons of toilet rolls or something similarly daft.

It seemed I would never get out of Colony Pol/Mil but of course I had been put there for a reason: I had been posted in my first tour at every station along the Frontier and was aware of the geography our side and theirs. I also understood the sensitivity of the border and how there were cross border contacts at many places along it: from Lau Fau Shan in the West to Sha Tau Kok in the East.

I moaned as much as I could and eventually was posted out. I had asked to go to a busy urban police division to get more experience and do some of the real police jobs that my old squad mates were telling me about. This banter had occurred at the Hermitage Single Quarters at the bar on the top floor. The residents there were young police officers and members of just

175

about all of the various government departments. The quarters were an improvement on the Inspector's single quarters on the divisions and the food was not bad at a restaurant and bar on the top floor. If my memory serves me correctly, I was there for about 6 months. I went out with a couple of lady residents but never got involved seriously..

I moved out when I was posted as a patrol Inspector to Wong Tai Sin Police Station (WTS). WTS was one of the new stations built in the early 60's. It covered a large area of resettlement estates. These had been built over the years to house the thousands of people who flooded in to Hong Kong from China after the Communist takeover. They had come in trickles, one by one or groups walking across the hills or swimming across the colony waters; they had come in floods, thousands swarming across the border sometimes pushing the border fence down. Sometimes they were allowed to leave other times they risked death or arrest from the PLA guarding the closed area on the China side.

In the early days these estates had been just a basic dwelling; small with communal toilets and water supply. They had improved over the years and today (2013) some are on par with some private housing. Then in 1969 they housed around 65% of the population, today the figure is higher with improved Government low cost housing.

The division included the resettlement estates of Wong Tai Sin (Upper and Lower), Tung Tau, Lok Fu, then up the hill was the newer Tsz Wan Shan; to the east was the nicer Choi Hung and Ping Shek Estates; then there was San Po Kong, an area with old fashioned tenements shops and factories and the San Po

Kong Magistrates Court. There was Diamond Hill with stone dwellings and wooden squatter type huts. Thus plenty of space for me to walk around with interesting places like the Wong Tai Sin temple, Morse Park with its football pitches and recreation grounds, the market at Choi Hung and if you wanted to view the City you could take a land-rover up to Tate's Cairn (Repeater/signal station) Post to check the duties.

I recall I lived in the Inspectors mess on the station, where there was a dear old chap: 'Cookie' who was a dab hand at a fry up or even greater cuisine. He only had one ear so it was important always to address him on the correct side. I recall most of my work was clearing obstructions and ensuring the men patrolled their beats. Sometimes I would be given an address to raid for drugs or gambling and I would be alert to street gambling. The Royal Hong Kong Jockey Club (RHKJC) had the monopoly on betting in Hong Kong and if you wanted to have a flutter you had to go to Happy Valley Race Course. Then there were no RHKJC betting shops all over the place. It appears the leaders of the community were against extending this; apparently the Chinese were not a people to gamble! As you can imagine many of these leaders had an interest in keeping the vast empire of illegal off-course betting continuing. Sadly, as I was to learn, some of the overheads needed to run this 'necessary' public service included pay offs to some in the local police.

Then there was, for those who didn't want to spend more than a few cents on a flutter, the Chi Fa ticket. A Chinese type lottery. Don't ask me how it worked. It was very Chinese. As you may have guessed once the Jockey Club started their off-course betting with shops in every district, the illegal business started to fall away. I like to think that the formation of the

ICAC in 1974 did much to stop this and most other types of organised corruption.

I let it be known that I wanted to develop as a CID officer. My dear friend Bob Brooks, who had served in London's Metropolitan Police and with me in the NRP was already a respected member of the CID and his tales certainly whetted my appetite for life as a Detective. I had been informed by superiors that it would help my chances in getting into the CID if I had Court experience. Accordingly I asked to become a prosecutor and so went after about 4 months at WTS to North Kowloon Magistracy where I became the prosecutor before the Number 1. Court Magistrate, Tim Bewley esq. I really enjoyed this sort of work. Number 1. Court was the busiest in the Colony. It dealt with all the cases form Mong Kok, Sham Shui Po and for a time Kowloon City Divisions. The morning would be the hundreds of pleas from the hawkers, gamblers and the like. Hundreds of people sometimes. The afternoon would be the contested cases, again usually of the minor type. The more complicated ones going to the other 8 or so courts in the building. Sometimes I would take cases there and would be up against paid defence lawyers. My boss as OC Court was my old friend from Ta Kwu Ling: Mike Harris. I learnt much from Tim Bewley and my time at Court but it was only a few months before I was off to join the CID at Sham Shui Po Police Station.

I mention that after leaving WTS I had managed to find a place to live off of a police station: at 137 Waterloo Road, Kowloon Tong. Which was a three-storey house standing in its own grounds complete with two trees but facing the main road. It was a great place housing about five of us single police inspectors usually with service of at least 4 years. We were looked after by a Chinese lady who had school age daughters. They had fled from China some years before leaving the father back in China. She was an absolutely marvellous cook: pastries, roasts, cakes you want it she could do it. Some years later I met her in Hong Kong after she had emigrated to the USA. I understand she had started a pastry cook type of business doing very well for her self and family. Who says the Chinese are not the world's most natural capitalists?

# 14. Good Afternoon Vietnam!

My police career starts in the Criminal Investigation Department; my short attachment with Superintendent Setterfield in the NRP I don't count. I was now really going to get busy.

Criminal Investigation Department/Sham Shui Po (CID/SSpo) was led by the Divisional Detective Inspector (DDI). He was an experienced officer of Senior Inspector rank. This would be re-graded to Chief Inspector later in 1972 when Senior Inspector became an advancement rank after a number of years qualifying service, not one gained, as was Chief Inspector, by the promotion process. His number two was the OC/CID, an often long in the tooth senior inspector who had not passed his promotion exams to Chief Inspector. Then there would be about 6 or 7 Inspectors who would command teams of usually one or more D/Sgts and between five and ten D/Police Constables, depending on their roles. There was an Anti Triad Squad, Crime Squads, a Pawnshop team, Patrol Squads, a Factory team and other specialist squads.

The old rank of Corporal had been re-graded to Sergeant by the new Police Commissioner Mr. Charles Sutcliffe who had spent time in Africa. There was then one Detective Staff Sergeant who was the senior detective other rank in the Division, which also included the Sub-Division of Shek Kip Mei. This rank would be abolished a short while later in the reforms to help stamp out corruption, which was perceived to permeate in some of the units in the Force.

I was assigned to command an Investigation. I would have a D.Sgt, a J.I. (Junior Investigator), who was a DPC and an English speaker who helped me with reports and files, along with 4 or 5 DPCs.

In those days only other ranks who had a red strip under their service number displayed on their shoulder were English speakers, most had very little command of the language, as I was to learn quickly dealing with the numerous cases that came in my 24 hour on duty period.

My squad would work a three day cycle: 24 hours on, taking all the crimes referred by the uniform Duty Officer downstairs in the Report Room to us upstairs in the CID offices. There could, on a bad day be anything up to 5 cases per DPC to investigate: upwards of 25 plus cases. These could be crime arrests, by the uniform and CID officers, cases which would have to be prepared for Court the next day or routine non arrest cases like thefts, assaults, pick pockets etc., which needed further investigation. A real major case – a homicide, rape etc. – would go to one of the specialist crime squads and if it was really serious and we were lucky it might be taken over by one of the Kowloon District or Police Headquarters Units.

In any event life as an OC Investigation team was hard work. You rarely got much sleep and usually slept on a camp bed in your office. The second day you were following up the reported cases and preparing, in regard to arrests, for any court hearings. There was also the dealing with the masses of queries that came from your immediate and more senior bosses away at Kowloon HQ. You rarely went home on Day 2 until late afternoon. Day 3 was supposed to be off but that was a joke. You frequently had to follow up your reported cases by attending Court or finishing the paper work. Your DPCs were expected to use Day 2 and 3 to investigate their cases and submit investigation reports.

I cannot recall any special cases I was involved in. The investigating teams were very much for initiating a criminal investigation, charging when the case could be dealt with soonest but leaving crimes that needed longer investigation to the DDI, OC/CID and other teams. There is in my mind a rape case I dealt with, remembered in particular because I received my first Commanding Officer commendation. This involved the rape of a small girl, 9 or 10 years old. She was very bright and was able to guide us to the place in WTS area where she had been taken and raped. I remember the trial at the High Court when she pointed at the accused a Chinese man in his 20's in the dock. A convincing witness which together with forensic evidence ensured the man was convicted. The sentence was I believe, it does not sound credible today, only 3 years.

My social life at the time was again typical of a single kwai lo young policeman: to drink in Tsim Sha Tsui area, usually with my old mate Bob Brooks in Joe's Bar. Although sometimes I would spend an hour or two at the 'Bug's Retreat', the bar at the Mong Kok Police Officer's mess.

Time flew by at SSpo. I don't know why but it was time to move, perhaps they decided that with all the tourist European victims of crime in Tsim Sha Tsui (TST) I would be useful there. I could more easily take the statements in English and deal with the Hotels etc. My work again would be OC Investigation Team and I would work as before a three day cycle: Day on, Day clearing up, Day off (?). My junior investigator, (J.I) in reality my office DPC, would be a really helpful bright DPC. He had a daughter who was anxious to go to the UK to study to be a nurse and I recall I did help with advice about London.

TST Police Station my new workplace was an old building going back to the 19th Century, probably one of the first police stations in Kowloon. We shared the building with the Marine Police whose Control Room and Headquarters was there. Their Watering Hole: The Mariners Rest was situated in a tiny room on the first floor, hidden away under the stairs. Some real characters would frequent there: Regular Marine policeman Uncle Charlie Fisher and Auxiliaries, (part time marine police) with all manner of backgrounds and stories. As you can imagine I was not slow in becoming a member.

I have mentioned Uncle Charlie before when I shared accommodation with him for a short time at quarters in Tai Po. He was an old 'matelot' from the Royal Navy and there was talk he was a descendant of the famous World War One Admiral of that name. But his gait, manner of speaking and general demeanour was much of the lower rather than upper decks. As a seaman who was probably the ablest of the launch commanders in Hong Kong's navy: the marine police whose fleet at one time had up to 166 boats (See government publication: 'Hong Kong 1994') included large Command Launches with crews of two Inspectors and 30 or so other ranks. Uncle Charlie, as his crew called him, even when

184

addressing him after the customary salute: 'Morning Uncle Charlie Sir!' When at sea, his uniform was not the regulation Khaki shirt, shorts, socks and black shoes, but these had been adapted to suit Charlie's and 'local' conditions to: regulation shorts, a white vest-singlet, red short socks (his trade mark) and plimsolls, Oh! and I nearly forgot: a uniform peak cap always on the back of his head. I am not saying he always used traditional West Country nautical terms of praise like: 'Me hearties'. But you expected him to. A first class man of the sea, well able to get along on the ship and in the water. A story which has gone into Royal Hong Police history was the tale of when Charlie fell off the back of Launch One (one of the two big command launches) while he was having a pee. The launch hit a wave and Charlie fell off. The tale goes the launch was miles off Hong Kong Island to which it was returning. As the stories are told the distance gets further and further away; versions go that he even fell off near Peng Chau others say that it was Kau Yi Chau, in any event Charlie swims to Green Island, at that time used to store non military explosives and guarded by some of our Pakistani police men. Charlie clambers up the pier and is met by one of the men on duty who say: 'Wah (or words to that effect) Uncle Charlie Sahib!' They get on the radio to Marine Control to report their find only to be told: Uncle Charlie is in his cabin and cannot be disturbed. Charlie himself clears the matter up, the launch returns to Green Island and Charlie has a shower and a beer on the launch. All to be taken with a pinch of salt? I say not; Charlie was a larger than life character, well liked by his men and colleagues, good at his job and with plenty of 'bottle'. He was also generous; I recall at my wedding he gave me a red packet with $500, quite a fortune in 1977.

My boss was the OC/CID/TST; Taff Hughes a great guy who was helpful in getting me into the swing of things, one of my other colleagues was a Pakistan Inspector whose nickname was Isa the Squeezer. There was certainly a buzz in Tsimsy. The Americans were involved with their folly in Viet Nam and so Hong Kong, Tsim Sha Tsui its bars, whores and entertainments was a favourite place for servicemen on R (rest) and R (recuperation) from Viet Nam and for the sailors on shore leave from the US 7th Fleet.. I would often do patrols of the bars either with a couple of DPCs incognito or with the SDI/TST and his uniformed officers. Believe it or not there were bars in Humphries Avenue which were for brothers only: no whities were allowed. The bar girls all wore dark make up and wore black wigs. Perhaps foolishly I would go into one of these bars to see what they would do to this whitie! I would show my warrant card and then search many of the servicemen inside. They were often fond of carrying 'soul brother' umbrellas, which had handles that pulled out revealing an 8 inch blade. There was a fine black Chief Petty Officer called Chief Johnson who was attached to the R and R office who could be called upon to assist in awkward cases. I must say I felt sorry for many of these servicemen who by their numbers seem to be favourites of the Draft Board. There were stories that there were parts of some of the US war ships which had 'no go' areas for all but the soul brothers.

There were some of their Army brothers who after RR and happy times with their new 'Afro' hair do and complexion Chinese sisters were in no mood to go back to the joys of helping Uncle Sam bring freedom and democracy to South Vietnam. I recall an occasion at Kai Tak Airport when a 'platoon' of them of sufficient size and numbers refused to leave the departure area and board their plane to return to duty. Larry Able, the commander of the airport police was called to the scene to talk to the brothers. Larry was 6 feet 5inches and a gentle Englishman. 'Come on Chaps off you go, you can't stay here.' This was met with much anger and protest with: 'Hay Whitey, you from Alabama?' To which Larry replied in his very English voice: 'No actually I am from Hereford.'

And it must have fallen on deaf ears as the group remained firmly where they were: anchored to ground and its fixtures. Larry's attempts were followed up by a Regimental Police Sergeant from the Welch Regiment. I mention he was regimental police not a red cap from the Royal Corp of Military Police, whose gentlemen were generally less polite and a little bit more aggressive. The Welsh sergeant was about 5 feet 5 inches and with his broad Welsh accent followed Larry with: 'Oh Boyo's we can't have you here can we, you will have to go and get on your plane, you've had yer holiday now, behave yerselves.' The brothers clearly sensing that the Welsh Sergeant was certainly fairly harmless ceased their disorderly clamour whilst Larry and those in the military went off to get 'qualified' help which came in the form of Chief Johnson, all 6 feet plus of him. He was able to talk to the brothers, calm them down and eventually persuade them to accompany him out of the airport. I understood that he took them to the British Army prison on Stonecutters Island, although I doubt that the brothers knew at the time that they would end up in an army 'nick.'

The reports my team dealt with seem to be centred a lot on disputes with some of the Indian tailors, tourists having their handbags and pockets picked, assaults on and by visitors and tourists. One case comes to mind was the assault on Joe

Redmond, the owner of Joe's Bar Cameron Road., who was glassed by an airline pilot. Perhaps foolishly I got too involved with the case and was very angry when counsel from our Legal Department allowed a prominent member of the private bar to persuade him to drop the charges and allow him to have his client placed on a Good Behaviour Bond. I complained to my CID boss at Kowloon PHQ but I realised later that I should not have taken the case to the magistrates court.

I enjoyed my time at CID/Tsimsy. But it was again time to go. I learnt that I was now qualified to be promoted to Senior Inspector and was wanted to act in that rank at the New Territories Pol/Mil up at Sek Kong.

During my time at CID/TST my dear Mum visited Hong Kong. She stayed with Bob Brooks and his wife Marilyn at their quarters at Eade Road, up in North Kowloon. She had a marvellous time, although with my duties I did not see that much of her. Dear Marilyn really looked after her as did their Amah, one of the old school Chinese pig tail and black pongee domestic servants. I would often visit them all at Eade Road for Dinner and managed to take Mum to all the splendid eateries in Kowloon. She really developed an affection for Bob and Marilyn and I had such fond memories of this and shed a tear when I think of dear Bob now gone over 15 years.

NT. Pol/Mil was situated in the Sek Kong Army Camp which contained the HQ of the 48th Brigade. The Brigade consisted of three battalions of Gurkha infantry, Gurkha Engineers, Gurkha Transport Regiment, a Light Artillery Regiment of British Soldiers and an armoured squadron from one of the Calvary Regiments. I have little memory of what I did there as the Police Duty Officer. I recall there was an army opposite number who was rarely in the control room. All I remember is the journey I had to take there from my quarters in Waterloo Road. I had a Vespa scooter and would ride through North Kowloon, Tsun Wan, then over the Tai Mo Shan Mountain then through Pat Heung to the Sek Kong Army Camp. When on day shift it was OK but at night the mountain road was pretty hairy. But I was not there long, a couple of months at the most. I was then given a really good command namely the Sub Divisional Inspector Sha Tau Kok (SDI/STK) an important border station. As described before I had spent a short time there in my first tour of duty both attached to the sub division and when involved with EU/NT. There was the main station and two police posts. One in the Sha Tau Kok village and the other on top of Robin's Nest, the mountain over looking the Mirs bay and the North East end of the border. Also on Robin's Nest but further back was an army Observation Post which had been there long before the troubles of 1967/68.

The area was still tense from the troubles of 1967/68 and now there was always a battalion of the army stationed in the closed area, predominantly at the eastern end of the frontier.

The sub division covered an extensive rural area and some of the most scenic and inaccessible villages. These were situated on the STK Peninsular. They were typical Hakka villages, some were in the hills and some along the coast overlooking Crooked Harbour and Double Haven. The biggest of those in the hills was Wu Kau Tang, which had in my time a population of 750 plus (my estimation). There was in the village a monument to those who died in the East River Column. That brave and tough guerrilla unit I have already referred to. The biggest on

189

the coast was Lai Chi Wo with a population of around 500. These villages were then inaccessible by road. To get there you had to walk for most of the way along paths, some concrete some dirt. The other way was to come by sea; for us in the police by marine police launch. There was a road going part of the way from the STK Police Station to Luk keng and the villages that were along the coast of Starling Inlet. Around the time I was there this was extended to Wu Kau Tang and not long after it was possible to connect up with the road at the Plover Cove Dam and then on along the Tin Kok Road to Tai Po. There were probably about 30 villages on the Peninsular, including those at and above Luk Keng and facing the Inlet.

Then there were STK's Islands: Kat O (Cooked Island in English), which was more like a small town with its own school and electric company, both of which I was involved with. I opened the power at the official Opening of the Kat O Electric Company; it must have been winter of 1972. I also presented the prizes at Prize Day of the School. A lively place then with an interesting history of sending pearl divers to Western Australia in the 1930's.

*Above; Me opening Kat O's Electric Company, I think it worked on a couple of old marine diesel engines, and (below) of me receiving or giving a prize. Was it at the school or the Electric company? Now I am not sure.*

191

I was to put a small unofficial post on Kat O to augment the visits and patrols by the marine police and to keep an eye on activities in Mir Bay and the continuing flow of illegal immigrants (refugees) swimming across the Bay from the Chinese side.

The other populated Islands were Ap Chau a tiny Island with comparatively resettled boat people (I may be corrected on their origin), no more than a hundred or so. Then far away 10 or so miles close to the Chinese side was Ping Chau. There were villages here but the population was just a few old people and dogs. There was no police presence from STK then. It was visited by marine police and I did not consider it was my responsibility until told otherwise. The residents of Kat O and Ap Chau would travel home by a Kai Do (small motor boat/ferry from the pier in STK Village which went for about 150 yards into Starling Inlet and was a continuation of San Lau Steet the road which ran parallel with a drain that acted as the border between the Chinese and British sides. The street had three storey buildings which looked over the road and the drain.

In the STK village there was also a wooden hut area occupied by boat people and non traditional Hakka villagers. There were a number of these Hakka villages within the closed area which ran approximately 3 kilometres deep at STK; outside the closed area going down the main STK/Fanling Road to Ku Tung, near where the Military built road up to Robin's Nest started, there were further such villages. So what a splendid place to work and explore: scenic hikes, excitement sometimes in the STK village, trips across to Kat O or the villages on the Peninsular and then up the hill to Pa Kung Au Post to observe to activities the other side.

There were few memorable events during my year or so in the job before I went on my second end of tour vacation leave.

In the first few weeks I bought an ancient US Studebaker car. It did about 8 miles to the gallon and it cost a round of drinks just to turn the engine over, understandably, apart from being fun to drive it did not stay with me long. After just a few weeks I sold it for about $500. I replaced it with a similarly daft idea: A 750 twin carburettor Norton Commando which was capable of a speed of 120 MPH. A great bike and the best one I ever had. I had been a motorcyclist in my earlier youth; the biggest bike then being a 500 twin BSA.

The Norton was to put me hospital about 6 months into my time at STK. I was riding back along the STK Road from the Fanling Officers Mess when I failed to notice the bend at the Wo Hang Bend. Apparently I was out cold lying in the road to be found by Gurkha's in a Landover going back to the STK village. I was in hospital for a few days with concussion, my third experience of such a condition: the first was when I fell off my bike at Holly Park School, the second was putting down disorder at Mufulira in 1963.

I was soon back at work with an order from 'Spade Face' Mr Rose the Assistant Commissioner of Police New Territories to sell the bike. After that it was police transport to take me to the Fanling Depot.

It was when I still had the bike that I had cause to stop and attend a drowning case which had occurred at a village just down the road from the Station. I was on my way to the Fanling. A little baby had fallen into one of the ponds/pits used to water/fertilise the paddy. I got him out and started to breath into the little child's mouth and waited for the ambulance. I breathed hard and pressed the child's chest for what seemed ages. There were gurgling noises but alas when I handed over to the Ambulance men they said after trying with a respirator gadget that it was too late. I saw the poor Mum and felt distraught, but resumed my journey to Fanling Mess.

I have mentioned that the situation on the border at the village was usually tense. You never knew what would happen with the other side. Loud speaker denouncements of the filthy Hong Kong British were not so common as they were at the end of the 60's but they still took place. Glaring faces of hatred from the PLA soldiers some times accompanied by stone throwing was not uncommon, but to be fair this could often be in reaction to some of the antics of British soldiers on duty in the village. Units with a reputation for toughness, without mentioning names, sometimes taunted their opposite numbers by pulling faces and making remarks, which may or may not have been lost on the Chinese soldiers. It was therefore always a relief to know that the Gurkhas were on border duty this month. They were well behaved and disciplined.

But rocks could be hurled at us when we were doing our job. I recall one event when I had to get an arrested disorderly man down from the pier, along San Lau Street and back to the village post. It was easiest to carry him firmly in a fireman's lift. As I did so I was just waiting for a few rocks to come my way

194

but I got him out of their sight and back to the post without being hit.

I was there for the Christmas of 1972 and Chinese New Year of 1973. I recall how cold it was that winter. There were reports of thin ice on the tops of the mountains; to keep the duties manning the Closed Area road barrier just below the Station happy I set up – especially for the night shift – charcoal braziers. I didn't mind if the men, a corporal and two Pcs used same to warm themselves and maybe cook themselves a chicken wing. ('But for Goodness sake be alert for any of the top brass doing a night visit')! I would occasionally bring back something to warm them up from the Better 'Ole!

Chinese New Year meant fireworks; and don't forget since 1967 and the bombs it was illegal to possess, store sell, buy, let off or have anything to do with them. In China of course it was not and they produced tons of them; with shops just across the border selling them.

The nearer you got to the border the less seriously HK people took the law prohibiting fireworks. There were some nights when it was like the first day of the Battle of the Somme. The Governor had a retreat at the Fanling Lodge and understandably our NT commanders were beginning to feel embarrassed by the apparent lack of law enforcement in the NT. Our orders were do something.

Fireworks were coming across the border. My roadblock duties at the barrier below the station and the patrols in the villages were told to be vigilant. One day, a week or so before New Year, a man was stopped at the road block duties. He had more

195

fireworks than just for his own or families use and he was clearly dealing in them. He was brought to the Station for questioning and charging. My orders to the Duty Officer were to find out where he got them. He was not co-operative and said they came from a friends. I was convinced that they came from the village and there was a lot more, considering the noise we had all been experiencing locally these last days. He would not say anything to my officers so I thought I would talk to him. He came into my office saying they were only for himself, family and friends. I said words to the effect I don't believe you and banged my fist on the glass top of my desk. To my surprise and to his horror the glass shattered and he said 'OK!' I'll take you where I have stored them'. I forget exactly the words said! Accordingly he lead us back to the village and pointed out a building which was right on the Chung Ying Street. The entrance was on our side but the rear window looked out over the Chinese side. I cautiously went in and saw it was a floor 200 or so square feet stacked with fireworks. A lorry load; at least a ton or more. It was a delicate task to remove all with the PLA soldier looking in at us through the window. But all went off without major incident. The bosses at NT HQ were delighted; so we were doing something to show the writ of the law runs through out the land!

The Border Road went all the way about 12 kilometres from the STK village through a valley between the Mountains on the Chinese side and on ours past the large village of Li Ma Hang in Ta Kwu Ling's area then on to that police station Ta Kwu Ling ending at just before the Man Kam To crossing. I would often patrol as far as our boundary with TKL: Li Ma Hang then hike up the 1000 or so steps to the PKA Police Post. I would do this at different shift time and sometimes in the evening or early morning. The purpose was to check the alertness of the duties but also to help with morale. Once a month there would be a special a Post Chow and I would bring up the steps in a ruck sack some beers and join them for dinner. Occasionally I would stay the night and in the morning watch the glorious sunrise over Mirs bay. The setting, the quiet, the noise of the birds, the view below into China: Wah! Peace, perfect peace!

What must it have been like that terrible day on the 8th July 1967 when the Corporal I.C Post had seen the PLA soldiers moving up to the border the other side. I understand he passed sitreps (situation reports) to Fanling Pol/Mil., calmly and clearly. I often wondered later if he ever got a gong for it? In the British Army he most certainly would have.

On some of these border patrols I would ask the OC of the Military on Border duty if he would like to do a joint Pol/Mil patrol with me. One occasion that sticks in my mind was when I took three soldiers from the Irish Guards along the border road then up the steps to PKA Post on further up to the top of Robin's Nest and the old Military OP. It was a stiff climb but they were OK. I learnt that they were two 'Papes' and one 'Prod.' One from the North, one from the South and one from Liverpool. 'Do you all get on?' I asked. The troubles of Ireland in mind. Oh we are all mates says them. It showed me it was physical: the place where the walls were built that caused the bitter division, away from the place there was friendship. Surely we should all refuse to tolerate the intolerant!

It must have been early spring 1973 when time came to leave STK to go on long vacation leave. I had no local leave since coming back in early 1969 so was really leave happy. I was sorry to be leaving the men and the local people I had got to know. I think I left with a good record although one black mark stays in my memory. One evening when going off to the watering hole I realised I had no cash. I thus borrowed a 100 or so dollars from the station impressed account in my safe. I had done this before always paying it back the next day after I had been to the bank or cashed a cheque. But calamity! Who should do a surprise visit early the next day but the 'Four Eyed Snake': Mr Illingworth the NT Police Commander. He checked my safe as is procedure on such visits and found the impressed account and register not up to date. I explained but he noted it in the Visits and Inspections Register: Naughty boy.

He could not have held it too much against me as in 1976 he had me back in the NT District as SDI/Yuen Long. I handed over to my successor: Dave Deptford another ex NRP man. I mention that there would have been some continuity as I would be leaving behind one Inspector who was OC. Posts. Two who I remember being there for a while were Phil Layton and Steve, S.P.Corrick. The former later in his career got prosecuted and the latter got a commendation. Phil Layton I remember was unable to wear boots!? Thus he was unable to do any real patrols and could only do office jobs like those he aspired to in the CID. Corrick you couldn't keep him away from walking the hills.

I flew to Singapore where I visited and took gifts to the brother of one of the Sergeants at STK. From Singapore I went by sleeper train to Bangkok. There I had a few days visiting the Japanese Death Railway, the bars and the sights. I then flew to Kathmandu in Nepal where after a few days sightseeing I boarded a coach of the Penn Overland Travel Company to take me to England.

# 15. The Hippy Trail Home

I finished the last Chapter with me boarding the overland coach for London. That was to take me on an adventure in its self: From Nepal over the mountains then crossing the plains of India, going up to Kashmir and a short stay on a house boat, then into Pakistan, Swat, the Khyber Pass; Afghanistan, Kabul, Kandahar, Herat; Iran (Persia), Tehran, Ishfahan, Hamadan, Tabriz, the Caspian Sea near Gorgan; Turkey, Lake Van, Erzurum, Diyarbakir, Gaziantep, the Mediterranean, Goreme, Ankara, Istanbul; Greece, Thessalonika, Athens; Yugoslavia (Still one country then) Dubrovnik and Split.

At Split I left the bus to fly home to join a Senior CID course with the Metropolitan Police starting in a few days at Peel House, London.

My adventures on the overland journey would be a book by itself. Perhaps now it is suffice to give my general impressions of the countries I visited.

In **Nepal** I was shown around by a Nepalese policeman who had been to HK and knew my colleagues. The country was poor and undeveloped. Katmandhu was the only large town/city which had a beautiful setting with the Himalayas in the near distance. There were different peoples some looking more as Indians with dark to lighter skins and others like the familiar Gurkhas with lighter more mongoloid features. A religious country with stupas and Buddhist's signs and statues everywhere. Ruled still by a king. The British and the recruitment of Gurkha's were still an important part in the culture and economy of the country. The first Gurkha's were recruited soon after we had thrashed them in a war in 1818; 200 years to date of loyal fantastic service to the British crown.

**India:** A material desert but some say a spiritual paradise. I suppose that is correct if you count the temples, the unwashed holy men, the disgustingly filthy Ganges, the eating habits, etc.. I am sorry to say I found little to like about the place apart from the relics of the Raj (well I am a grandchild of empire!). The arrogance and intolerance endemic in a caste system which treats some in the community as serfs: untouchables. The hierarchy of caste seemed to  permeate even in 1973, through the whole of society: know your place, don't let your impurity cast a shadow on mine. Any official we met, whether in the bank or at a customs post, made it as difficult as possible. It helped with the latter to oil the palms. A stamp in my passport was obtained cheaply on payment of my smart ball point. Believe it or not, especially looking at the situation today, when we crossed the border into Pakistan things were better. There were no terribly deformed professional beggars made like they were deliberately by their demonic masters. It was not necessary to avoid barriers placed on the roads and to pay tolls to local landowner/officials to proceed. Stones were not thrown at the bus. Again believe or not it was easier getting a local beer in Pakistan – London Larger (brewed in Lahore) – than it was in most parts of India.

**Pakistan** was not as now! The Swat Valley was beautiful with the mountains and almost a Swiss like atmosphere. The people were friendly. I visited a couple of the old cantonment Raj

Churches and visited the graveyards. The stones were interesting: Captain Smith age 26 died of the flux, Mrs Brown wife of Lieutenant Brown died of the flux! What ever the flux was it certainly took its toll on British soldiers, their families and servants of the Raj. A gravestone in Peshawar mentioned a young officer killed by brigands.

At one of the churches I was shown around by an Indian Christian man who kept an eye on it. He told me how even then things were getting more difficult for Christians. Then there was the Khyber Pass where at the small settlements just about every type of weapon was copied and sold. Some I think would have blown up on discharge.

**Afghanistan** and the road there over the mountain was something; rugged hills and proud people. In some you could see the blue eyes of the descendants of Alexander the Great who passed this way well over 2,500 years before. The roads were surfaced and in good condition. I understand one of the great powers had built the Kabul to Kandahar stretch and the other rival Kandahar to Herat. We stopped at small a hotel and guesthouse and were impressed with the people who served us. We had demonstrations of local music and dancing (men only). There was even a Chianti( red wine) developed by an Italian concern outside Kabul. The wine was new but drinkable. There was a supermarket in Kabul where you could even get familiar UK goodies of the type from 'Marks and Spencer's'. There were certainly, in Kabul and Herat, good looking women who were not totally veiled. The country was still then a constitutional monarchy under King Zahir Shah. He had tried to introduce liberal reforms and one wonders how Afghanistan would be today if he had not been ousted from power in a coup. Which occurred whilst he was in Europe for medical treatment a few months after we left the country.

He had tried to unite the different tribes/factions including the communists, Muslims: Sunni and Shia.

**Iran**. Over the border into Iran. The Shah of Persia (Iran), Mohammed Reza Pahlawi, was still the "King" of the country. To many he was trying to bring his country into the modern world with comparative liberal policies especially in regard to education and women. His Literacy Corps which "encouraged" the well educated youth to serve the country by going to the rural and poorer areas to bring literacy was not popular with some of the more well to do middle class. There were also many, especially among the religious "Ayatollahs" of the holy City of Qom, who opposed his western secularization and his closeness with the USA.

My view based on over a week touring the country was the country was definitely moving forward. The people in the cities appeared healthy and content. The woman were attractive, their faces not hidden, with for the most part, at least in the cities, wearing western clothes. There was a local beer, available and drunk in all the places we visited. There was a Persian culture and music which the Shah was patronising. We went to a concert of really lovely Persian music at a concert hall in Tehran where the audience could have been in the Festival Hall, London. There were in the large towns nice coffee bars and restaurants run often by the Armenian community. A group whose faith was evidenced by a plethora of churches with their ghoulish paintings and statues. I liked Iran and was saddened with the overthrow of the Shah in 1979 and his replacement by the new Shah: Ayatolleh Khomeini, who to me evidenced the thinking of the middle ages.

**Turkey.** A great country, full of history, culture, scenery, attractive people and then very much a secular state with its eyes very carefully on the excesses seen in the Wahhabi jihadists busy at work from Saudi Arabia spreading their disorder. The Turkish Army was the guarantor of a democratic secular state. But I ask now (2013) for how long?

I must mention the food. It was a joy to go to small town local restaurants and visit the kitchens to chose your dishes.

**Greece**. We were there not long. I preferred Turkey. But of course, its culture, history, scenery, especially those mountains with the monasteries high up in those inaccessible places, were memorable.

**Yugoslavia**. Another four days and I was off the bus at the little airport at Split and on my way to London. My only memory of Yugoslavia was Dubrovnik. A lovely walled town with much history. The country was then still one; not divided into what became 6 or so separate States. Marshal Josip Tito was still ruling the country. A country he had made after uniting the six or so peoples after the war. There had been much bitterness especially with the Nazi Germany created state of Croatia and its Utase fascist army being responsible for killing thousands of Serbs. Tito's death was the catalyst for the wars which eventually destroyed Yugoslavia.

For what it is worth! Many have forgotten their history. The Serbs certainly don't deserve, what has appeared to be the predominance of blame, for the atrocities that have have occurred in those countries since Tito's death in 1980.

Back in England and just time to say hello to Mum and Dad before I start the Senior Course at the Metropolitan Police Detective Training School at Peel House, Pimlico.

I forget now how long the course was; it must have been at least 8 weeks. It was centred on law and procedure with some emphasis on the Judges rules and the interviewing of suspects and witnesses. The lectures were primarily from the regular staff. I note from the course photograph there were, with the Commandant and his deputy, nine instructors of inspectorate rank. Besides these we had a large number of lecturers from outside: Policemen and experts in the forensic field. There were practical exercises involving the searching for and collection of exhibits. A crime would be staged and the students would perform as suspects and interviewers. I recall once I was to perform as a criminal suspect. The staff instructed us suspects not to give in: admit, at any cost. We were given a script and were to keep to it, not giving anything away despite the pressure of whatever form. I showed I would be a useless perjurer as it was only 20 or so minutes that I agreed to tell my student interrogators the truth. Their technique? 'Come Dave don't piss about, let's go for a drink'. That didn't go down well with the instructing staff.

I found the course worthwhile and learnt much. The lecture from the forensic scientists and officers from other police units/forces and similar law enforcement bodies were interesting but the only one that sticks in my mind now came from a Superintendent of the British Transport Police. He told us how they dealt with the hooliganism on the trains carrying 'away match' football supporters. You recall this is the 1973. He would put his men in plain clothes two to three at a time and "physically deal' with any yob who was misbehaving. I recalled Sir Percy Silitoe's time as the Chief Constable of Glasgow who brought order there just after the war with the return of servicemen with their souvenirs. The hooligans knew who was giving them a hard time, plain clothes or not.

I became very friendly with some of the staff who took me around and introduced me to working CID colleagues outside. I learnt that some things were not so different to the CID in HK. The Met CID was described as a firm within a firm. I was asked by one Detective Sergeant: "Dave, do your 'guvenors' like a drink?" meaning do they take a few bob! I would reply, 'Yes we have police officers messes where we all take a drink', knowing exactly what the Sergeant meant. Sadly I learned that the Met needed sorting out. There was organised corruption in some units: West End Central was the best earner, with Enfield the worse. I understand that a clean-up occurred, but after things had begun to do so in HK with the ICAC. Later I found it ironic that some of the Investigators who came to HK in the mid 70's to staff the ICAC had come from the Metropolitan Police CID. Oh well, it takes one to catch one.

There were a few course outings. The one I remember is the trip by charabanc to Hastings by the sea. A real piss up, beer in the back of the coach, stops on the way; just like a works outing. The Hastings Police looked on us with disapproval but there were no arrests!

*Students Of The Initial (Senior) Course, 27th July, 1973.*
*I am standing at the back again, just to the left of the central window frame.*

The rest of the leave I spent with my family. I recall I did some touring around England and Scotland and visited my old mate Jock McRoberts up in Tarland, Aberdeenshire. I had decided that the time had come to look at property in England. The old medieval town of Ludlow, Shropshire had taken my fancy and I had hope that my parents could retire there leaving the complications there were in London sharing their home at 7 priory Villas, Colney Hatch Lane with my sister. By my next leave in 1976 I would have bought Westminster Cottage, a listed property, a small three storey town house in Bell lane, Ludlow.

The other memory of that second leave is using a private gym in Bloomsbury.

I returned to HK on the Autumn of 1973 and was posted straight away to the post of the Divisional Detective Inspector, Sham Shui Po (DDI/SSP). You recall I had spent some time here as Investigation Team Detective Inspector. Now I was the boss. A large CID command, in one of busiest divisions in the Force; three to four thousand reported crimes a month. I had over a 150 detectives all ranks both at the main Shamshuipo Station and up at Shek Kip Mei. Not long after my posting Governor MacLehose visited us at CID/SSP. He seemed happy how we had got our new Intelligence section going and had re-organised our squads He had just taken over and we were in for some welcome changes to come in the immediate years.

The structure of Divisional CID had been altered in the time I had been away from the CID. We now had the familiar Investigation Teams, but also Crime Squads and Action Squads. The latter were supposed to be for ACTION! An idea I recall of Mr Richard Quinne, a man who later was to ensure I was not promoted to Superintendent. 'Thank you Mr Quinne the best thing that happened to me'! They were to get crime arrests: Loitering, unlawful possession: the more minor street offences. They were also to do raids and help control the triads with membership of a triad offences. Mr Quinne was in charge of the Kowloon District CID and was known for his fixation with figures and crime arrests. He even instituted a race with the different CID divisions to see who could get the most crime arrests. The more crime detected through arrests there was the better the detection rate figures looked with  all the more serious undetected crimes. Quinne's policy was stated cynically on the wall of the Bug's Retreat in Mong Kok Police Officer's Mess: 'One undetected serious robbery (there had been a major

Goldsmith armed robbery) does not affect my statistics at all'. Oh well! He was to go on to greater things and sits today, I understand, as a member in the House of Keys, the Manx Parliament on the Isle of Man.

I was to be at SSPo for two years before Quinne moved me to CID Kowloon Headquarters.

It was, as boss of the CID/SSPo, an extremely busy and stressful time. In the first few months there was a gang murder in the fish market; a murder in the Mei Fu Shan Tsuen, a private estate, involving five youths who broke in and killed an old man; later there was an armed robbery on a Cash in Transit Armoured Van plus all manner of minor and serious crime. Some, but only very few, would be taken over by P/HQ or K/HQ units, as was the case with the Armoured Van 'blagging' (Robbery). All serious cases that required trial on indictment at the High Court by Judge and jury (in HK usually 7 to 9 jurors) would be handled either myself or the OC/CID. There were a few crimes that were straightforward but were triable only on indictment. One of these was Buggery: sexual intercourse with man or woman via the forbidden orifice. It was still a serious offence punishable with life imprisonment. The days when it would become fashionable then compulsory, sorry joking, were to come! A uniform beat patrol officer had caught two men misbehaving in a staircase. The OC of the investigation took the case papers to Legal Department to be wrongly told that it was a matter for District Court, a lower court where trial was by a Judge.

I realised the advice was wrong. It was only triable on indictment. The OC and his team were keen to pass the case to someone else; such cases were unusual and they were getting some ribald banter from their colleagues. OK says I, I'll take it to Court. The older man got three years and the younger two years. I recall the mother of one spat in my face outside the Court. I felt so sorry for her.

As DDI I was often in the High Court as OC Case and occasionally to give evidence. On one such occasion, a triad gang chopping in which a youth was killed and there was a confession. I was questioned during a *voire dire* (a trial within a trial) proceeding for three days, in which it was standard practice in our criminal evidence and procedure system to decide the admissibility of evidence before a Judge alone. He would decide if it was safe to go to a Jury and in regard to confessions he had to be sure that the statement had been made voluntarily. The counsel who cross-examined me was well known for his ability to defend his clients with a vigour which some said verged on paranoia. His boast was: 'I eat policeman for breakfast'. Looking back I was amazed that some Judges allowed him the licence they did. There was talk he was a homosexual, OK today who cares, but then as stated above sodomy was still criminal offence not as some say nowadays a qualification to get on. But now having been myself a defence lawyer for over 25 years I admire his dedication to his client and the dexterity and determination he displayed in exposing every hole in the prosecution's case. It was a truism, perhaps an overstatement to say a Detective learnt more during a trial he was involved in than a whole week at the Detective Training School.

During my evidence on the second day in the witness box, having asked me the same questions over and over again from the first day, he suddenly put his fingers in both ears and poked his tongue at me. I couldn't believe it and exclaimed to the Judge: 'My Lord' and pointed at the counsel. 'Get on with your evidence,' said the Judge not turning a hair, 'We all know Mr.San.....ty'.

The trial continued before the jury after the Judge had made his ruling and the youths were convicted. I remember at the end of the trial the counsel burst into tears and said: 'Yet again has an innocent man framed by the police.' The jury looked amazed and I was annoyed with what to me was theatre.

My court appearances gave me a taste for criminal advocacy. I saw how many counsel were the opposite of the gentleman above. They did not appear to try hard. They were not effective in cross-examination and didn't even understand evidence and procedure. I can do better than that I thought to myself.

Perhaps a word about the armoured van robbery case which I mentioned before I got involved with my court appearances. It was near Christmas. We had three major call outs that day: to the fish market, the armoured van job and a serious gang chopping up at Shek Kip Mei. After going from the Fish Market we all rushed off to Cheung Sha wan Road where the Van had been attacked. I was with Fatty Chung who was OC of the Intelligence Unit, Lam Mun Cheung the OC. CID and their teams. We took the Van Guard, still carrying his shotgun, to show us what had happened. He led us to a staircase and in a very agitated voice told us how he had held the gun as the attackers came. There was a BANG! He fired the shotgun! It narrowly missed me, but one of the rounds pellets took a piece out of Fatty's ear. I went away in a daze hearing the cry: 'What's happened to the Boss'. We took the shotgun from the guard. All right! We should have done that first! Fatty went off to see to his ear, it was still attached, only a nick, whilst I went off to Shek Kip Mei to see the OC/CID/SKM and deal with the gang chopping.

In 1974 saw the formation of the ICAC and a traumatic time for many in the Force. Sadly its leadership had at best tolerated corruption, at worse indulged it and in a few cases was part of it. But it was the lower ranks who were to take the punishment. The Lords of All: the Detective Staff Sergeant Ones: Mr Lui Lok and Nam Kwong and others like the Staff Sergeant Chan Tsz Chu, said to have his hand in drug protection, were to flee. They never faced prosecution. Chan Tsz Chu went off to America to run an Undertakers Business in New York and the other two to Taiwan. Although hard at the time to accept that the sins of the mighty were being laid on the not so, I realised things had to change. I welcomed the fact that in a short space of time – some said it was as abrupt as a light switch – organised/syndicated corruption was no more.

Whilst ICAC was busy at work with the CID in the other Kowloon Divisions. We at SSP could breath freely, our boss a true gentleman Mr Keith Lomas the Divisional Superintendent had kept the Division clean with his tight firm but fair leadership. He would not tolerate any hanky panky.

As can be appreciated the formation of the ICAC and its operations in its early days caused havoc in the Force. There were so many raids on police units and arrest of officers that it was becoming difficult to properly function as a service. There was much anger amongst the rank and file about what was happening and the attitude of senior officers, notably the Commissioner, Mr Brian Slevin. It was as if these personalities had no idea what had been happening under their watch. It is always easy to look at things differently decades after the event and say: they may have been bad commanders but there was no excuse at all for the corruption of their subordinates. In any event in November of 1977 a number of police officers showed their anger and demonstrated outside the ICAC Head Quarters. There were pictures in the papers at the time of ICAC Officers with raised fists toward a provocative group of policemen. At around the same time there was a demonstration involving hundreds, perhaps over a thousand policeman showing solidarity at the playing field of the Police Club in Boundary St, Kowloon.

The Government was concerned. Was there a rebellion in the Force? Governor Sir Murray MacLehose could not have had much faith in Commissioner Slevin but something had to be done to re-assure, what I consider were most of the loyal but ill led junior police officers, that the ICAC would not finish them off. The Governor declared an amnesty: Investigations already begun would continue but an amnesty, excluding heinous crimes and a few other exceptions was given for offences before 1st January 1977.

There was now no excuses. The force from the top to the bottom would not tolerate corruption with in its ranks. It was also a signal for other equally dirty practices in the Hospitals ( Amah's Tips),Fire Services(Charges for delivery or not of water),Ambulance Service( Charges for delivery to hospital) and the Public Works Department. (well you name it, the sky was the limit).

Sir Murray was our greatest Governor. Hong Kong has much to thank him for: the ICAC and his handling of the Police "Mutiny" was one of them. It is generally considered that we have today one of the cleanest of Governments in this part of the world. I hope that our closeness with our new master: the PRC and its culture of government will not alter that.

My hours of work, many today would not believe. I would leave my quarters, then still living at 137 Waterloo Road at 0630, and be in the my office at 0700 to take the morning report from the OC Investigation Teams at SSPo and SKM. I would then face a barrage of questions from K/PHQ: They never seemed interested in the relevant and important and questions asked were sometimes inane,so daft as to invite any answer that came to mind: Was the victim a watchman or a caretaker (Vitally important no doubt to some), how tall was he etc. etc. This after you may have been up all night on a major case and keen to pass on things the powers should know.

I was getting tired of the statistics game and the attitudes of the likes of Mr Quinne who I recall once, during a kidnapping of a baby case, asked me if we had, after hours of interrogation, 'REALLY' interrogated the prisoner. A very tired me, we had been up for about three days on the case replied: 'Do you mean have we really tortured the man yet, Sir?'

We did make an arrest in that case but I was not very happy with it. The prosecution was based on circumstantial evidence and a confession statement. I handled the committal proceedings at the Magistrates Court but it was defended by a respected leading barrister who persuaded the magistrate that the evidence was too unreliable, relying much on the confession, to commit for trial at the High Court. I was disappointed because of the flack that would now come from CID/Kowloon/HQ. But in some way I was relieved I could see problems coming in a later trial. I was not totally convinced that we had arrested the main culprit in the case. Years later when I was a barrister myself I asked the defence counsel in that case if he thought our man had done it. He said : 'Don't worry David you had the right man.'

I have fond memories of the men I worked with: Steve Dunn who went off to join UK Customs and Excise; Chris Keeping who still lives in HK; Fatty Chung Ho Cheung who loved his booze and gourmet food and didn't make old bones; Benny LAU Wai Ming who became like me a barrister and joined, for a short time, my chambers, and LAM Mun Cheung a **real** Hong Kong Chinese Detective who was, like many in similar positions everywhere in the discipline services, indispensable and wouldn't and couldn't be promoted

Most of my time as DDI/SSPo I was quartered at one of the married flats above the Station; it was a floor up from my office. I was thus on easy call and able turn out during the night. This worried my dear old Dad who in the Autumn of 1974 came with Mum to stay with me at the Station. He would hear me going out in the early hours of the morning not to come back until sometimes mid day. He knew I was armed with my service revolver. The station could be a noisy place and I realised later that they would have been more comfortable in a Hotel. But they did have a good time. The Chinese are so respectful of old people and my men were so kind to them. Godfrey Pang Shun-mei, one of the new Station Sergeants who had helped me in particular with the baby kidnapping case, showed them around. Today, an oldie myself, I look back and say how pleased that both came and saw how responsible my position was. Both knew I always wanted to be a policeman and why was I doing the job now.

*My Mum and Dad, taken during their month long stay with me at Shamshuipo Police Station. I recall Dad could never get used to me being called out at all times of the night and the noise that came from the CID offices below where I would be working, briefing my Detectives and ensuring suspects were being properly dealt with.*
*I think Dad would have been 67 and Mum 65.*

Mr Quinne had another man for DDI/SSP a chap junior in service to me who I did not know: Ben Munford. He took over and I was sent off to CID/Kowloon HQ. I was to be the cold case officer and the OC/Kowloon/Homicide. I was given a bright English speaking D/Sgt. and a small squad. Apart from an infanticide case in which I was able to offer some ideas to a divisional crime unit, ideas which led to an arrest and prosecution, I can recall little as to what I did there. It was a cushy job, however; none of the crazy hours and pressure of commanding a big Divisional CID formation. It thus gave me time to do some courting with my lovely Diana Cheung Yee-fun, my future wife and mother of my two children. I had met her during the last few weeks of my time at SSP.

# 16. Affairs of the Heart

Diana was to be the first regular girlfriend since Marilynne Kent. I was not terribly confident with the fairer sex and had a negative opinion about myself in regard to my abilities to impress and win them over. There had been a few ships that had passed in the night and in regard to some of the English women I saw in Hong Kong I was afraid to develop any relationships. I knew that I was going to be in Hong Kong for a long time. The few dates that I had found time for since arriving had been with Chinese girls. They certainly, with their nice figures, always smart clothes and demure natures, appealed to me. I had a fear of loud women. My sister, poor soul, had given me enough experience of that, with rows and arguments with my parents. I certainly was not a Romeo and unlike many of my friends did not spend much time collecting scalps either with visits to Houses of The Foolish or with regular, frequent and different dates. If I fancied someone I was really going to make a go of it and would not give any misleading impressions. My Dear Mum had been impressed with the Chinese friends I had and had said how delighted she would be if I could find a nice Chinese girl.

Diana had been out for a short time with a European Inspector before. He was a decent chap and had said what a nice girl she was just before he left Hong Kong. I had seen her on social occasions at the Restaurant and Bar of the Ho man Tin Government Quarters in Kowloon. I was given a flat here when I moved out from the DDI/SSPo's quarter at the Police

219

Station. I was not on 24 hour call every day of the week, like I had been at SSPo, so had time to take her out. I would often pick her up from work. She worked at the men's department of the big department store: Sincere's, at Shuen Wan. Where I had first met her to talk to when I was buying shirts. She lived a little further on from there in Western where she had been born. She was total HK as was her mother. Her father had died years before but she had a brother: Ah Keung and another half brother, her father having two wives. There was a grandmother living in Macau whom I visited once with her.

She really was a beautiful girl, quiet with a lovely nature, and could she look gorgeous when dressed up! She had been educated in Chinese and her English was not fluent but with my Cantonese and her English we had no trouble communicating. I recall outings with colleagues from her Sincere's to the beach or dinner functions. After we had been going out for about 6 months she would spend the weekends with me staying at my flat. I decided I wanted to spend more and more time with her and when it became time for me to go on long leave I asked if she could get leave from work and have a holiday with me in England. She had not been abroad before, only travelling to China with friends from work during the tail-end of Chairman Mao's time. (He died 9th September 1976).

I went off on end of tour leave early in the summer of 1976. I would again make the most of my time and fare by, this time, touring the USA. I travelled with a police friend: Dave Ronald who had worked in the CID at Mong Kok and was another regular of the Bug's Retreat. We flew to the Philippines and then across the Pacific to San Francisco where we boarded a Greyhound Bus which took us via the south west: Arizona,

New Mexico, Texas, New Orleans, Orlando, Disney World up through the Carolinas to New York and home via British Airways.

Home for me now was Westminster Cottage, Bell Lane, Ludlow, Shropshire. An old Medieval Town guarding the Welsh Marches. Saint Lawrence – its parish church – was the biggest parish church in the country. My mother and father had moved up from London a year or so before and Mum was already into the life of the church and the town. My Dad, however, I felt missed London, the football and his biggest source of discontent immigration: with the town all English there was no one to moan about. Ludlow is a very pretty town situated on the River Theme. The cliffs above the river and the Hills to the East and West made for fine views and great walking country. I was very happy with the move although, as my friend and best man at my wedding Steve Stephenson, who was a Ludlow local, would say: you would not be accepted as a local until your family had been there for aeons. To the north up the A 49 was the county town: Shrewsbury, another town full of history and not terribly far from my birthplace Wellington.

I had been home for a couple of weeks when I went down in a hired car to pick up Diana from the Heathrow. My parents, mum in particular, were totally delighted with her. She was so typical of a Chinese then: filial and respectful of older people and so anxious to help in the home. Mum I could see was so proud of her and when I said I might marry her and settle in HK for the rest of my career she gave me 100 per cent approval. Dad also said what a sweet girl she was who being a HK local would be an ideal wife. I have on my study wall today a treasured picture of her looking lovely with my Mum and Dad outside Westminster Cottage.

I took her around the country and we drove up to Scotland. I have a memory of visiting Bob Toal a fellow Hong Kong cop and a friend at his home in Coatbridge outside Glasgow. And to my best mate Bob Brooks, his wife and mother at the family home at Burnt island, Fife. We of course later went to the bright lights of Birmingham and London for yum chas at the Chinese Restaurants there. It must have been a month she was with me. I took her back to Heathrow with the idea of getting married very much in my mind.

*Some photographs taken of Diana during her visit. Previous Page; the lovely one outside the cottage with Mum and Dad. Above, standing by the river in Carlisle on our way to Scotland.*

*Feeding the pigeons in Trafalgar Square.*

My leave finished and I flew back to HK early Autumn 1976 and was posted to Yuen Long as the SDI/YL. I was happy with the posting as my previous tour had been all CID and I thought a period in uniform may help my prospects for promotion. This despite Quinne letting me know he would do his best to prevent this course. The Divisional Superintendent Yuen Long – my boss – was Uncle Ernie Common. A man I liked and got on well with. He had a liking for the amber nectar and was a great supporter of mess life. Under his charge the Yuen long mess thrived as a place for the officers of the division and friends from the Fire Services, the Army (The local Captain of the Royal Military Police) and civvies to meet for a few jars and the occasional formal mess dinner.

My command was 180 or so uniform men and women. I had an assistant (ASDI/YL) and about 5 or 6 Inspectors, three were British lads living in the Mess. Yuen Long then was little more than a rural market town and the villages serving it. It had a Post at the head of the Yuen Long Creek which flowed into the Shum Chun River to the north. The town would eventually be city size but then it could not have been more than 9,000. The 30 to 40 villages within the sub-division, which stretched from the border with Castle Peak in the west to Pat Heung in the East, probably contained a population of less than a 19,000 thousand. Small indeed for HK.

Our duties were general watch and ward: keep an eye on the hawker situation, always a problem in HK; be alert for illegal immigrants from across the border; keep up pressure on any vice activities drugs and gambling and deal with disorder. My experience in the new Territories showed that the people on its west side, mainly Cantonese Punti were a lot more difficult to handle than those in the mainly Hakka east side. A vice raid in a village could easily erupt into a confrontation with the Police. Some of the villagers did not want their activities disturbed. There were occasions in my new command when I needed to talk to the village leaders and let them know that obstructing the police would be firmly dealt. A platoon from the Police Tactical Unit (PTU) could be posted to their village/s. I have no recollection now of any thing untoward happening during most of my watch as SDI. Down the road at Pat Heung, however, where Paul Croft was the SDI, There were two really

225

traumatic events: A Kowloon Motor Bus (KMB) coming down Route Twist (The road linking Tsuen Wan with Sek Kong) had a break failure at the bottom and ploughed through a shop/restaurant. On another occasion a spectator stand collapsed during a show in the Sek Kong camp killing and injuring a number of people.

I got married on the 5th February 1977 at the Yuen long Registry Office. Diana looked gorgeous and from the photographs I looked over-weight and clearly not deserving of such a lovely girl. The reception was in the Yuen Long mess. Steve Stephenson ex NRP and colleague from my time in the CID/Kowloon was the best man. Brian Gravener, some would say the European doyen of Hong Kong's Oriental Crime Fighters, gave the bride away. Bob Brooks was there, a little miffed that he was not the best man. Their three wives were there looking lovely. Grace Stephenson and Marilyn Brooks remain good friends long after both their husbands have passed on. The two ushers included that lovely character Bob Wilkinson, the only man given a field promotion: he was promoted to Chief Inspector without passing the qualifications because he was so respected and liked by everyone, from station labourer to Commissioner of Police. A gentleman at a time when there were none too many in Hong Kong's finest. The other was another such gentleman who commanded the Pat Heung sub-division down the road from Yuen Long: Paul Croft.

Dear Bob did not make old bones; perhaps his addiction to smokes and the booze didn't help. That and his over generous and sensitive nature. Paul, thank goodness, after many downs, including loosing his dear wife is still with us. He has just

(Summer 2013) taken over as president of the Hong Kong chapter of the RHKP Association.

*Those closest to us; best man Steve; then between the happy couple Brian Gravener, the doyen of Hong Kong's European Detectives; Diana's best friend; her cousin Annie and husband policeman John to the left of the group.*
*What a fat sod am I and how gorgeous is Diana.*

The wedding day was a great occasion marred by the news on the day that my dear Mum had passed away at the small hospital in Ludlow. It certainly was terrible: our marriage on the death of my mother. God! How I wept. A Chinese wedding dinner had been prepared when Diana would put on her traditional red wedding dress and our Chinese relatives, her mum and brothers, and friends would attend. This had all been planned and we decided to go ahead with it. My place as the groom would be taken by Steve and I would fly off immediately to attend the funeral which followed within a day or so of me landing.

She was cremated at Shrewsbury and there was a service at her Church, St Lawrence, Ludlow. Her ashes were to be put under a stone in the church graveyard.

Oh such sadness. I have never got over losing her. I wept and wept hiding outside Ludlow Castle. Poor Dad. He was now up by himself at Ludlow. He had had a colostomy and I was worried about him. My sister went back to London and Dad's brother and wife to their home on the south coast. I returned to HK.

Ever since that sad day I have blamed myself for not giving a thought to making sure Mum and Dad were invited and could have come to the wedding. I fear I did not. I was so wrapped up with myself and the new job. I excuse myself now by saying it was only a few months before that Diana and I had been with them at Ludlow. Mum died, apparently of aneurysm in the brain. Could this have been brought about by not attending the wedding: Her joy, excitement and concern. It certainly is one of the crosses I now have to bear.

229

I was only in England for a week and had to get back to work, which continued as SDI/YL performing uniform duties. I was a year more as SDI/YL before the DS Ernie Common and powers above, including the NT Boss Mr Illingworth transferred me within the division to DDI/YL.

I was back in the CID, commanding all units within the division, including those of its sub divisions: Yuen Long (YL), Pat Heung (PH), Castle Peak (CP) and Lau Fau Sha (LFS). My number two at YL as Officer in Charge of CID was Paul Chung Kwai-fat a Hakka from the Sai Kung area and the son of a man who had business connections with the fishing industry at Aberdeen and beyond. He was well educated in the UK and extremely bright and was a Senior Inspector. There were two or three other Detective Inspectors and depending on work levels, I would sometimes post one of these as OC/CID/PH. Altogether I had about a 100 plus officers of all ranks, a smaller command than at SSPo with nothing like the volume of crime.

But just weeks before my return to CID and still SDI I was involved with a crime which must be on the record books.

To the south of the sub division there were the hills and the Tai Lam Chung reservoir. There was a hike which took you along the Tai Tong Road south through villages then over a hill by way of steps and dirt track until you came to the reservoir, the bigger hills leading on further south towards Tsuen Wan. At weekends the track would be popular with young hikers. One day a gang of youths laid an ambush on the track near the foot of the hill. As the hikers, usually in groups of 4 or more arrived at the steps they would rob them at knifepoint. They continued robbing for some hours. The area was remote and it was not the days of mobile phones. The robbery should be on the record books because there must have been a hundred or more victims. At least 40 came to make a report at YL and others were located through appeals to the public. The crime was in my area and as I was not yet in the CID the investigation was not my responsibility. Paul Chung and his team did a good job identifying the robbers and collecting the evidence to convict them.

The scores of witnesses were required to attend identification parades held at the YK Station. I, as a Chief Inspector, was authorised to conduct these parades. Again it must have been a record: 60 or so victims eventually turned up. It certainly was not an easy job to have so many suspects, we had five, and so many victims on a parade. Logistics: the actors to form the parade and the location of the viewing room were problems. We got started and the victims filed into the parade one by one. It took the best part of the day to complete the parade and was well into the evening when we finished. The robbers were all identified by most of the victims. They went quickly to Fanling District Court where Henry Daniel the magistrate, but with his District Acting Judge hat on. convicted and sentenced them. I believe (It is 35 years ago) they got 4 years, although some would have been juveniles and gone to Training Centre. Today they would have gone to the High Court.

We learnt after, that some motivation to do the robbery had come from a movie going at the time. It was about a gang who had robbed cinemagoers. It showed them going along each row of seats stealing at knifepoint from each spectator. Our robbers had certainly used a similar modus operandi. By the time they had been convicted I was the DDI. I recall I inherited a solved murder case which still need to be prepared for Court.

I have said that YL did not have the volume of crime of SSPo. But it certainly was not sleepy hollow. Most of the major triad societies were well represented in all the villages. The notorious and influential Sun Yee On being prominent and active in Castle Peak. The ownership of a 'deng uk' (village house), a scheme where every male indigenous villager was entitled to build and own his home, had created unearned wealth. A deng uk was permitted to be of three stories, covering an area of 700 plus square feet. These were supposed to be for the owner's habitation. But many got around the restrictions and turned the houses into three flats and made a tidy sum selling each one. Many of these sons of the village did not even live there anymore and had emigrated to the UK.

The bars in Kam Tin were built and originally used by Her Majestie's Soldiery at the Sek Kong camp nearby. They started to be used by the young locals most of whom had some sort of triad background. Things got out of hand one night and a youth was chopped to death. This was when I was still SDI/YL. Once I had taken over as DDI I decided we needed to show our presence in the Kam Tin and its bars. There must have been around 8 bars then, some rough, some less so, but all under the influence of someone not in lawful authority. They employed bar girls, most from town and some needing care and protection. I called most of my men back, notified Paul Croft about what we were to do, and then set off to raid all the bars and places of ill repute. We certainly shook the place up. We arrested about 60 people needing two police lorries to get them back to Yuen Long. They were arrested for Suspected

Involvement in Triad Activities. There were cries later, after complaints had been made to the Complaints Against Police Office, about what evidence I had to justify so many arrests, although we did charge a number for triad offences and arrested a number who were wanted persons.

I was required to submit a report as to what I had done and why. Uncle Ernie Common my boss supported me. I explained that the area was getting out of hand with the homicide of the youth before and unreported cases of extortion on shops and bars. I took full responsibility for what I had done and would do it again. I add here that Kam Tin remained a proper place to relax for a long time after. I did apologise to one man who I had arrested and perhaps I had overlooked. He was a merchant seaman who had been a little under the weather through drink and was a decent man.

I was involved with a number of cases which I took to the High Court. Some I had become directly involved in the Investigation. In those days it was practice for the DDI even if he was a non-fluent Chinese speaker to take the statement on arrest and on charging under caution from a suspect. This being done through and interpreter. It had also become the practice, at least from my experience, to record such important procedures on a cassette recorder. I recall I did so with an arrest of a son who had killed his father in Castle Peak. The case did introduce me to a prominent member of the community who I was surprised had links with the Sun Yee On Triad Society. The son was charged with murder and originally pleaded not guilty. Once the trial started he changed his plea to guilty after his confession was ruled admissible. I ponder now if it would have been today; such statements have to be in the language of the maker notwithstanding the taker has some command of the language and has a first class interpreter.

Another case that comes to mind was a rape. It was not a stranger on stranger but one where the man knew the girl. He was charged and taken, as was procedure, first to the Failing magistrates court, where I objected to bail. I was concerned: it was a serious case and the parties were from the same area. Henry Daniel after a plea from counsel granted bail. Some weeks later there was a report of a man hanging in a YL village; sadly it was the rapist.

One of the saddest cases I handled at YL was the manslaughter in Castle Peak of a pre-school infant. She was one of three children of a perfectly outwardly normal middle earning Chinese couple. Her siblings were healthy school children. She was like the runt of the litter. She had been starved, beaten and neglected until her small body could take no more and she died. I fought hard to get her parents charged with Homicide. I recall the legal Department were for a lesser child abuse charge. I recall both mother and father were charged with manslaughter, one going to prison. I had always admired the Chinese for the emphasis they put on family and children and this was an extraordinary case seen alas in cases more often in other cultures.

Life was good at YL. I was happy with my Diana. Uncle Ernie Common was a good boss and I had a hard working likeable OC CID in Paul Chung. Paul lived in the flat above me within the YL Station Compound. He had a lovely English/Swedish wife and a young baby daughter. My own daughter was to come on the 16/4/78., born in Queen Elizabeth Hospital. I awaited her arrival first at the Hospital then at the La Bamba Bar In Tsim Sha Tsui. It was there I got the news. Diana was fine and the baby: Alfreda (after my Dear Mum) Emily an absolute Joy. Poh Poh, Diana's Mum, helped the first few weeks at our quarters in YL as Alfreda and her Mum settled in. Her cot was in our bedroom and as she grew it was nice to wake up, the pair of us, to see Alfreda standing in the cot looking over to us. I would take her sometimes over to the Officers mess where she would sit on the bar with Uncle Ernie sometimes cradling her in his arms. Paul Croft, Bob Wilkinson (SDI/LFS) and others would make a fuss of her and her rival, Paul Chung's little girl.

*Our gorgeous baby Alfreda:*
*A chubby Dad holding the lovely bundle at her 'first moon' party*
*held at a restaurant in Yuen Long.*

*And with Mum on the same occasion.*

But sadly things were starting to happen that would change my family's life.

I had let myself get too large. I had always weighed in at 220 pounds or so but always convinced myself that walking the hills kept me fit enough. Life with the Officers mess centred on the bar and sundowners plus good living was taking effect. One weekend I decided on a long hike. I took a vehicle to the top of Route Twist on Tai Mo Shan Mountain and then walked along the ridge above the Sek Kong Valley to the path that led over the hill from Tai Lam Chung to Yuen Long. The last part up the steps caused me some difficulty. I had a minor pain in my chest but didn't worry about it and carried on as usual for a few days. Colleagues and Diana said I should go to the Families Clinic at Queen Elizabeth Hospital for a check up. I saw a New

Zealand Doctor called Wong, a Chinese with roots in that country going back to 19th century. He took my pulse: 'Dave! You have got no pulse!' Apparently it was going so fast he could not feel it. I said I felt fine so he sent me home to come back for tests, which I did. The heart was racing and was irregular.

I was hospitalised and ended up having electric charges bounced on and off my chest. It was like being hit in the chest with a sledgehammer. The doctors tried on two separate days to get my motor firing properly and on the second day the pulse slowed down, although was still irregular. I was monitored by a machine next to my bed and could hear my heart going: da,da,da,da,tit,da,da,tit,tit; in any event all over the place. My carburettor was blocked and the motor was misfiring all over the place. I could hear it. Turn the bloody thing off! I said.

I was discharged after a week, fit for work and returned to my job as DDI/Yl. I was not myself but was determined – before I left CID/YL – that I would write a full report on the crime and triad situation in the various towns and villages of the Division. I thought it would be a good idea to map out literally the strengths and locations of the various unlawful societies: together with known personalities involved. This I did and forwarded to NT HQ. I was surprised when much later I learnt that no one there seemed aware of the report. Things get lost and/or such intelligence may already have been on file!?

In regard to my health I let the thing wear me down. The doctors had said I must take my pulse regularly and report to Casualty whenever it went irregular and was beginning to have cardiac neurosis. But I went off on leave with my dear Diana and baby Alfreda. She must have been 15 or so months old. I decided to see a specialist in England and hoped the long vacation would restore my confidence and health.

We went home via Ceylon and hired a car and driver to tour the country. I remember we could not get milk formula for Alfreda so she subsisted quite happily on bananas. There was a lot to see and enjoy: the beaches on the north east and south coasts, the game parks, the high lands with the tea plantations and colonial hotels, the old town of Galle, the holy city of Kandy and of course the capital Colombo. Our driver was a lovely chap who really looked after us and kept us safe in what unfortunately was a poor and badly governed country.

The flight from Colombo back to London was in a British Airways VC 10 and I recall how ill I felt on that flight. I was starting to develop phobias and unnatural fears: flying, enclosed spaces goodness all manner of things. My poor Diana what had she got into marrying me. In the UK we made for my home in Ludlow. My health had not improved when I saw my poor Dad. He was not looking after himself although seemed to be handling the colostomy bag quite well. I realised that he should not be by himself and it would be best if he returned to live, for a while at least, at his home at 7 Priory Villas, London. N11. I had decided this after we had made a trip up to Scotland to visit and stay with a friend of Diana, who had married a Scottish soldier. It was here that Alexander was conceived, so he had some affinity to Scotland! We came back to Ludlow and then took a short pre-Christmas break on the Mediterranean in Tunis. We were booked to fly back to Hong Kong at the end of January via a few days stop over in Kenya.

*Me leaving with Alfreda for the last time my house: Westminster Cottage, Bell lane.*

*The only photograph of my father with his granddaughter*
*taken in Ludlow just prior to us leaving.*
*It is also the last picture of him.*

We took my Dad back to his house at 7 Priory on our way to the airport. His presence was not apparently welcomed and sadly I left him there with no other choice. He could not live by himself; it was his house. I couldn't take him back to HK; my health was poor and after a visit to a Harley Street specialist I was not sure if I would be fit to continue my career in the Police. The report from the specialist said that with my neurosis it was unlikely I would ever be a good prospect for regular employment. Oh how wrong he was.

We returned to HK and I was sent as senior Instructor to the Detective Training School situated at an old RAF Building above Choi Hung in Kowloon. We were given a quarter in Eade Road, North Kowloon, right at the top of Waterloo Road. We could sit on our balcony and watch the planes as they flew passed just yards in front of us as they banked sharp right to turn and land at Kai Tak Airport. I understand it was regarded by pilots as a tricky manoeuvre.

It was a good quarter, we employed for a short time an amah who had worked for Bob and Marilyn Brooks. She was a marvellous soul. A traditional black and white amah. The filipinas had not yet really started as domestic helpers and these single ladies from Shun Tak up in China, who had been part of the domestic culture in Hong Kong for probably as long as it was there, were still very much around. She could cook anything: pastries, cakes and her ironing was as if done by the laundry department at the Peninsula Hotel. Sadly she did not work for us for long as we were to leave Hong Kong soon.

I had tried to do something about my phobias and had seen Bill Green, a forensic psychiatrist who had given evidence in one of my High Court cases. He kindly saw me a few times and advised I started to gain confidence through muscular tension and exercise. It sounds strange now but the idea was like in a 'Charles Atlas Course': tense your muscles then release and continue to do so, this to be coupled with aerobic exercise. I started long distance running.

But it was along time before I got right. My instructions from the cardiologist were ever in my mind: if your pulse goes irregular report to casualty at the hospital. This I did at least twice to be kept waiting for hours and then admitted when I told them my doctor's instructions. I was detained barely longer

241

than a couple of days. Poor Diana! All this and the fact that she was carrying Alexander, who had been conceived on our visit to Scotland.

I continued my duties as an Instructor at the Detective School. It was not far away, only a few stops on the new MTR line. But even this underground journey caused me stress. I was able to manage my work which consisted of lecturing very junior and senior Detectives, Inspectors and other ranks. I would write the scripts and produce realistic criminal plays. There would be victims with the necessary faked injuries and blood. The scene of these crimes would be prepared offering clues and lines of enquiry. The Judges Rules and the questioning of suspects and witnesses was an important part of the course. The boss was a decent chap, but a man who I thought was ill placed as the Commandant of a detective training school in our urban and complicated Hong Kong. He had come like a number of similar new officers from one of our remaining possessions in the Pacific who had arrived, apparently as 'new blood' to help the force restore its confidence. They were called the 'Coconuts'.

*Me as chief instructor and a course of detectives at the Royal Hong Kong Police Detective Training School.*

My own confidence declined, the pulse taking and trips to Casualty were taking a toll. I realised that I had best be out of the Force. Clearly even if I got better I was not going to get on. I had passed all my examinations for promotion to Superintendent, including, the paper 'E', which some said was difficult to pass. And I had passed the Senior Promotion Board held before a Senior Assistant Commissioner Browett. Mr Quinne stopped my promotion. I knew as long as he had influence I would never be promoted and I would be stuck in the heavy working rank of Chief Inspector. I decided to leave the Force and start a new career as a Barrister at law. I was assisted with this endeavour when a Medical Board decided I was not a good prospect to continue working as a police officer and should be retired on medical grounds with a pension.

# 17. Alfreda, Alexander and Aberystwyth

Alexander our son was born on the 4th June 1980 only a few months before I was to leave Hong Kong and fly off to UK to start my studies at the University of Wales, Aberystwyth, Wales. Dear Diana and the two babes were to join me later when I had sorted out our accommodation. She was to stay with my best man Steve Stephenson and his wife Grace in Kowloon.

Before we left Alfreda and Alexander were taken the short distance down Waterloo Road from Eade Road to Christ Church, Kowloon Tong where on the 31st August 1980 both were baptised. I still have the Certificate of Baptism for Alexander Charles; the one for Alfreda Emily is not to hand and I have some recollection of Alfreda keeping it. Alexander's Godparents were Mr and Mrs Henry Daniel and Mr R. J. Stephenson. Henry Daniel had been the Magistrate at Fanling and had been a friend for much of the time I worked in the New Territories. He was a member of the Fanling Police Officers mess and was good company and a friend to a number of its members. I say a friend; this friendship did not extend to his relationship with the Police and he could be a bloody nuisance in Court. He was one to throw out cases when he found the evidence unreliable and certainly could never be called like some of his brother magistrates: A pro police bench. His wife was a Chinese lady from North Borneo. Stephenson (Steve) was my best man who I had known since my days in the Northern Rhodesia Police. A dear friend and a brave and admired policeman.

Alfreda's God parents were Steve's wife Grace, a lovely albeit tiny Chinese lady, Bob Brooks, a fine Scotsman from Burnt island, in the Kingdom of Fife and his wife Marilyn from Welsh Wales. Bob was my best friend. I had known him since my time in Africa and was particularly fond of him and Marilyn. He certainly enjoyed a drink, knew his whisky and sadly didn't make old bones. Marilyn still lives at the old Brooks residence in Burnt island a home occupied by Bob's parents before they died. I stayed there in earlier days and got to know Bob's dear Mum. Her Scottish breakfasts, with their 'puddins', I can still remember with pleasure.

The Certificate of Baptism has a message on the second page:

'A member of Christ, the child of God and an inheritor of the Kingdom of Heaven' together with 'A prayer of St Richard'

Thanks be to thee my Lord Jesus Christ,
 For all the benefits which thou hast given me,
 For all the pains and insults which thou hast
 borne for me.
O most merciful Redeemer, Friend and Brother,
 May I know thee more clearly,
 Love thee more dearly,
 And follow thee more nearly:
  Day by Day. Amen.

I include the above as a reminder of the prayer I used to recite to my two young children as part of their bedtime prayers when we lived at Aberystwyth. I recall that Alfreda could recite it from memory.

It was on the 26th September 1980 that I kissed them all goodbye at Kai Tak Airport. Kevin Sinclair a reporter from the South China Morning Post was there. Also many friends from all working ranks in the Force who I had worked with during my 16 years in the Force. Kevin an old friend and generally a supporter of working policemen was there to take a short interview from me and take photographs. This was subject of his column: 'Conversations' published in Sunday's Post on the 28th September and entitled **Danger: Officer under strain.** A copy of which I have framed, rather ostentatiously, on the wall in my study. I felt very sad to kiss my daughter and Diana and shake the hands of those dear mates who so loyally had served with me. I was going into a new life. I had not really lived in the UK since leaving in 1962 to go to Africa.

I landed at Heathrow and made my way by train to Aberystwyth. During my last visit I had made friends with my tutor to be: John Baxter, who like me had been a mature student. He had helped me gain admission. My family and I needed accommodation and he put me on to the right people. For the first month or so I lived at a bed and breakfast place in the town. There were other students there and a very nice Welsh lady ran the place. It would of course only be suitable until Diana and the children arrived. After which the University would give us a student married quarter that was right on the sea front near the pier.

I met Diana at Heathrow on or around the 11th of October. I was proud and to some extent ashamed when I saw her emerge from customs and immigration with bags and the two babes. She had a long flight: 17 or so hours and must have been truly whacked out. She carried Alexander in a sling on her front and Alfreda similarly on her back. I said to myself: What have I done, a lovely Chinese girl from Western in Hong Kong coming to a foreign country with a different culture and language which, where we were going, was very 'Welsh'.

I had hired a car from a local pub and I have little memory of the journey. Diana must have been tired out what with feeding Alexander and Alfreda. It must have been a 5 hour drive to Aberystwyth. We arrived totally shattered and moved into the university flat, which was fully furnished. Our own stuff from Hong Kong and from Westminster cottage would come later when we would be given a slightly better unfurnished flat by the university. There was plenty of room, it was austere but not uncomfortable and would do until we had our own place. We were to be in student accommodation for well over a year before we bought our own house.

The flat was in Marine Parade on the Promenade just around the corner from Pier Street which leads onto the sea front and the Aberystwyth Pier, in all its glory, just to our left.

Almost next door was a Chinese restaurant run by the Chung family from the Lam Tsuen Valley in Hong Kong. My dear wife became good friends with one of the wives there. A lady with four sons, their English names begin: A. B. C, with the last one D and the English, or should I say Scottish, name Duncan! She also had one daughter. They were really nice people. Duncan was about the same age as Alfreda, so our families had much in common. I remember that some days I would walk the two little ones to a play school at a church near us. Diana would be home with Alexander. Our friendship with the Chungs remained over the years and it is only the last few years since my Diana died that we have not seen each other. Although I am still sending Christmas cards.

Our finances were not good. A 38 year old mature student with only a limited police pension and savings to live on. The house at Ludlow was empty and locked up. My father I had left with my sister. I wanted to sell the place but there were difficulties with my sister and/or her daughter in allowing my father, who was joint owner, to sign the sale agreement. She wanted a share in the proceeds and the return of the furniture in the house which I had bought for my parents and some of which I had shipped from Hong Kong. Thus there was no question of me selling it and buying a place for us to live. We would have to remain in rented university accommodation; until goodness knows when.

My personal tutor at the University John Baxter had been helpful to us: he had got me registered as a local student; not as an overseas student. Which I could have been with all my time abroad. This saved much in fees. I was keen to get this paid by the local authority. I was a property owner in Ludlow paying rates and also now was a resident in Aberystwyth, Ceredigion, Dyfed. I thus might be able to apply to both respective education authorities for help. I thought that as a UK citizen I might qualify for a grant to pay the fees and living expenses. This was the norm then for all UK resident belonger's.

My application to the Education Authorities was turned down. I had been too long away and did not qualify for a mandatory grant. I was disappointed. It was going to be difficult for us to live, especially with our house in Ludlow in limbo.

I got work as best I could, but as my studies progressed I found I had little free time. I was determined to get a top law degree and so was a diligent student carefully dividing my time between my family, my lectures and tutorials at the University. I was able to get some cleaning jobs: cleaning at a hotel and a Wimpy bar in the town. I wrote to my old master: the RHKP for help and they kindly offered to help pay for some of my text books.

I also started what turned out to be a lengthy exercise: an appeal against the Education Authorities' refusal to offer me a grant. This included writing to my members of parliament: Geraint Howell the Plaid Cymru MP for Dyfed and the MP (whose name I have no memory) for South Shropshire. I followed these letters up with visits to the Houses of Parliament where I met the MP for Ludlow. If it was his intervention that got me a discretionary grant I don't know, but I was awarded one. My fees were also to be paid. What a relief! I wrote to the authority and the MP thanking them and assuring all that I was determined to justify the award.

The degree course was to be three years. All lectures and tutorials to be held at the campus up the hill from Aberystwyth at Penglais. Each year there would be 5 subjects. The first year I recall was criminal law, constitutional law and contract, the others have escaped me. There was a mock just before Christmas 1980 and, as could be expected I flew by with the criminal law. Professor Andrews our lecturer said: 'Well David, that's to be expected.' Thus I was surprised to find with the first years results out that for some reason criminal law had become my worst subject. I realised later that I was finding it difficult to find the wood in the trees. I was too diligently reading all the cases which were on our reading list and was missing the main points. I later learnt as a lawyer to focus on the issues: don't get lost with all the waffle! In any event I showed I was up to the mark to continue into the next year.

We were outsiders so it was difficult to make friends. I did however have help settling in. A local doctor: Dr Lloyd who I had first met when he was attending a masonic dinner at the hotel where I cleaned and served. I didn't speak much then, but later he became our family doctor. He was a senior mason and knew I was a very junior mason from HK. He took me under his wing and took me around a number of lodges in the West Wales area. He was everything good about masonry and helped me to advance to my next degree within his lodge, after my own Lodge: Star of Southern China in Hong Kong had given dispensation.

We lived on the sea front for what must have been nearly a year. I bought an old Marina car which was held together with 'polyfiller'. But it got us around . At weekends we would have family outings to places like the Dovey Estuary to collect cockles or to Devil's Bridge Falls and the lovely countryside around us. Sunday we would go to St Michael's, Laura Place, the local Anglican church. As it was Sunday and Ceridigion was dry with the pubs closed we would sometimes motor down to Machyhlleth where they had not voted for drink free Sundays. There was a place on the way: The White Lion, next door to the

Black Lion in Talybont which did really great lunches and had a garden. When it became time for the Ceredigion voters to vote on Sunday drinking our rector Bertie Lewis said: 'I hope you all are going to vote to keep us dry on our Sunday'. I had to say: 'I am sorry Bertie but I can't miss my few pints of Banks's beer before our late Sunday lunch'. But I was a supporter of the Church. I even got confirmed there at the age of 38. Alfreda got involved with the Sunday school and Alexander the crèche. Another Chinese restaurant belonging to another member of the Chung family was right across from the church and Diana would some times go there.

I remember our first Christmas 1980. The children were very small: Alexander was only 6 months and Alfreda 22 months. Poor Diana; never complained and went about looking for ways to improve our income. I forget how she did it but even in the early days she managed to earn a few pounds at the local Wimpy bar; selfishly I have no idea how she coped. But I did manage with the help of Mrs Chung from the Restaurant next door to combine studies and baby sitting.

I recall the winter of 1980/81. One morning Diana reported to me that the sea outside our front window on Marine Parade had frozen. 'Don't be silly' said Old know it all: 'The sea has not frozen since the 18th Century'. But sure enough it had and the beach and promenade was in four feet of snow. I am sad to say I don't have many memories of our time at Marine Parade. I recall the family would walk along the prom and visit the short pier.

Diana got involved with the foreign wives group at the University and through a friendship with the wife of an Indian

252

research student became excellent at making chapattis and other dishes from the Sub Continent. We made do and she never moaned or pressed me for money.

After I had taken my first year exams: five subjects. What each was I have now little recollection: criminal law, contract, constitutional law? I took the family for a fortnights holiday on the Costa Brava landing at Girona airport. It was a cheap package tour full of 'Brits' of all shapes and sizes looking for budget booze and food. They are a few pictures of us riding donkeys with me with a wispy beard perilously holding Alexander between my legs. I recall the beard stayed for about a year then fell off one day when I was doing my regular lengths in the University pool. Then it was back, after a trip around the houses: Girona/Luton/Cardiff by air then a bus to Aberystwyth and a vacation job as night hall porter up at Penglais student accommodation.

Summer jobs for me and Diana's part time jobs were certainly needed to keep us going, at least until we knew what was going to happen with the Ludlow house. The jobs which came, sadly gave me little summer holiday time for the family. But dear Diana used her friendship with the Chung family to explore the town and particularly the cockling beds on River Dovey Estuary. I went a few times. It was great fun filling the buckets with the fresh cockles. The Chinese will never miss an available food source, especially if is from the sea. They are also green fingered and Mr. Chung's ability to grow vegetable at his house, five doors down from us, was commendable.

My job at the Hall was from evening to morning. I was responsible for cleaning all the common areas of the hall: Both male and female lavatories, the staircases and floors and for being on call to deal with any incidents with the residents. As it was for much of the time out of term, the accommodation was used by mature students and people on special courses or on holiday terms with the University. They were an assortment of mature 'professional' students, holiday makers and interesting people doing short semesters. The state of the toilets often determined the type and quality of the occupants!

I started the new academic year at the end of September 1981. I recall that towards the end of that academic year that funds had improved enabling us to think about buying our own home. A new home and a new car. We bought a blue Fiat 128. Diana had started driving lessons and it displayed for a time an 'L' plate. I had gone with her on her first test, telling the examiner I would be needed to translate from Cantonese to English. OK, I know what you are thinking: you were to give the right answers. Well it did not work. Diana got so nervous with me sitting in the back behind her and the Welsh examiner, that she missed a corner and drove on the pavement, thus earning a failure. Don't come with me again she said angrily as we got out the car. And I didn't; a few months later she passed her test. She was certainly a better driver than I was.

My second year '81/'82 at University was uneventful. I worked hard during the day on the assignments, attended all the lectures and tutorials. I would try to combine family, work, pleasure and exercise. Most days I would go for a swim at the college pool doing my laps, routinely a mile plus. I would also on good days go jogging, covering not infrequently five plus miles around the lovely countryside. I was worried about my irregular heart and was determine to keep my weight down. I

254

had seen Doctor Lloyd at the beginning of 1981 about my condition. I had told him how I had been invalided out of the Police Force and instructed by my doctor in Hong Kong that I must never drink alcohol again. He took my pulse and said: 'Yes, you have an irregular pulse and so does about 40% of the town if you were to stop them in the street. 'Go and have a couple of pints of Banks's mild beer it will do you the world of good, but we will wire you up to a monitor for a week to see how you get on.' And have a couple of pints of that splendid brew I did. It is still my favourite beer: a malty brew with a hint of hops and only 3.5 alcohol. I wore the monitor for a week and went back to see Dr. Lloyd. How is it I asked? It's irregular but you are OK he said; carry on with your exercise and enjoy a few pints. This really restored my confidence; clearly Dr Lloyd knew his patient. I became really fit and became a strong distance runner and swimmer.

Doctor Lloyd had been particular kind when dear Diana had a miscarriage in our second year back and had to stay for a short time in Bronglais Hospital.

I would study in the evenings at home but would always eat with the family. Diana was a first class cook and there was not much she couldn't cook. Weekends would be a roast which she did superbly. I recall going to the butchers in the town one Saturday with the family and asking for New Zealand lamb! The Welsh lady, who we got to know, nearly threw me out of the shop! Sunday was always church followed by dinner and sometimes an afternoon drive. Saturday was shopping in the town and or the supermarket up at Waun Fawr. There were many nice drives: to Devil's Bridge about 15 miles; along the Afon river to the Cwm Rheidol reservoir; the coast road along to the cockle beds on the Dovey estuary. There was a narrow gauge railway from the Aberystwyth station to Devil's Bridge which was not cheap: one of the Great Little Railways of Wales. But it only cost a platform ticket to look at the steam engines!

I said above that things for the second year at University were uneventful but they certainly were not for Great Britain and in particular its colony in the South Atlantic: The Falkland Islands. I remember how many of us from the Saint Michael's Church gathered in the church hall to pray for all those involved in the conflict, our servicemen in particular, for there to be peace. It was May/June 1982 and two Royal Navy ships had been lost. The nation was concerned. The meeting in the hall was strangely moving. I called myself a Christian believer then as I do today. I enjoy church, the message of the love of God, the hymns and the company of others of a like mind. But at the time I was suspicious of those termed 'Charismatics' who were into the spirit; hands in the air, rapture and all that! We started to pray, about 25 of us, at about 7.30 am. We were still there at 10.30. I felt as if a warm glow had come over me dispelling all doubts I had about my unbelieving; inexplicable became explicable. Those three plus hours were as if fractions of time, seconds, minutes. When I got home, we were still at Marine Parade, Diana looked at me and said 'What's happened'. It may sound mumbo jumbo but she could see I had had a religious experience. Ever since then I have always tried to attend church every Sunday wherever I am and at church festivals. I also understand what praying in the spirit and in tongues mean. To certain friends who have known me for years I can hear you now: 'Is that really our Dave!'

I took another lot of examinations for the five second-year subjects. I forget what they all were: tort and international law ring a bell in my memory; I found the latter really interesting being very much an international political historian. After the examination it was time to earn some money. It was I recall another summer as night porter at the student accommodation at Penglais. I have little recollection what I did when not sleeping in the day to be ready for work. It can't have been very good for the family. I know it was still church on Sunday. But I do recall that just before the new-year started at the end of September 1982 we had a holiday in Malta. Diana had made friends with a Maltese lady who encouraged us to visit there. I can see from Alfreda's British Airways Junior Jet Club Log Book that we flew off from Birmingham Airport on the 2nd September 1982 and returned on the 17th September. I recall that during the trip we stopped some thieves who were breaking into the car we hired. The Maltese Police were not interested. The friend of Diana entertained us to a meal at her lovely home in the capital Valletta. She told us of the places to visit. One day we took the ferry over to the other island Gozo, another day I swam across Saint Paul's Bay. We also attended on Sunday the Anglican Cathedral. We stayed in a self-catering apartment.

Diana had met this Maltese friend through one of the associations for overseas staff and students of the university. She made some friends who were from Hong Kong, one girl in particular we kept in contact with when we returned to HK years later. She would attend meetings and social gatherings organised for married families.

The children not so much babies now at 2 and 4. Alfreda would on our return start in the baby class at Comins Coch junior school (4 to 11's.) Although I recall she had started going to a state funded kindergarten at a school at the end of Park Avenue when she was just three. Comin Coch school was just a couple of miles down the road from Waun Fawr where we purchased 42 Maescenion. Which we were able to do because by the time I had come to the end of the second academic year my father had died and as my Ludlow property had been owned by me, mum and dad as joint tenants I was free to sell as sole owner. I recall now that he died in the late winter/ spring.

It was a detached family house with a study for me, two bedrooms, a lounge and a small kitchen where we ate, plus a garage and small gardens spaces front and back. The mortgage payments I could meet with the grant money, savings and what we earn t. I arranged with the local Pickfords removal company to clear the Ludlow house of furniture. Some of the old cheap furniture had previously been sold through an agent at Ludlow. The rest: nice stuff which I had purchased in Hong Kong or in my travels from India I collected and helped bring back to our new home. I was given a special rate by Pickfords because I was a student and had done part time work with them before. We were then in a much more comfortable state to finish my last academic year.

The house was on a modern estate. Some would say most of the homes were standard 'Barrett' detached houses, three up and two down with garage and small front and back gardens. If I may say such the people were for the most part middle class, with some from the university. Our friends the Chung family were a few houses down. There was an open park behind us where I remember a bonfire was lit on Guy Fawkes night. All Waun Fawr residents would bring fireworks to the delight of all, children especially.

It was walking distance for me to the main university building at Penglais where the lectures and tutorials were held. There was a path which went down from Waun Fawr down the hill beside the university complex to Llanbadarn Fawr where there was another Black Lion pub. It served my favourite tipple: Banks's mild ale. I would visit here in the evenings about 9pm, usually twice a week, never going over my limit of two pints. I would then walk up the steep hill back to Waun Fawr. I would always say goodnight and say prayers – as my mother had done with me – with the two children, who shared a room and who were always in bed by 7pm, 8pm at the latest. Diana was a loving but strict Mum.

I studied hard in my last year as I was determined to get a first class honours degree. But this was wishful thinking. I recall my friend and tutor John Baxter had said that there had not been a first at Aber for years. They didn't give them away like some of the more ancient stone and honourable centres of learning. I recall the examination hall and the tension I felt. These were the examinations which would really count and decide if I was good enough to pursue my desire to practice law at the bar. The final year was the usual 5 subjects although I only remember Trusts and Legal History. The latter I enjoyed, especially with my interest as a political historian. I was also required to submit a dissertation which I had done early in the last term; this would count for the degree together with a moot I took part in during my second year.

In the moot I was counsel for the Republic of Argentina against Great Britain and Northern Ireland before the International Court in the Hague in the matter of sovereignty of the Falkland Islands. I researched the case thoroughly and considered we had a good argument. I learnt then that you don't have to believe in your case to stop you arguing it vigorously, persuasively and fairly. The Falkland War intervened and I recall the court (staff and student) did not deliver a judgement. I was told by my tutors, however, that I had delivered a convincing case.

My dissertation was The English Constable at Common Law. The idea was to trace his origins as very much a creature of the community. We had no national police like countries in Europe and our modern day police constable traces his origins to men like the parish constable and the town watch, officers who were often inefficient and some times bumbling figures of fun. Things progressed with Sir Henry Fielding's Bow Street Runners of the late 18th and early 19th century. The modern police forces, first the London police with the Metropolitan Police Act of 1829, were creatures of Sir Robert Peel who was also responsible some years before for starting the Royal Irish Constabulary. But unlike Ireland, England was not to have a national force. It was to have individual and independent police forces for cities, large towns and counties, each with their own chief constables and watch committees to supervise them. They were to be very much of the community not the state. There was some minimal responsibility with the Home Secretary. Like the Metropolitan Police, these forces would also be created by Act of Parliament. The English were always suspicious of the State Police that they could see in countries across the Channel.

I obtained a top two/one, with which I was happy. One girl, another mature student, got a first. The first one since 1901, well not really!

With my time at University finished I now had to decide where I was going. I had worked closely with barristers in my time as a Detective Chief Inspector in the CID in HK. I had seen some who were good and some who were hopeless. I recall a murder case I had inherited from a colleague in which I was OC case. It involved a deaf and dumb boy who was found standing over a dead shopkeeper at a village stall in Yuen Long. The evidence was all circumstantial with some forensic contact evidence. I felt sorry for the boy as he tried painfully to give his testimony in the witness box using sign language and an interpreter. Reliable testimony I thought not. I had hoped his counsel would have been able to explore the case and the doubts that there must have been. And to convince the jury it was unsafe to convict him for murder. I had my own doubts as to the accused's necessary guilty intent to kill. But then again it may have been the law then that it was murder if the killing was in the course of a felony: robbing the store. In any event I was not impressed with the counsel involved who I recall did not stay in Hong Kong. Sadly I understand the boy's appeal to the Court of Appeal was dismissed.

I started the procedure to register for a vocational course with the Inns Of Court School of Law at Grays Inn with a view to taking the Bar examinations which after so passing would qualify me for the next step: becoming a pupil. Then it was 6 months as a pupil in a set of chambers where I could learn but not earn anything followed by a second 6 months where I was able to earn professional fees. Then eventually hoping to find a set of chambers which would have me to practice law in England and Wales. Once enrolled for the Bar course I had to apply to one of the Inns to become a student member. I applied to Gray's Inn because I understood it had some historical connection with Wales. I then looked for work to help pay for the next year. When I would be again a mature student, this time without the benefit of a discretionary grant from the education authority.

But now was the time to earn some money and if possible have a break with the family before I started work and then moved down to London to start my year at the Inns of Court School of law at Gray's Inn London.

# 18. Raising the Bar

My time at the university finished at the end of the Easter term, around the last few weeks of May/June. It was then waiting time to graduation in July. I recall I took the family on a short weeks holiday to the Isle of Wight. I have no recollection of taking our car. I do remember being on the top of a bus on the Island pointing out the road signs to the two children. I was pointing out the black 'Bends Ahead' signs telling them they were to warn us there were black bananas on the road ahead. OK, hardly educational but it gave us something jolly to do as we sped along the country lanes. We stayed at a guesthouse at Ventnor on the south side of the Island. It was again selfish me! You remember I took the family: Mum and baby Alfreda all the way up to Nuwra Eliya in Ceylon to try a pint at one of the only places in the world, apart from Guinness, that brewed dry stout! Well Ventnor had Burt's Brewery with antecedents going back to the middle of the 19th century. Alas it is now no more. Then early summer it was still running and producing two delightful mild beers. There were 8 or so Burts' pubs in and around the town. Alas not enough to keep it going. A micro brewery took the name many years later again, I understand, to fail. We had a nice trip. I swam in the sea off Ventnor. We went on the Ryde to Shanklin train, saw the coloured sands etc. and then returned to Aberystwyth for me to start work at the Clarach Bay Holiday Village.

Clarach bay was the bay next north of Aberystwyth and was about three miles walk over a cliff walk. I recall taking Alex

263

there on walks. He was barely three, so I carried him on my shoulders and arms. My job at the village was, at first lifeguard/cleaner at the indoor swimming pool. I quickly got on with the Bourne family who owned this and another such business down at the next bay a few miles away at Borth. The boss asked me to act as doorman/bouncer at the nightclub/bar as well. This job, at three pounds an hour was a vast improvement on 1 pound 50 pence at the pool. The two jobs helped us a lot, but unfortunately the hours were not good: Pool in the day, night club in the evenings. I tried to keep Sunday free for church and family. The Borth business was Brynowen Holiday Park. I worked there also the following year at their outdoor pool.

The night club job was OK. I got friendly with some of the visitors who were for the most part from the English Midlands. They would either own or rent caravans/chalets in the village; some would come from outside. All were suppose to show membership cards unless I knew them as resident/owners. There were occasions when lower orders would come to the club, who clearly were not wanted. I was always firm with them and ignored the threats that sometimes came at me. The word seem to get around that I was ex-army or police and this helped my image as one with whom not to tangle. I was always careful not to drink on duty and it was only after we had started to close that I had a night cap. I did have a 6 or so mile drive home. It was usually lively in the night club with a resident band and sometimes floor show.

The work must have run from the middle of June to September when I started at the Inns of Court Law School. I recall I was so busy with the jobs that I overlooked graduation day which was on or around the second week in July. I picked up my graduation certificate later from my old tutor John Baxter at the University.

Although I couldn't attend graduation day when the certificates were presented I did attend the day earlier, after we had received our results, when we obtained caps and gowns and had our photographs taken.

*Me suitably attired outside the old college of Aberystwyth University.*

*Another, perhaps a clearer view with me outside the main block at Penglais.*

It must have been some day in September that Diana drove me to the Aberystwyth railway station where I kissed and hugged all three and got the train for Euston. It was a five hour trip with a change of trains at Wolverhampton. I had already joined Gray's Inn as a student member but needed to report to the Inn at Holborn WC.1. Here a very helpful secretary of the Inn, a Ms Chadderton assisted me in two ways. When I told her of my background and needs she suggested I write to one of the Inn charities to see if I could qualify for some financial assistance. There was one in particular that was for mature students like myself who had served HM in the overseas service. She advised how I should write to them: I recall it was called the Bands Award, which I did. She also gave me some addresses that had been used by students of the Inn for board and lodging. I was fortunate on both counts. I was awarded about a thousand pounds which was of much help with my London lodging and travelling expenses.

One of the addresses : 46A Hillside Road, Muswell Hill. London N.10 was just right. It was at the other end of Colney Hatch lane where I had lived before. My landlady was a widow, Mrs Margaretta Woods, a German whose husband had been a professional violinist. I had a nice comfortable bed in which I would spend much time during the winter cold, as there was no real heating in the room. Mrs Woods liked to be called Nana and I was to use her place for the two years I was qualifying in London.

We became very good friends and when things got really tight in my second year there she was good enough to excuse the rent when I had problems. She would provide breakfast and evening meal. She had a number of student lodgers before and for the first year there was for a few months a student from Saudi Arabia. Nana had been to Saudi Arabia as a guest of this chap: veils, burkhas and all! I was familiar with Muswell Hill as it was here in my teens I had courted my girl friend Marilynne Kent who married my friend Barnard Humphris. There were two cinemas at Muswell Hill and a 'new' pub: The John Logie Baird. The inventor of the first publically demonstrated television system shown down the road at Alexander Palace and the first colour TV tube. It was also a pub used by mum and dad when we lived at Colney Hatch lane.

I recall it was some time in September that the academic year started at The Inns of Court School of Law, which was situated within the precincts of Gray's Inn, Holborn. The nearest tube station was Chancery Lane. The whole area, with Lincoln's Inn not far away and the Inner and Middle Temples down at the other end of Chancery Lane at which was also situated the headquarters of the Law Society, had an atmosphere of legal learning. You could feel the history with the ancient signs, marks and buildings. I would get the 212 bus from Muswell Hill to Finsbury park where I would catch the tube to Chancery Lane.

I forget now the syllabus but to be called to the Degree of an UTTER BARRISTER by the Honourable Society of Gray's Inn you had to pass the Part 1 and 2 of your Bar examinations and then you had to attend at your Inn and dine, I think it was, four times each dining term.

The idea of the dining was to mix with your fellows, junior and senior members of your Inn. I recall we would have to be robed and would then sit on forms in the Great Hall of the Inn often with counsel and judge members. The idea was to make conversation and learn from what you heard. It was also a good exercise in manners and decorum. I recall that Gray's Inn provided wine with the dinner to each mess, other Inns were not so fortunate and had to pay for such luxuries; me thinks we also were served a bottle of port per table. Some students found the dining requirements a burdensome duty. But I enjoyed them. I did not have a lot to do in the evenings, the food was not bad and the atmosphere in the ancient hall was something to be experienced.

The academic part of the qualifying at the school of law was based on lectures, similar to university, and practical exercises. There were certain key subjects that one had to pass and a choice of others, non key. My LLB degree from Aberystwyth had most of the key subjects so the course for me centred more of the practical. We were taught how to do pleadings both in civil and criminal law. I remember evidence civil and criminal procedure were compulsory key subjects and I chose conflicts of laws and laws of the European Community as my optional subjects. I recall that we had also tutorials; the only learned teacher I recall now is one Mr. Emmins, who was particularly good at explaining criminal procedure. I bought his text book. There were also visits to barrister's chambers and to the High Court in the Strand where we would be involved in practical exercises and moots. Lunch would be in the school canteen or a sandwich from one of the sandwich shops in Chancery Lane.

There was a Christmas break when I returned home to celebrate with the family. The cost of the train and the short weekend meant I only got home about once every 4 to 6 weeks. There were no mobile phones and I don't recall using any phone at Mrs Woods. I seem to remember ringing home from a Muswell Hill call box at weekends. I was always excited when the train pulled into Aberystwyth railway station usually on a Friday evening. Diana would be there waiting with the car outside with the children hiding under the seats. They are such lovely memories. The weekends would be special, church as usual and a great Sunday lunch from Diana. I, to this day, feel guilty that I neglected the family with my determination to qualify at the Bar.

I forget now when it was examination time. I have no certificate to hand from the School of Law evidencing that I passed my exams; only the certificate from my Inn certifying my call to Bar, as mentioned above. This states that I was called on the 26th July, 1984. I recall the examinations were much earlier and I had dined a number of times after the examinations were finished and before being called to the Bar. This calling was done formally with a ceremony in Gray's Inn when a senior bencher presented us with our certificates. I have a photograph of me looking young and of proper size in a gown in the gardens of the Inn. It was a fine day and I recall there were snacks and drinks. This must have been call day.

*Me with a group of young attractive Gray's Inn students, wearing for the first time their bands and gowns, in the library of the Inn.*

*Me at the garden party held in the grounds of the Inn.*

I have little recollection of my fellow students of the time. I did get involved at the school with the Lawyers Christian Fellowship, which met regularly. I remember two Chinese girls who attended, one from England whose Chinese clearly was not her first language and another from Singapore whose Chinese was. The former later came to Hong Kong to work in the Director of Public Prosecutions department. She eventually married a friend and colleague at the Hong Kong Bar. In the time after the exams and being called I made efforts to find chambers who would take me as a pupil. I also needed to arrange for my next years London accommodation. Mrs Woods had kindly said she would be helpful as far as rent was concerned. I wrote to a number of chambers and had some help to start with from my Inn mentor: a practising member of the bar who had agreed to mentor a number of recently joined student members of the Inn.

I eventually found a place in a common law set of chambers in Gray's Inn Square. My pupil master was Leslie Blake. He had been a late starter at the bar like myself. He was primarily dealing in criminal law although I do recall accompanying him to the Royal Courts of Justice in the Strand for other matters. I have recollections of what was termed in the profession as the Bear Garden: the place where scores of lawyers would assemble and in a very Dickensian manner wave pleadings about for use in the adjacent Masters Court. Leslie was unusual in that he 'spoke' and wrote that ancient and mysterious language Sanskrit. Again I have no recollection of when I started six months pupillage with Leslie. You will recall that to qualify for practice I had to have performed at least 12 months successful pupillage. The first six was to assist and learn form my master and the second six likewise but I could under this master's tutelage accept briefs and earn fees.

I have records now of my second six months which was at 4 Paper Building, in the Temple where my pupil master was John

Harwood Stevenson. These show I was with John from January 1985. I know that for the summer break of 1984 I worked again 6 plus weeks for the Bourne's at the Clarach Bay holiday park night club and as life guard, this time at the open air pool at their other resort at Borth. I presume therefore that I must have started with Leslie at Gray's Inn Square as early as May and had a summer break whilst I worked for the Bourne's.

The summer job was much like the year before. This time I was out in the open in the day time at the pool returning home for dinner to get changed and put my suit on for my evening job at the night club. We needed the money. I had to fund our home at 42 Maescenion and my digs in London. There was no indication I would find a second six months pupillage let alone one that would give me any fees. Again Diana was so understanding, hard working and patient. She still managed to earn a few bob at the school as a dinner lady. We had no time to fit in a holiday this year, 1984, hence our one day off a week was special.

After the summer job it was down again to London to stay with Mrs Woods and my start as a pupil to Leslie. I have no memory of any particular cases I did with him. I do recall spending my time in the Gray's Inn library doing research and drafting the occasional opinion or pleadings. He was a very nice man and sympathetic to my position. But I could see it would be difficult getting a second six months with him or his chambers; I was therefore ever looking ahead. His work was mainly Crown, County and Magistrates Court. Although I do have recollections of going with him to the Royal Courts in the Strand. My evenings I spent working at Mrs Wood's doing work for him or writing to various chambers about a second six months.

There was the occasional meeting with the Lawyers Christian Fellowship, but my age, I was now 41, meant I did not fit in that well my younger fellows. I did become friends with the two Chinese girl students, one from Malaysia and the other an English Chinese that I mentioned above.

I also kept fit; I would use, as I did the previous year, the local swimming baths in Hornsey Road. At weekends hail, snow or sunshine I would go jogging, believe it or not, I would often run from Muswell Hill through Highgate Woods down into Hamstead then through the back roads to Regents Park then on via Oxford Street to Kensington Gardens where I would take the tube for home. It must have been at least 10 plus mile run. I would stop half way at Swiss Cottage and do a few lengths at the swimming pool there. Other weekends I would run from Muswell Hill via Southgate and Cockfosters to Potters Bar, Hertfordshire, again a 10 miles jog.

After work at the chambers I would sometimes spend a few bob at one of the pubs near Gray' s Inn at Lambs Conduit. One was a Young' s of Wandsworth pub selling really lovely beer. I recall their 'Winter Warmer' a brew to keep the cold at bay on a cold autumn or winter day. It was here that I ran again into my old friend Barnard Humphris. He was then working as a detective chief inspector just down the road at Holborn police station. He would be there with some of his detectives having a drink.

Christmas 1984 was at home and very much church centred. I always love the Christmas message and the carols and hymns. I know Diana made sure we had a great festive feast and the whole family had a jolly time.

Alexander's fourth birthday was on the 4th June. I would have been busy with my limited pupillage practice with Leslie at Gray' s Inn Square and Diana would have organised the party for him and a few friends.

By the summer of 1984 both children were at school at Comins Coch which was a couple of miles down a country road behind us at Waun Fawr. Alexander now at 4 would have been in the first infants class and Alfreda at 6 in primary 2. Both would have taken part in the Christmas nativity. I have a memory and a photograph somewhere showing a very shy Alex and Alfreda with some sort of festive head dress.

After Christmas it was back to London and a report to my pupil master for my second six month: John Harwood-Stevenson. I consider I was very fortunate to be with John in a fine, well respected set of Temple chambers at 4 Paper Buildings in the Temple. John must have been about 12 years older than me. He had previously been an ordained monk in the Benedictine order and a teacher at the famous catholic school, Ampleforth in North Yorkshire. He had lost some of his faith when reforms in the Catholic church had done away with the use of Latin in the different masses. He had come to the bar a learned and academic man speaking Latin, ancient Greek, some of the Slavic languages and others more familiar. He had a huge head, a pleasant but powerful voice and was certainly a counsel who clients and judges would listen to.

He was a hard task master and made me do much for him. We would often work late in the evening in chambers. He alas, despite his success as a barrister, never had any money. I would sometimes find myself paying for the taxi to court. He had a better practice than Leslie and we were sometimes in the Old Bailey. He seemed not to turn away work and I recall we dealt with a number of family law cases. His lack of funds he attributed to his foolishness with women on leaving his monastic life at Ample forth. He had married one lady because he thought she was pregnant only to find that she was not. He had divorced her at much cost only to marry another whom he likewise divorced. He remarried the first one and lived with her for a time. There was a daughter with expensive riding tastes. Thus his money went, as he said, to pay for his follies. He worked hard to pay his women, so I was able to learn much.

He took me one day down to darkest Brixton where he was to buy a tiny flat in an area where most of neighbours were rastafarians. I said to him: 'You can't live here Harwood'. 'Oh no' said he, 'these are very nice chaps', pointing to a group who would have put the fears up many, including members of London's finest.

I was fortunate in not only learning much from John but also in that I was given a number of my own cases, by the chambers clerk of 4 Paper Buildings, for which I was paid a fee.
I still have my Oyez diary for 1985 and have recorded in brief the cases I handled from my coming to 4 Paper Buildings in January, 1985. I see that already by the 10th January I was earning 40 pounds for withdrawing an appeal at Bow Street Magistrates Court. The next day I was junior to a QC, just for

the day at the Old Bailey, for 55 pounds. Things were looking up. My diary shows for January I had six cases for which I was paid, plus a few which show no payment and a majority where I accompanied Harwood robed and acted as his note taker. The cases were a cross section of practice: e.g. Chelmsford Crown Court, Tower Bridge Magistrates Court, Slough County Court etc. February followed with a day long trial at Camberwell Juvenile Court for which I got paid 86 pounds. From January to the second week in July when I said farewell to Harwood and 4 paper Buildings I must have at least 4 or 5 of my own cases each month. My biggest fee was for defending an Indian man for drunken driving and failing to report an accident. He was found guilty by the Feltham magistrates and fined 100 pounds on the first charge and 250 on the second, in addition he was disqualified for 18 months. I was paid nearly 300 pounds! The case started at 10.30 am and finished at 7.00pm the same day: 18th June.

It certainly gave me the appetite for more work at he bar. But my enquiries at 4 Paper Building for a tenancy were not encouraging; there was another pupil who had been there longer and who had better connections. I had been away from England since the early 1960's. I got the impression they would let me stay a bit longer than 6 months until I found my feet but I realised I was going to have to look around for perhaps life as prosecutor linked to one of the police forces. I recall also that the new crown prosecution service was just starting and that there might be opening there. In any event by April 85 I realized things were not going to be easy for us.

I therefore considered it would be a good time for Diana and the children to return to Hong Kong for a holiday to see their grandmother and perhaps even their great grandma in Macau as well as Diana's brother and sister in law (Kaufoo and Kaumo) in Hong Kong. In the month they were away I would continue with my pupillage and look for work. I took them to Heathrow on the 21st April, 1985 and they were to be away for a month The month or so they were away I had a busy time at Court. I must have had 6 of my own cases and was in court with Harwood for most of the other time. Diana and the children returned on the 26th May, 1985 and I drove them back to Aberystwyth in our Uno.

With the family away I had made enquiries about a job. I had an interview with the Thames Valley Crown prosecution Service. The man in charge was an ex colonial police officer but I recall we did not get on that well. He seemed either unimpressed or overwhelmed with my exposition of my time as an oriental crime fighter. I had seen, after they came back, an advert in a legal journal for lecturers at The City Poly technical College in Hong Kong. It was a new college, not in existence during my time in HK. I had never heard of it. They were looking for law lecturers to teach law for diploma courses. I was somewhat wary of going back to Hong Kong, especially with my health problem and we had been away five years; was it fair and proper to for us all to start again there? I did, however, have an interview which went well and a medical during which the doctor said my blood pressure was that of a 20 year old and that the irregular heart was not a problem. He had been made aware of the reason for my discharge from the police force.

From my notes I see that on the 25th July 1985 I saw my old friend Gordon Hampton walking in the Temple grounds. He was a well known respected solicitor in Hong Kong. He had acted for policemen in trouble and frequently was against us when he defended some of those we had charged. I had been against him as prosecutor in a number of magistrate court cases. In Hong Kong at the time police officers acted as prosecutors, and in the more important criminal cases the O.C case himself would handled the hearings, trials and committals for trial at the High Court. I had always found him an honourable opponent, wise, clever, thorough, and as helpful as the rules and code of his profession allowed. He was often successful and on such occasions I may have a coffee with him in the court canteen when he would explain what was wrong with our case and how we may had erred in the way we had dealt with the evidence or handled a particular witness. I saw nothing wrong with this and consider he a taught me much which helped me as a police detective and court prosecutor.

I told him of my position: young family with no real prospects ahead other than the HK teaching job. He told me that he was in England to qualify for the Bar! He wanted to become a total advocate: a barrister at law, one who had access and right of hearing in all the courts of HK, all the way up to the Court of Appeal. His solicitors firm with its considerable litigation preparation work he would leave, concentrating on what he loved: advocacy in court.

He had already set up a chambers in Hong Kong with a number of other barristers and was looking for the right people to join.

My understanding at my interview for the teaching job was that the college encouraged their legal staff to be involved with 'live' practice in Hong Kong. Gordon said that would be ideal. You could join our chambers and also fulfil your teaching duties at the college. It was almost about the same time that I contacted the agents of the college in London. I have a note mentioning a phone call to City Poly the same day: 25th July. I also have a note saying I confirmed the job on the 2nd August. It was therefore off to HK again to start the new academic year which began in September.

Diana was pleased to return and the children were excited, although perhaps with Alfreda 7 on the 16th of April and Alexander 5 on the 4th June they didn't take it all in, especially as they had only just come back from there.

There were jobs to be done: letters to write to utilities, DHSS (we had to cancel our child benefit). Inland Revenue, estate agent, solicitor (about selling the house at Maesceinion), the bank, insurance company, local council etc. I also wrote thank you letters to friends: Rev Bertie Lewis, the rector of St Michael's and Dr John Lloyd. Then it was selling things we didn't want. I had to sell the car, which we did and handed it to the buyer at the airport on our day out. Some of our nice wooden furniture, chests tables etc. I took to my friend John Turner to look after. John had been one of my bosses in the RHKP. He lived at Yockleton just outside Shrewsbury.

I also had things to do in London and in particular say farewell to Mrs Woods, my landlady for two plus years. But I was extremely cheerful as was the family and I recall we had an outing in the countryside near Maescenion in the month of July to give us some nice images of the Welsh countryside to take away back to Hong Kong.

I have a recollection that we started the process to sell 42 Maescenion and that it was in hand as we were preparing to leave. Then there was the rest of our household goods and furniture to pack and deliver to the shippers. I have a note saying I paid Pickfords. My note says we all went to London on the 24th August where I went through the process of selling the car and taking our baggage.

We finally left London from Gatwick Airport on the evening of Sunday 25th August on Cathay Pacific, business class (the first time we had every experienced such luxury and joy!), arriving in HK on the morning of Monday the 26th to be met by Ms Rita Fung an officer of the Estate Office of the college.

# 19. Wheels within Wheels

Leaving the UK again for a new career and life in Hong Kong was a big challenge for all of us. At least we would be on familiar ground with food, language and culture. It would be a place where the ownership of anything mechanical to take you around was not necessary. The public transport system was and is, since the 80's, first class: air-conditioned buses, mini-buses, under and over ground trains and cheap, comfortable taxis. Private cars were for those to display and evidence their position, wealth or to put it in Chinese terms: their face.

I would need no car in Hong Kong. And can say from then until now, at the time of writing July 2013, I have never owned anything for wheeled transport except for the wheelchair I bought for my dear and lovely wife. This was after the poor soul so tragically suffered a stroke during an operation on the 5th February 2001 at the Prince of Wales Hospital. This was to place an implant in her brain to help with her Parkinson's disease. We used it often, on long hikes around Shatin and up the Shatin river, sometimes as far as Ma On Shan, until she got cancer of the stomach in 2006. Eventually after about four months she died on the 15th August at the Bradbury Hospice up at Au Kung Kok Shan, above Shatin.

Thus for over five years we had good use of it. And those long hikes kept me fit.

An appropriate time perhaps to pause here in the chronology of my life with a chapter about my wheeled childhood to my wheel less age of 42.

I have a dim recollection of owning a metal scooter in my infant/junior days but by the time of teenage hood I had a Rayleigh 26 inch wheel, straight handlebar, old fashion, no gears, bicycle. I recall that this was the vehicle that was involved in my first 'road' accident. I was a second, or was it a first year student at Holly Park Secondary school for the children of 'gentle folk.' I am not sure if I was hastening along the large playground down the slope to freedom out side. I may have been intent on escaping from some of the more senior Neanderthals who were after my cap, bag or anything to throw in a puddle or over a wall. They were not averse, either to doing a bit of thumping. We were not allowed to actually cycle on the school premises, so, for one who has always meticulous about following the rules, I was scooting. I had my foot on the one pedal without my leg over the saddle. I was thus technically not in breach of the law and had a good defence if reported to the higher authority. I fell off. I was unconscious and helped by dear Dr Popjoy the music teacher and Mrs Warren from the primary school next door. She had been my primary school teacher. I woke up, I don't know how soon after the 'prang', in the Barnet General Hospital, about 5/6 miles up from our home. As explained previously it was around Guy Fawkes time: early November. I was little worse for wear and resumed my 'studies' and the bullying that went on with it. That is, until dear Mum came up to the school. I feel she did this reluctantly as in her day the rough and tumble of school was part of being educated: a certain amount of scar tissue strengthened rather than weakened body and character! Wow! I hear people say how cruel. Don't forget readers the higher orders were paying fortunes to public schools at the time for their sons to be thrashed regularly not just by masters but by senior boys. Then there was fagging. No wonder that things went on there?!!

My next bike I bought myself on the hire purchase from Oscroft Brothers bicycle shop in Friern Barnet Road. It was a brand new BSA, drop handlebars, three speed derailleur gear, smart with red and gold colour. I bought it with my paper round money and would use it at 6.30 in the morning, wind, snow, rain, hail or shine to take me up Friern Barnet lane, Manor Drive and beyond. Sunday and Friday were killers with the extra Sunday papers and supplements and the Friday Radio Times. But my bike was a part of me. I used it a lot for school, errands and pleasure. A bunch of us would cycle weekends and holidays all over the place; Southend and back in a day, Brighton on one occasion. There were easy and frequent rides around the next county, Hertfordshire to places like St Albans and Hatfield. We went down to Maldon in Essex to visit my greengrocer boss Mr. Saunders, who had a caravan there. There was the big trip I did with two friends: Roger Crouch and Michael Bradshire. Michael and myself had 'ordinary' bikes which we had bought ourselves. Roger had a bike and a half: one with ten gears, two cogs on the front drive wheel and five on the rear; it was feather weight, made in Italy, drop handle bars, lights the lot. His dear Auntie had bought it for him. The first day we made it to Swanage, which is across from Poole and Bournmouth and must have been at least 120 miles from London. At Swanage, after finding a bed at a hostel/bed and breakfast, we went to a local pub. We were about 14 or 15 there the kindly locals gave us to try some of their local scrumpy cider. Kind yokels that they were, they saw us leave after not so long staggering back to our bicycles and sleep. I recall a few 'aaaaaaahs I think that learned um' as we walked out.

We cycled on the next day stopping for the night at Bridport. I have forgotten now our next stop. I do recall we crossed the River Ex on the ferry and cycled past Torquay. We visited the Lizard Point and then after a night stop nearby went on to Penzance in Cornwall. It was here that Roger left us. He had things to do back home; that is what he said! But we thought that perhaps even with his special bike, his legs were beginning to weaken and the thought of some of the hills to come in North Devon on our way back may have been a bit too much. He went home on the train and Michael and I continued for another 4 or so days. We cycled then to Lands End and then north along the coast  to Bude where we stayed for night at a very nice lady's B and B. The next day we by-passed Illfracome and went on up the steep Porlock Hill, a one in four incline, even Olympic athletes could not get up without dismounting. Then further along the coast, via Lynton and Lynmouth to Minehead where  we stopped again for the night. I forget our route back from there to London, Devizes rings a bell. We must have been away for a total of 8 or so days. I recall we would often see the miles fly by as we got in the slipstream of a lorry or coach, going at least 50 miles an hour. No helmets, knee guards etc. in those days. I suppose today Mum and Dad would have been done for child abuse allowing their offspring to take such terrible risks. Then there was: being away from home, with all those paedophile vicars and priests who were apparently all over the place pouring out their unnatural desires on all and sundry. OK if their 'partners' were adult, nothing was unnatural then or was it? All that Mum said when I got back was: 'Did you have a nice time son.'

Before I move on from push bikes I should mention the trades bike I use to ride to deliver green groceries for Mr Saunders at his shop just across the road from us at Halliwick Parade. It was usually Saturday when I worked all day at the shop. I would serve, stock up the fruit and vegetables and was also the delivery boy. During the week I would only work some evenings, usually the busy time: Friday. The trades bike was a heavy thing with a large carrier on the front supported by a 16 inch wheel in the front; the back wheel was a larger 26 inch. All manner of green groceries would be piled onto the carrier, separate orders for customers each in a box. There were also heavy items like hundredweight sacks of potatoes for large families who could not carry them home. This was the late 50's; few people had cars and supermarkets were only just starting. It was the time of rows of local shops: bakers, butchers, fishmonger, grocers, chemists, greengrocers, oil shops, sweet shops, news agents etc; each one provide a living for the self employed and large companies like Boots and MacFisheries. Many of these provided apprenticeships for young school leavers. Those who didn't go to grammar schools or colleges left school at 15. A friend of mine who I was in competition with for Mr Saunder's delivery boy job went on to become an apprentice fishmonger at the local MacFisherie's. Can you see the young of to day doing such jobs? But to be fair they properly don't exist any more. It was not easy peddling up Friern Barnet lane with a hundred weight plus load in the carrier; not infrequently such was my mighty thigh power that I would shear off the cotter pin off the crank on the chain wheel. I would deliver the order and take the cash giving change if necessary from my cash bag. In the first week I was short on my float by quite a few shillings when I finished my round.

Dick (Mr Saunders) was not happy, he thought I had taken the money. But goodness no, I didn't want to lose the job and was really puzzled how I had mishandled the change. It was the age of pounds, shillings and pence, halfpenny's even; there were no magic phones, pocket calculators then.

When I was about 15 and a half I bought a 125 cc BSA Bantam motorcycle, but I still kept my bike. I don't recall the circumstances of buying the Bantam; it may have been new found wealth from my building labourer's job which I did when still 15. As mentioned before I was amongst other things a hod carrier and foundations digger for a small builders firm who were engaged in constructing a huge posh home for the well to do in Hamstead Garden Suburb. I recall using my new wealth to 'do up' the bike: painting the frame, new aluminium mudguards, plus taking the engine out and re-coking the cylinder heads. Where did we, my mates and I, do this? It was done in the front room of 7 Priory Villas, to the chagrin of poor old Dad. Why he allowed us such freedom I am not sure. I do remember Mum saying: 'Dad said It will be alright if they are careful and put paper down'; which we did! Damage to the room was minimal and the furniture left intact. I was not yet 15; 16 was the age that you could get a licence to ride a motor bike. It didn't matter what cc they were: mopeds 50 cc up to the masters of the road: the 1000cc Vincent. I rode it when finished, with its new red livery and silver aluminium mudguards, around the blocks near home. My memory now has no adventures to tell about this bike and so I am sure that it was only months in my possession before I sold it. Bigger bikes were to come and I still had my bicycle which was always in the hall leaning against the wall causing problems like taking the wall paper off with its handle bars.

Not long after my short ownership of the Bantam I noticed across the road from the main entrance of Tottenham College, at a motorcycle show room, a particular fine machine that really took my fancy. It was a Douglas 350 horizontally opposed twin-engine motor bike. Douglas Motor Cycles went out of business in 1957. It must have been 1959 that I was inspecting the machine. It was not a 'Dragonfly', their last model but an earlier model called the 80 plus. It's special feature was a really large front brake, with fantastic stopping power, also the way the frame hung low with the horizontal opposed two engines gave it excellent road holding. You could really chuck the bike around leaning over on bends and almost touching the ground with your knee. It must have been at the end of my first year or the beginning of my second at the college. I forget now how much it cost but I had enough for the down payment and persuaded my dear Mum to sign as guarantor of the hire purchase agreement. I assured her with my part time jobs I could pay the seven or so shillings a month payments. It may have been more. In any event I had the wonderful machine for just over a year after which a man from the credit company, or was it the showroom, came to re-possess the bike. I recall he was very polite and nice to my Mum who apologised profusely for causing him and his company trouble. But it was a marvellous year. A great bike; I would roar up Colney Hatch lane wearing my chequered cheese cutter and a pair of mark 8 goggles down over my eyes. Wah! did I think I was something. I had no helmet, although promised Mum and Dad I would get one when I could. Helmet wearing for motorbikes was not yet the law. Nanny was trusting baby with his toys and knee-pads, elbow pads and special bicycle helmets even, were not yet in her mind. I recall using the bike to go to college and to take out

Marilynne, although I recall for a short time we were not together. She had found, albeit not for long, another fella.

It was at this time that I went on a camping holiday in the Lake District, Cumbria. I had been there about three years before on an Outward Bound Course. This time I went with Mike Bradshaw and another Mike who was slightly older than us and had done or was doing his National Service. I don't recall if I took the bike, whose registration number was either UMT or SNO. I remember one of my bikes was called affectionately 'UMTI' (as in Dumpty who fell off the wall). I mention this Mike because it was from him I bought my next bike:(UMTI?) A BSA. A.7. 500 cc twin cylinder machine. It had a plunger rear suspension and unlike the Douglas had only one carburettor to supply both engines. It was not as sporty or as good at road holding as the Douglas although its engine was much quieter and less likely to leak oil. I recall I had the bike until a few months before I went to Africa in February, 1962. And had it for most of the time I was courting Marilynne. She was comfortable on the back, although I remember one disaster when I asked her to hold the bike up while I did something, only to be careless taking it back whereupon it fell a bit(!) catching her lovely leg on the exhaust pipe. I forget what her Dad said.! I used it a number of times to go to the coast. Once going into Brighton with Marilynne on the back we were stopped for speeding by Brighton's finest, I think that's all it was; I paid the fine through the post. A group of us, Marilynne and all, went on our motor bikes to Beauleigh in the New Forest to the annual jazz festival at Lord Montegue's estate. It was camping, we couldn't afford anything else, including the charges to go into the festival. But it was fun enjoying the atmosphere, the beer, the forest ponies and what we could hear of the music from within or without Lord Montegue's place.

My friend Barnard who at that time was still a cadet in the Metropolitan Police had become a proper, passed the test, motorist. And had acquired a fine veteran or is it vintage Morris 8, or was it an Austin something, in any event it was a smart little car, one that you had actually to drive. It had knobs and levers on the dashboard which would have confused even the most uptodate youth of today's electronic age. He like me was a man with simple habits: we both smoked 'Petersen' pipes and liked to taste as many of the fine and different brews that were then coming on the marker after the great consumer rebellion, lead by the Campaign for Real Ale (CAMRA), against the big five or was it six national breweries. All the marvellous brews which differed so much across the country for the various regional palates were being finished off and replaced with pasteurised, highly carbonated keg packaged fizz beer, more commonly larger. CAMRA had been very successful reminding the Englishman, alright including those up across Hadrian' s Wall and Offa' s Dyke as well, of how marvellous and varied our beer was. God! We must not descend into the appalling sameness of the USA, where all the beer tastes the same and is ice-cold and fizzy like pop. (I must say now: 2013 there has since been a similar revolution in the USA and it is no longer that land of uninteresting fizz).

Barney would drive us around the Home Counties, sometimes as far as Oxfordshire visiting some quaint pubs and tasting as many brews as we could manage. Barney was a police cadet and not long before that he was issued a truncheon was and able to beat people up, so had to be careful. He rarely had more than 6 pints but as we did journey far there was plenty of time to let its affects dissipate (only joking). On one of our educational tours we visited Stonesfield, not far from Woodstock in Oxfordshire where we saw the old cottage of Grandmother Tolliday. She had worked at Blenheim Palace, Woodstock as a 14/15 year old girl and I recall she had told us how she had to curtsey before Winston Churchill, who must have been a similar age to her self.

You recall I have said in a previous chapter how Barney drove me in his splendid machine to Gatwick Airport on the 28th, February when I flew off to Northern Rhodesia to join a very tough paramilitary Northern Rhodesia Police (NRP).

I had no vehicle there when I was training at Lilyai or as a cadet at Ndola. When I was posted as an Assistant Inspector to Mufulira I was required to take my driving test to drive police vehicles. The licence issued also covered me to drive my own vehicle. I still have that licence with me today. It is a green cardboard fold-over booklet of six pages. The second page has my photograph, a young spotty youth in the grey summer working dress uniform shirt. It is dated the 26 'Sep' 1963 and shows I paid a fee of one pound (It was still pounds shillings and pence in Rhodesia) and was valid for any private motor vehicle not included in classes A-H above. I won't bore you any more. A-H was nearly everything except private cars and light goods vehicle. I was thus OK for police land rover/Jeeps, saloons and 3-ton troop carriers. I am sure on the troop carriers, although some NRP pensioner may say: Oh no you weren't. Well, Oh yes I was!

I drove the land rover patrol cars most shifts, although I liked to keep an eye on the men sometimes surreptitiously of foot. There were also concealed patrols to catch housebreaker/burglars in the European and African townships. During disturbances when we were tooled up in riot gear and the windows were covered with screens I would often act as driver or sit along side my friend driver Constable Chisengalubway ('Chisenga'). He was a real character, steady and loyal. Although to be fair in this regard he was not alone. I had been pulled out of a number of dangerous situations by other similarly loyal and steady African policemen. But when he stood in front of you making a report or taking orders you never knew if he was really looking at you: one of his eyes always looked over your head to the right whilst the other looked almost straight at you but to the left. He was a good man to have around when the mob started rocking your vehicle. Especially when some of the younger members of the car crew who were on the roof of the vehicle, their feet held through the front windscreen by me, started to fire their tear gas guns. 'Old Chisenga' loved his native beer and seem to judge his officers on their ability to drink as much as he could and still be sober enough for work.

As soon as I had my licence I went to the local Barclay's Bank, in Mufulira High Street to seek a loan to buy a private car. It was for an old Mark 1 Ford Zephyr, six cylinder, powerful motor whose body work was not too bad. We didn't seem to have rust problems on the Copperbelt. It cost 50 pounds, that's all! But the miserable bank manager, after pompously interviewing me, declined to give me a loan. I therefore borrowed the money from an older colleague. I used it for work to drive from my quarters in the police camp down the 5 or so miles to the Central police station. I also used it on mess outings to Ndola and Kitwe., It was over a hundred and twenty plus miles to Ndola and about the same to Kitwe. We thought nothing of bombing along at silly speeds, albeit on the good, surfaced Copperbelt roads, for a party at one of the officer's messes there. What went for parties I hear you asking? Well alas, there were not many single girls and most of the local mums kept their shy and sensitive daughters away from us. It may sound strange today, a criminal offence even, but it was not done then to court the African girls. There was one, however: Penny Chileshi, a really beautiful girl who was a sister at the hospital. She was from a very good African family and had been educated in the UK. A cultured, well spoken, and educated young woman who quite a few of us fancied. But available only for proper and steady relationship with the right man of whatever race. His education and background seem to be what mattered. Oh well, some of us could do joined up writing!

The horny ones in the mess went across the border into Katanga in the Congo and then if they had a few days holiday up to what was still called Elizabethville.

At Mufulira there were some nice African ladies of the night, especially Ndebele girls from Southern Rhodesia. I understand that some of the more foolish risked getting charged under the disciplinary regulations for going with these good ladies. Explanations of exchanging stamp album's, night language classes or sitting for portraits etc. were not generally entertained, at least that's what I am told.

My time with the NRP finished at the end of summer 1964 when I returned to England a place I still recognised without the huge cultural change that was to come later with the massive influx of people from the Middle East and South Asia. Christian churches then, although with falling congregations still had more attending them than Islamic mosques. A fact that would change significantly by the 2000's, when the call to worship would be for hundreds of thousands throughout much of the land.

Back in England as I have explained previously I went to work for the nationwide security company: Securicor. It was as a detective/investigator in their Detective Division based at Swan House in Chelsea. I had bought a Ford Consul, Mark 1, an old model, not as powerful as my Ford in Africa, but not bad for a run around. I am not sure then what regulations were about for compulsory testing for second hand vehicles; maybe there were none. In any event I don't think, with its barely robust bodywork, it would have passed any examination. This would have been especially so after I crashed into a traffic bollard in Hamstead Road just outside The National Temperance Hospital. This was only a short way from where I had picked up my dear Mum from work. She worked as milliner at a workshop down the road near Goodge Street. I was full of things to tell about and hit the bollard. I told the police, always helpful, it was knocking off time, that I had swerved to avoid a dog. A black one! Mum was shaken up but I took her across the road to the hospital. Thank God she was OK. But when I had righted the car and got home Dad said: 'What the bloody hell have you done with my wife!' I recall the car was afterwards poorly but functioning. In any event such was my job with the Detective Division that I was usually away on an assignment and didn't need the car. When I was in London I had the use of a Mini Minor from the company pool.

On the 10th of April I flew off to Hong Kong. On the plane were at least three old comrades from the NRP.

In my first tour of duty in Hong Kong I did not buy any vehicle. For the short time at Ta Ku Ling Police Station on the Sino/Chinese border, before I was hastily transferred for upsetting the Law Fong commune the other side, I rode one of the station bicycles. These were sturdy, painted grey in the then police colours, navy blue for all vehicles was to come with a Commissioner called Sutcliffe some years later. I would use the bike to cycle along the border road to visit my two posts : Kong Shan and Pak Fa Shan. A night patrol with the moon out alone in the quiet with my carbine or sterling gun on my shoulder was memorable. There was then no huge city of Shen Zheng the other side. The biggest building was further west and was a two storey customs post, that is what we thought it was. When there was no moon a night patrol could be quite wary and I often wondered if I would bump into a PLA soldier who had sneaked across the footbridge and gate in the fence at Li Ma Hang, for a dare or perhaps to visit one of our village girls. The ride should not have been difficult as there were no real inclines. But like my trades bike, with Mr. Saunders the greengrocer, I was forever shearing off – with my mighty thighs – the cotter pin. This much to the displeasure of the transport corporal whose job it was to keep all wheels moving.

I recall I passed my police motor cycle test and thus when I was transferred towards the end of my first tour of duty as SDI/LFS I tried to use the station motorcycle and side-car. I have a photograph of this fine machine with my dog Jomo sitting in the side-car. Alas I could not steer it around corners so sent it back to the transport sergeant at Yuen Long Headquarters for a scooter. This I used when too lazy to walk the 5 miles to my post at Nim Wan and to patrol along the Ha Tsuen Road to Yuen Long officers mess where important conferences were held. I even remember taking the scooter on a few occasions down to Tsim Sha Tsui, Kowloon. It was always important even on your leave day to be able to come back at a moments notice if I was needed at my command.

It was not until I was posted to the CID in Kowloon at the end of 1969 that I bought a vehicle. It was a brand new Lambretta or was it a Vespa; 150 cc and able to carry me around on and off duty. One of my bosses was Tim Fitzpatrick, a lovely fella, but like many Celts, he had a weakness for going on 3 day benders. He was a popular, able officer and always had a few minders around to ensure he didn't come to harm. He called me D.I. (short for Detective Inspector) Verity: seeking truth and good on his bike around the division! The scooter was useful and I rode it in all conditions, unlike a car, parking was no problem. But one day when I was working in the CID at Tsim Sha Tsui Police Station I lost it. I reported the crime to myself. I was the reserve CID inspector on duty and ensured the crime was properly recorded in the Crime Complaint Book (CCB). Those investigating the crime i.e. me and my team were not very efficient, as I found the scooter two weeks later parked in one of the side roads outside a 'Hasty Tasty' food stall. Which was where I had left it; Alzheimers disease was already at 27 starting to affect me!

I had the scooter when I was promoted to Senior Inspector which must have been around the end of 1971. This rank I obtained after passing promotion examinations and a promotion board. The rank was re-graded soon after to chief Inspector, whilst the senior inspector rank remained to be one obtained not on promotion but on advancement after 6 or so years qualified service in the rank of Inspector. I was posted to the New Territories Pol/Mil (Police/Military Command Headquarters) at Sek Kong Army camp. I would ride my scooter there from my quarters at 137 Waterloo Road; a route which took me over Route Twisk ( short for Tsuen Wan/Sek Kong), which because I was working shifts entailed day, evening and night riding. It was not an easy ride over the steep winding road of Tai Mo Shan, especially in the dark.

I was not long at Pol/Mil and was soon posted to what was a cream posting: Sub Divisional Inspector Sha Tau Kok. Here I sold my scooter and really moved up in the world with an ancient US Studebaker car. It must have come from the early 50's, with a huge V. 8. engine and room for six large American passengers, eight Chinese!. I would start the mighty engine up in the compound of the station and you could hear and feel it drinking the petrol. It must have needed half a gallon to start it up. The trip down to Fanling Railway station where I would drop some of my men off after duty whilst I went of to Fanling Depot to the mess, would need about a days wages of fuel. I realise that, perhaps it was not the car for me when one evening on a visit to the iconic Better 'Ole pub I reversed it off the pub car park over the adjacent railway platform and half way on to the railway track. I had mates in the Royal Military Police. The Betta 'Ole had been famous since the Korean War 1950/3 as a place for our soldiers. At the height of that war there must have been two divisions of our troops going through the NT on their way to fight the Chinese and the North Koreans. I always thought it strange that just across the border 3 miles up the road were the self same Chinese. The RMP called out their engineer mates from REME and soon to arrive was a gigantic breakdown Scammel recovery vehicle; better used to helping tanks in distress. My monster was pulled up from the track none the worse for wear. But cost and parking difficulties dictated that I sold it, or did I give it away, anyway it was no more to be seen bombing along the STK Road around the Wo Hang bend to the STK police station.

It was time for two wheels again. I was always a biker at heart and who held the motor car in contempt. Oh the power of roaring off at the traffic lights leaving all the toffy-nosed Porshe drivers with their mouths agape, or the joy of seeing them all with their blood pressure rising as I weaved in and out to escape the jam with no end. I had had two powerful bikes before but never a 'Roll Royce'. The iconic Vincent 1000 was a collector piece and certainly no longer available anywhere, least of all Hong Kong. There was, however, the Norton Command 750 twin. I saw it for sale at a showroom in North Point and bought it. A great bike: at a 100 MPH was just warming up, although I realised as the local police chief of Sha Tau Kok I had to set an example: always in a helmet, obeying the traffic rules, courteous to others on the road etc. But as good as it was it did not have the road holding of my old Douglas. One evening returning from Fanling Depot I did not make the turn at the Wo Hang Bend and went into the side of the big rock there. I had my helmet on which took the brunt of the collision with the rock. I woke up in the Queen Elizabeth hospital having been told I had been picked up from the road by a passing Gurkha unit on its way for duty at STK village. 'Spade Face' the supremo boss of the NT police (DPC/NT) came to see me and said: You have got to get rid of that bike, or words to that effect. So I did.

I have memories of a motoring holiday around the West Country and into Wales with my Mum, Dad and sister. I had bought a good second hand Humber Sceptre car. I recall it must have been in 1973 when I was on leave from my second tour. That was the year I attended the Senior CID course at Peel House with the Metropolitan Police. The trip continued on there for us as a family: plenty of arguments about where to go and where to eat. But I must have managed to maintain discipline by threatening to leave offenders behind.

When it was time to go back to Hong Kong I left the Humber with George who used it in his mini cab business.

I returned in the summer of 1973 and as I have already said was posted to what was the most difficult and strenuous posting I had in my career in the Police. But it was a time when I did not buy a vehicle. My command at CID. Sham Shui Po (SSP) and Shek Kip Mei (SKM) must have been not far off 150 men all ranks. The government had provided us with a single Mini. I could with my not insignificant bulk just get into the front seat. There was room in the back, with the front seat pulled back, for a small prisoner and a standard size detective. My other unit up the road at SKM did not even have a Mini. Luckily in the early days at least we were able to hire suitable vehicles from local garages. Which we did by cutting down on our own little pleasures.

It took a significant change in the 'culture' of the police force after the formation of the ICAC for us to have official transport, equipment and proper rates of pay and allowances.

I finished my third tour of duty what must have been at the end of 1976. I returned to UK and stayed with my parents at our new home at Ludlow in Shropshire. The only car I had then was a Triumph Herald I had bought really cheap as a run around for the local scene. It had its hubcaps stolen one night, although the local police convinced me that they had fallen off. I recognised the 'keeping the crime figures down' culture was not confined to oriental crime fighters. Crime figures were used for all manner of things, none of which from my experience served any purpose except to support promotion for senior officers or politicians. These could use them up or down depending how the fancy took them.

Only after a few weeks of use the engine gaskets decided to blow or do that which renders the car kaput. So it was a hire car for me to take my lovely Diana up on a trip to Bonnie Scotland.

Back in Hong Kong it was posting to SDI/Yuen Long for a year or so then back into plain clothes as DDI/YL. I bought my last set of wheels in Hong Kong here at Yuen Long: white/dirty cream colour beetle VW. What a car; you just put petrol into the tank and it went forever. I can't recall putting oil in or anything for lubrication and I never found the radiator! It had holes in the exhaust and I remember one occasion when I was taking a prisoner back with two of my detectives. The prisoner was taken with the noise from the exhaust only to be told, (was it by me or my detective?) that the VW was a special 'Q' car: one able to travel at astonishing speeds and do things

301

which standard cars could not. Always good to keep the underworld confused and ever wary of Hong Kong's Oriental crime fighters!

The last vehicles in my life were those I had during the 5 years I was back in the UK studying law and qualifying for the bar. This included the three years I was studying at the University of Wales, Aberystwyth and the two in London at the bar school and pupillage. For the whole of those 5 years the family was based in Wales, even though for the last two I would be in digs at Muswell Hill, but would return home when I could at weekends and during the holidays.

We had only been back a few months when I bought the old Morris Marina. It served its purpose as a run-around although I have no memory of taking it much out of Aberystwyth.

The second was the Fiat 128, a much more respectable car and one in which Diana took her test. I have memories of using this car to take us on outings to Shrewsbury and Hereford which were two hour journeys. This Fiat was part exchanged for a brand new Fiat Uno which we must have bought around 1983. With me being away in London for the most of 83 to 85, Diana would have had the greater part of the use of the car. I recall we did no major trips although I did it drive down to London to catch our plane back to Hong Kong in the summer of 1985. There we handed it over to the buyer and took his cheque.

# 20. Under the Setting Sun

We were taken from the airport to the Holiday Inn in Nathan Road, Tsim Sha Tsui. I even have the room numbers which I noted down in my diary at the time: 816 to 818. I recall the children were excited to be in such a posh place. We were there until 16th October when we were given a staff quarter at B9. Sun Fair Mansion, Shiu Fai Terrace which is off Stubbs Road. Then it was just a short walk down some steps at the far end of the terrace, which was a cul-de-sac, to Kennedy Road and Wanchai.

It was a good location, quiet and away from the traffic on Stubbs Road. It was to turn out handy for us to use the steps to attend our new church: the Methodist church at the junction of Kennedy Road and Queens Road East. There was also a useful and regular mini bus service to take us from Shiu Fai Terrace to Admiralty and later for me to the High Court. Up Stubbs road about 10 minutes away on the regular service bus was Bradbury Junior School, one of the many run by the English Schools Foundation. The school would be attended by both children until they went on to secondary school at 11.

So Monday was resting and unpacking our suitcases. We had sent our household goods etc. ahead of us and these would not be here for a few weeks at least.

On Tuesday 27th August I made my way to the campus, if that is the right word. Because the City Poly of Hong Kong which

303

was brand new and had only opened the year before in 1984 had no grounds. It was situated in a large multi-storey centre in Mongkok. I have looked at recent maps and think it was at the Argyle Centre; I recall getting out of an exit at Mongkok MTR and going straight into the main entrance. I met my section head: James Collins a pleasant Welshman from Lampeter near Aberystwyth. He headed the then small legal section at the college. Not yet were they The City University offering degree courses but The 'humble' City Polytechnic College offering diploma courses. The four or five of us lawyers were there to teach law subject modules to support these. I recall I taught contract and tort as it related to business and legal method/constitutional law. Two of my colleagues: Robert Buchanan a man who had been teaching law at a college of further education in England and Malcolm Bell an Englishman who had spent most of his time in Canada as an in-house commercial lawyer for Procter and Gamble. Dear Malcolm is a close friend today, who I still see on his frequent visits to Hong Kong. Robert, notwithstanding that he had no court experience before, found his forte as a criminal advocate in jury trials at our High Court. He did this after he was called to the Hong Kong Bar and had followed me to join Gordon Hampton at the Chambers of James Kinoch.

I spent the remainder of August and September settling in at the Poly. There were interviews with the head of department Brian Nichol and the big cheese, the Principal. Then there were forms to fill in, claims to make and correspondence for me to write concerning our property in the UK. There were many staff meetings to attend and I was to learn that in Academia meetings are 'important' and occupy much time. I was required to interview students and prepare induction programmes and the courses I would teach; this included course manuals. I learnt very quickly that detailed lecture notes were expected as handouts by the students. It was not, as I was use to at university, just headings with reading references. Our students had to be spoon-fed. Perhaps I am being unfair; the lectures were given in English to students whose mother language was Cantonese and whilst some spoke and understood it well most did not. So there was plenty to do before lectures and tutorials started at the end of September.

I recall our first Christmas back in Hong Kong we spent with my dear friend Bob Brooks and his wife Marilyn. Bob was from Burntisland, Fife, Scotland and I had visited him at his home there when on leave from the police. I remember in particular his lovely Mum who served up proper Scottish breakfasts: black 'pudins', white 'pudins', bacon, the lot, all full of the best cholesterol. Marilyn was from Swansea, Wales. Bob I had known in the Northern Rhodesia Police and we were in the same squad at Training School here in the Hong Kong Police. He was a very fine policeman and spent time in the 'Bum Squad' (The Special Investigation Unit: SIU) as the officer in charge, formed first to investigate a homosexual who was using his position as a solicitor to 'corrupt' young boys. There were tales of him entertaining boys on his junk and putting them off the ship if they were not obliging. The investigation unfortunately grew when other homosexuals were discovered involved or were on the periphery. The Governor, I understand, ordered a full investigation into the involvement of prominent homosexuals in the Colony. Bob who was a humane human being did not like the job and there were powerful people who would not have liked him looking at them.

Sodomy then: sexual intercourse with a male or an animal was still punishable with life imprisonment. It was the early 70's and it was not yet fashionable as it was in the UK where it was later, by the late 80s, to become almost compulsory if you wanted to get on in certain jobs!?

Today things are very different and same sex marriages are being forced on communities in much of the western world. It is also not necessary to be a mummy and daddy to have children. You can have them manufactured for you!

It got him down and I told him to get out of it all and to get back to proper police work but he was the old school: given a job he would see it through. I said it would be better to sweep the whole thing under the carpet. I likened it to creepy crawlies under a stone: lift the stone but put it back. He retired early with, in my view, his health affected by the whole thing. He did not make old bones and died of cancer of the throat refusing to have an operation that would have destroyed his ability to speak. He was a great friend and a tough nut with a good heart. I am still in contact with Marilyn who still lives in the Brooks home at Burntisland.

In October I visited Gordon at his chambers which was on a floor of the HSBC building in Peddar Street junction with Queens Road Central. I recall there were only five barrister members there: James Kinoch, a man in late middle age who I did not know but had come from the UK to practice here. Wags would say of such people FILTH (Failed In London Try Hong Kong); Ian Poulson an Aussie who I knew from my days in the CID and his as crown counsel; Barrie Skeets, a Kiwi long in the tooth ex senior crown counsel, who I had shared a

Cantonese class with in 1965; Gordon my old friend and sparring partner and another English man Robert Forest who had been magistrate, who I had not come across before. They were willing to have me and were kind enough to allow me to be a member without paying any chambers expenses until I started to earn fees.

On Friday the 11th October 1965 at 10.00 am James Kinoch moved my call before The Honourable Justice Sir Alan Huggins at the High Court of Justice. James said, as is customary, a few nice words introducing me to the court. I was then qualified to practice at the Bar in Hong Kong. I would have right of access in all Hong Kong' s courts: Magistrates, District, High Court and Court of Appeal. After all these years I was proud and so was dear Diana who was there to witness the event. My children were also there and I have a picture of the four of us standing smartly and proudly outside the entrance to the Supreme Court of Hong Kong. Such an important event allowed a day away from school.

*The family outside the Supreme Court just after call,*
*and another of me standing proudly alone.*

My work at the Poly did not involve anything like 9 to 5 hours. I would, at most, have around 10 lectures a week with a similar number of tutorials. I had already prepared my first terms' course of lectures and work and I was in the process of writing manuals. Then there was research, to keep up to date with the law and procedures. The best way of keeping up to date as a teacher of law was to be involved with practising. It was with this in mind that I did get involved very soon after being called to the bar with some legal practice and court work. I made no secret of my membership of chambers nor the occasional briefs I was given. My seniors in my department were informed and I understood that guidelines on outside practice would be given in due course. They never were and my private work eventually caused such a misunderstanding that I left the Poly under some cloud after my two year contract had expired.

I have some notes which show from the end of October 1985 until my leaving in the summer of 1987 I was involved with around 2 to 3 cases a month. Most of these were relatively simple criminal cases requiring little preparation and in all fairness my involvement with them did not detract from my teaching duties to the Poly; if anything my contact with the profession enhanced it. The diary I still have for 1985 show I had criminal cases: drugs, triad, assaults and dishonesty in the Magistrates Courts, bail applications in the High Court and a family law matter in the Families Court. One case does stick in my mind and that involved the relative of Gidget, the wife of my old friend John Turner. You will recall he retired to Yockleton in Shropshire and was looking after my furniture. The man involved had been charged and appeared at North Kowloon Magistrates Court for trial on the 12th December, 1985. I forget what it was all about, in any event my note says that I managed to convince the crown counsel to offer no evidence and the case was dismissed.

Both children settled well in at Bradbury Junior School. Although dear Alex remained terribly shy. I have his school reports. The one for his first year class 1.H repeats what was said in his first ever school report at Comins Coch Primary School in Wales. <u>Bradbury</u> : 'Alexander is very quiet, reserved child who found it difficult at first to relate to his peers'. <u>Comins Coch</u>: 'Alec is a very quiet member of the class, and is very reluctant to participate in any class discussion.' This for me was a painful shyness which showed through most of his time at the junior School and worried me. Alfreda was not generally shy, although her reports show she also was reticent in taking part in discussions. Both got involved with the Sunday school at the Methodist church where we made friends with Willie and Sandy Halter and later Ian and Dorothy Brown and their children. Family outings involved going to the Tai Tam Country Park where we would go for picnics and football. My involvement with the children, I like to think did something to draw Alex out of his shell. And I blame myself that the first 5 or so years of their lives both children didn't have much time with me, what with my studies and time in London. And perhaps such a life for Eurasian children in a quiet Welsh town was not easy for them or their dear Mum.

I was selected to be Father Christmas at our Methodist Church one year. Looking at the age of the children that I know now as adults, it must have been 1990 when Ken Anderson was still our minister. He clearly thought my boozy red face and expansive girth fitted me well for the role of Santa. I remember vividly one dear little girl looking into my bearded face and saying as I gave her the present: 'I love you Santa!' Wow what a responsibility! I had to send all the children off with a real belief. The following years with John White as the minister there was no Father Christmas. Rather Scrooge like he said it detracted for the real meaning of the birth of our Lord. Oh well!

*Me filling the role of Santa.*

The summer holiday saw us on the 26th July 1986 going off on a weeks holiday to Penang, Malaysia. We stayed at hotel on the Feringgi beach. My only recollection of the stay was being stung badly on the back of my right thigh by some beasties as I swam out far in the Malacca Strait.

We spent the Christmas holiday, 1986 on another family holiday. This time to the Philippines, we flew out on the 23rd December returning on the 29th December, 1986. If my memory serves me correctly we stayed a Punta Baluarte Resort which I recall was on a hillside or Puerto Galalera which was on the beach. I mention two resorts because we went again to the Philippines the next Christmas holiday, this time from the 28th December, 1987 to the 2nd January. The only thing that strikes my mind is swimming with Alex in the sea on the Galalera holiday when he dropped his goggles into the water. They sank to the bottom quickly. We were in 20 feet of water. I took a big breath to dive down to get them. Goodness, I can feel my lungs bursting now! I retrieved and handed them back breathless saying: 'Son, you nearly killed me!' or words to that affect.

The other holiday had jeepney type run-around to take you to your chalets. I recall doing lots of jogging from the resort down to the town where there was a statue to the 'feudal' local landowner dressed in his anti Japanese military uniform. It stuck me then how much land was owned by so few. The post Marcos revolution didn't do much to change the power held by so rich a few over the so many poor. It seems that it's US inherited democracy with money for votes and almost tribal loyalties has kept the Philippines in a state its hard working women, in particular, don't deserve.

I note also from looking at one of Diana's old passports that we visited China twice during the 1987 and 1988 Easter holidays for four nights and two nights respectively. I have memories of us visiting Kwei Lin (Guilin) and seeing the fishermen with their cormorant fish catchers on the River Li and the background of the peculiar limestone mountains standing up like sentries looking over the lovely and unusual land. It was early days for tourism in China and local air travel was an experience. I recall us standing on the runway, as in a bus queue, waiting for our plane to land. Once on board it seemed seat belts were optional as many were broken and no longer fixed to the seat.

The other time was when we visited Peking (Beijing). I am sure we were they longer than just a few days as we did visit the Great Wall and also the Summer Palace. I do recall a walk down Wangfujing Street looking at the markets and shops and seeing that the old grey, soulless, state enterprise shops with their disinterested bored staff were still alive.

Alexander also went to Peking with Bradbury School in his last year, 3/1991.

And Diana, without me, took the children with girl friends to Peking and the Great Wall in April of 1990.

During my second year teaching at the Poly I was encouraged to apply to do a masters degree in law at Hong Kong University. This was a two year part time course. I was interested because it was a chance to study the Law of China. Under the communist tradition law was the business of tricksters and in general had no place in the system. Things were changing and I wanted to be up to date as the Giant started to awake. There were four subjects, two for each year. I recall Chinese law was in two parts: civil and criminal law; and commercial and business law. There were other subjects from which to chose two others. I chose travel law and company law. I have forgotten nearly all I learnt. Travel law interested me and the examination was in the form of a thesis which I did well. And it was only this subject that I ever put to use, when I wrote an opinion on the liability of a travel agent for a client.

The Chinese law I never used at all. Although I did find parts of it useful when I went in 1987 to visit a court across the border at Shen Zhen. That visit was done with my fellow masters classmates, one of whom became very senior in the Hong Kong Government. My memory of a hearing in the Appeal court concerned a hawker from Hong Kong who had obtained for payment some 'artwork' to take back to HK. He represented himself and was appealing for the goods, which had been seized by the authorities, to be returned to him. He spoke only Cantonese and so told the court, who told him the language of the court was the national language (Mandarin). There was no interpreter and he left the court after the judge, on a bench with two other folk with military hats, had said a couple of lines which the appellant and me took to mean: 'P.... off, you can't have your things back'. As he passed me leaving the court he smiled and shrugged his shoulders as if to say: not what I am used to in Hong Kong!

After the session at the Appeal court the class, I was the only gwai lo, went off to a traditional restaurant where a special menu had been prepared for us. It was exotic to say the least and most of the items, except the one that went for chicken, could not have been legally obtained in Hong Kong. Nay, it may have been we would have been committing offences to have tucked into same. I didn't try the pangolin or the 'one of only one hundred of its kind left on the planet' in oyster sauce, but the dishes certainly excited my colleagues. Who if they had had tails would have wagged them off. I stuck with a more familiar mutton, a bit strong, but then it was traditional and very local. From one of the herds who grazed the China Mountain and who usually cock their hind legs to pee!

As I said above I left the Poly under a cloud. Towards the end of my second year I had been taking more practice and in order to accommodate the odd morning at court which clashed with a class I asked Malcolm Bell to stand in for me. James Collins had to report these irregularities to the higher authority who it seems did not want their staff to practice at all and if they did to share the fees. Again there was no regime yet in place to permit this course. I recall after hearing our representations which I did with the aid of my friend Gordon Hampton, both Robert Buchanan and myself were not rehired. I was given no time to move out of the flat in Shiu Fai Terrace. The poly estate staff almost broke into the flat to move us out. I learnt later that it was the first and only time in my dear Diana's life that she used bad language. I was now free to develop my practice and bring up my family with this new uncertain career. On the 17th November 1988, into my third year back in Hong Kong, I was presented with my certificate Master of Laws, issued by the University of Hong Kong by His Excellency the Governor of Hong Kong Sir David Clive Wilson. It was a formal occasion and I was proud to be there: an old Hong Kong policeman standing before the Governor. As he presented it to and dubbed me a Master, he said: 'Well done David', with a twinkle in his eye, as if to say I know you. He had been close to Sir Crawford Murray MacLehose who was Governor from 1971 to 1982, when he had served for a time as his adviser. Both men were sinologists and diplomats, David also being a Mandarin speaker. Jock the Sock, as he was called affectionately or otherwise, was in my view Hong Kong's greatest governor. He had visited Sham Shui Po Police Station in 1974 when I had been in charge of the CID there and had spent over an hour with me and some of my men discussing our problems. He impressed me then and even more so during and after the so called Police Mutiny of Autumn of 1977.

*Our graduation class taken outside Queen Elizabeth Stadium.*

*The whole class with some staff members at our dinner afterwards.*

Sir Murray concerned with the widespread corruption that was rife in most of the government departments had introduced the ICAC (the Independent Commission Against Corruption). They were recruited much from the British Police and it was said, rather ironically and perhaps with no basis, that some of the recruits were themselves escapees from their own rubber heel unit: the police who police the police. But in any event Sir Murray was absolutely right to start the ICAC which in a very short space of time cleaned up the civil service, the Hong Kong police in particular. But he soon realised with advisers who knew situation on the ground that 'A Night of the Long Knives' in regard to the Police could have brought it to an operational stand still. He therefore declared an amnesty for those not under immediate and ongoing investigation for all misdeeds (It was not a blanket amnesty) committed before, if I remember correctly, November 1978.

As you can imagine there was opposition to such course and there were questions in the British Parliament. But Jock the Sock was a brave and wise man and I felt at the time most of the thinking public appreciated what he had done. The situation requiring investigation, arrest and prosecution involved so many government departments that sadly with the: Public Works Department, Urban Services, Police, Fire Services and the New Territories Administration perhaps being the most affected the public service would not have been able to operate properly for long.

Life came back to normal, after a short period when there was uncertainty as to the state of law and order. The police, most of whom had not been involved in any protest, let alone mutiny, carried on working. I have a good friend today who was Sir Murray's ADC and has been able to give me some idea of what went on in the corridors of power.

If I could use this time to sing Jock the Sock's praises in other regards: He introduced and really got going the Country Parks. Hong Kong scenically is not all concrete, in fact most of it is hills, mountains, islands which are for the most part uninhabited. There are delightful hiking trails, ranging for those with thighs of steel to those for families going on country picnics. In these areas all future development was prohibited, so we were to have a places where all could go: a green refuge away from the fumes, noise and traffic of the city.

It is only now that there is agitation, some from the leadership of the Heung Yee Kuk, the body representing the indigenous New Territories community who, with their eyes on the fortunes to be made with land and property, are advocating 'development' of the Country Parks. A look across the border can tell us what can happen: a tranquil farming community with the highest building, in my time on the border 1965-71 a three storey customs post, now a city of 7 million or more. 'Keep our Country Parks Green!'

Another of the many things Sir Murray really moved forward was in 'Public Housing'. Some of the early resettlement estates were little more that dormitories, with communal lavatories and wash rooms. There had been little improvement by the 70's. But under Sir Murray public housing with shopping centres and recreational facilities e.g. Sports grounds and district swimming pools really took off. OK I hear old Hong Konger's saying the Victoria Park Pool has been with us for ages, before Sir Murray, I would answer one of the few! The quality of life for the majority of people certainly improved in his over 10 years as governor.

We, all of us Hong Kong citizens, should be grateful to the Baron George-Brown. When as George Brown, Foreign Secretary he helped Murray, who was his private secretary escape disgrace and failure. By supporting him after he was in trouble when he left in a bank a confidential letter from Harold Wilson the Prime Minister to Lyndon Baines Johnson (LBJ) the US President written in 1967 during the American war in Vietnam. I mention this to show that he, like us all, was not immune, despite his status and station, from making mistakes.

Today we have much to thank him for. And if I could be so bold to say, at least some of what he did here in HK had some effect, co-incidentally or not, on improvements I have noted in the quality of life in China.

# 21. Early Tremors

From the summer of 1987 I was a full time practising barrister at law needing plenty of briefs to support my family. After being thrown out of the staff quarters in Shiu Fai Terrace we needed somewhere to live. I bought with a mortgage a flat in our next door building: No 8 A Mandarin Villa, 10 Shui Fai Terrace. I recall we paid 1.5 million dollars for it and lived there happily until we sold it, about the time Alfreda went off to boarding school when she was 16. Then we took advantage of the huge increase in property values and sold it. Diana with skill and canny wisdom managed to get nearly four times what we had paid for it. This gave us a real nest egg which certainly meant we would never really be short of money, as long as I could keep working. But just starting practice things did not look that good. There were ESF school fees for the two children, and the mortgage payments. The property at Ludlow still needed to be sorted out and when it was I intended to buy a property in Shrewsbury which I planned to be our UK base and home. In the event we never returned to UK to live and became total Hong Kong people. 8 was a lucky number and the name of the road went well with it to ensure good fortune there.

Not long after moving into our new home we went off on a holiday to Phuket in Thailand. I recall we went to the Club Med' facility together with Ian Poulson, his wife and two daughters. I recall coming last in the cross-country run. This contrasted sharply with the position of iron man Poulson. Not fast perhaps, but I was fit. My heart problem had scared me and since leaving the RHKP I had spent much time trying to keep the weight down with regular swimming and running. Since moving into Shiu Fai Terrace in 1985 I had started the habit of running – whenever I had a free day – up the Peak. I would run along Bowen Road up the steep hill that was Wanchai Gap Road along Coomber Road and then Magazine Gap Road to the Peak. It was a heavy pull needing 45 minutes up and 30 minutes down. Sometimes I would have a change and run along Black's Link, then on through the Tai Tam Reservoir to Stanley. Here I would complete my journey with two pints of Bass at the Smugglers Inn; then back on the bus to Shui Fai.

Even when I was working I would try to fit in a morning run around Happy Valley racecourse, combining it sometimes with a swim at Morrison Hill public baths. I ran to be able to enjoy a beer without fear of getting too large. I continued the regime of exercise at least until we moved from Hong Kong Island to live at Shatin, which was just before the handover to China in 1997. I still continued exercise but my running changed – after Diana had the stroke in 2001 – to long walks pushing her in the wheelchair. After moving to Shatin I would often use the Olympic size public baths there, trying to maintain a regime of 30 lengths (approximately one mile) a session. Then there was the pool and the large running area around the cricket pitch at the Kowloon Cricket Club where the family had been members since 12th May, 1986.

With Alfreda off to Queen Anne's School at Caversham in the Royal County of Berkshire in the late autumn of 1994, we decided to sell 8A No.10 Shiu Fai Terrace, wrongly as it turned out. This was to trade down by buying a small flat at Lyttleton

Road, Mid levels. I say wrongly: It was too small, poor Alex's room you could hardly swing a cat around. Our bedroom we had hardly any floor space from which to climb into bed. Why did we leave our nice flat? Diana was not happy and it was at the time of the move to Lyttleton Road that she started to show signs of the terrible Parkinson's disease that would so cruelly afflict her and change her and the whole family's lives.

I recall walking down the slope from church one Sunday when she started to drag her right leg. This got worse and she started to get terrible cramps. We saw privately a neurologist Dr. Lee, he was the brother of the famous counsel and leader of the democrats: Martin Lee. He diagnosed early signs of Parkinson's and she eventually was put a course of drugs, the dose increasing as the painful symptoms got worse. I feel as the condition got worse it was the drugs which were causing some of the symptoms, especially the terrible cramps.

The drugs did seem to help to some extent with the seizing up of the muscles. This seizing up would sometimes prevent her quite suddenly from moving. I remember one day walking near our home in Tai Wai, Shatin she suddenly stopped and then just as suddenly started to walk speedily down the road.

When we moved to Shatin we started to see the neurologist at the Prince of Wales Hospital a Dr. Vincent Mok who recommended she have deep brain stimulation: the placing of an electronic device in her brain. The brain surgeon Professor Y Poon told us the operation was risk free: there was only a 1% chance of a stroke happening. It happened and was the most horrible thing that has even happened to us as a family. Oh how I weep today for how she suffered afterwards; but more about this later.

We were certainly happy and healthy at Mandarin Villa. My legal practice took off and most days I was in Court. Early on I had a High Court trial involving a robbery which had gone wrong and the victim had been killed. There were two accused; I was for a youth and Robert Forest for the older man. It was through Robert's skill that he persuaded the jury to find them guilty not of murder but of manslaughter.

I do not have the date but it must have been the summer of 1988 when Gordon Hampton was briefed by Bernard Gunston to defend Captain Clement Couto. Mr Gunston had worked with Gordon when he was a solicitor and still worked in his firm Hampton, Winter and Glynn. He was the very model of a colonial solicitor, short and round, grey hair, cream linen jacket, always totally honest and correct. Captain Couto was one of Stanley Ho's jet foil pilots driving the punters the 60 minute dash across the South China Sea to Macau. I have the information still: there were three charges all relating to him driving his vessel dangerously, endangering life at sea and failing to stop and report a collision. It was a bright clear day, so I don't know what he and his crew were doing, perhaps gambling with cards or dice or busy doing something else, in any event they were not looking where they were going. They narrowly missed colliding with 'Mathilda' a pleasure craft on which were two foreigners and a Chinese coxswain. I recall one of whom, at least, fell into the sea.

It was to become Hong Kong's longest magistrates trial. The magistrate was Mr Maharaj a South African Indian with an Irish passport! I had helped Gordon prepare the case; our instructions were to vigorously defend it. The integrity of the Far East Hydrofoil Company was at stake. We put the Crown to strict proof and submitted mistaken identity; it was not jet foil Madeira! The trial went for over a week and was then adjourned for a few days to accommodate the court diary. I had already booked a holiday with the family to go to UK and stay at a farmhouse in Shropshire. Gordon and Mr. Gunston had not originally thought they needed a second counsel but after a few days of assisting Gordon out of court they decided he should have me, as a junior in court. So I started to assist in court. I did some cross examination of one of the prosecutions expert witnesses.

I took the family to Shropshire, where I spent a few days, then left them at this farmhouse on a hillside, 10 miles out of Shrewsbury. Diana had a car, so there she was, with the two little ones 8 and 10, sharing a hillside with some sheep. I returned to Hong Kong and continued with the trial. I returned to the family and the sheep when it finished about another week or so later on. I recall the trial went for over a month. Captain Couto was rightly found guilty. The trial gave me a nice fee; the refresher was 4000 dollars a day, no brief fee, but not bad, it was more than enough to pay for our holiday.

Mr. Maharaj's reasons for verdict were spot on, or so said the wise 'Somerset Maugham' Bernard Gunston. But we were instructed to appeal. I drafted the grounds and included everything I could find: duplicity, omission of material averments and the fact the Crown had not proved the required intention under the Indictment Rules. In any event The

Honourable Mr Justice T Bewley hearing the appeal made short work of our arguments and dismissed it.

He also took the opportunity to reprimand the two counsel involved at the trial. Gordon and Mr. Blanchflower for the prosecution; I quote from the record: "The Magistrate's task was made more difficult by the vast quantity of evidence, much of it unnecessary in my view and the acrimonious squabbling between counsel that took place."

I knew Judge Bewley when I had been his prosecutor at North Kowloon Court in 1969/70.

After the trial I returned to join the family in Shropshire. I recall we returned to our old haunts in Wales. I also started the process about buying a home in Shrewsbury. My intention then was to return to England sometime, either to retire or work. As things turned out I became totally Hong Kong in regard to loyalty and affection. When I saw how England was going in regard to its change of culture, I decided I would end my days in Hong Kong. I did buy a detached, three bedroom house at Copthorne, Shrewsbury during that holiday. But I never lived there at all myself; the place was always rented out, the rent paying the mortgage.

I recall I stayed with the members when chambers moved form the HSBC building in Pedder Street to Garden Road where we became Garden chambers situated for one lease of two years in Citibank Building and for one lease in the Bank of China Building. I left the chambers then when a number of new people joined and I felt I was not being given the correct position in regard to my seniority at the chambers. I went and joined my friend Christopher Grounds at Man Yee Building, at the western end of Central. We were there until they started to knock the building down when three of us: Chris and Luke McGuinnity and I decided to purchase 801 Yip Fung Building in D'Aguilar Street, where we were for five years or so. We sold it at a slight loss. Although small in space it served us well. And was with Chris and his chambers, through various names and buildings, until I retired, which I did in September 2012 from Convention Chambers at China Overseas Building 18th floor, 139 Hennessey Road, Wanchai.

I must have prosecuted and defended hundreds of cases in all the Courts of Hong Kong. When I started I was conscious of image and the need to dress and sound the part. Harwood Stevenson my old pupil master in London said to me once: 'David you have got to do something about your vowels, the punters don't want people who speak like they do!' I am a good mimic and can do most voices, so for a long time I tried to speak proper wif owt the London voice. And even in Hong Kong' s 30's temperatures I did the waist-coat bit. But it was not long before Dave (of the cops) with his new voice and stature had reverted to, almost, his old self.

You never expect thanks as a criminal advocate. Occasionally you feel satisfaction if you have got some horrible type convicted and relief when your client who was innocent, or should I say was less than guilty, is acquitted. But rare is it you are given an actual thank you. I have three: A young man for being acquitted for Robbery at the High Court, I managed to show that not only was the evidence weak but inadmissible; a mature man for raping his domestic servant and a youth for indecent assault of a young girl. I have the three plaques/trays displayed on my side- board.

I have been thinking about old cases recently with these memoirs in my mind. Some early ones come back. There was the case before District Judge Cameron in the old French Legation building at Battery Path, before the District Court, with its score or so of courts, moved to its new building in Harbour Road, Wanchai. I was defending a youth who was involved in a robbery in Sai Kung. I had only been in full time practice for a year or so and was keen for Alfreda to see what I did in court. She came to sit in court, Alex was too young. Some of the evidence as it came out I thought was too much for a young child to hear so I whizzed her out of the court.

In the event I managed to have the confession statement ruled out as inadmissible and the youth was acquitted. Judge Cameron I liked much. He was always his own man and not a 'company' man like some of his colleagues, who seemed to regard sentencing tariffs as straight jackets. But there were judges like Mr. Justice Joe Duffy, a man of the people, who sentenced looking as much at the prisoner as the crime and did spend time carefully explaining and justifying his sentence. I recall a drug trafficking case, when he showed compassion towards the youth before him and did not follow the strict tariff. The prosecution did not appeal but I never found the sentence in reported cases.

Some time later, the District court had already moved to Harbour Road, I was before Judge Henry Daniel. He was the godfather of my son and I had known him as a friend from my days on the Frontier when he had sat as a magistrate at Fanling

Court. He had been an honorary member of the Fanling officers' mess. But correctly he was not a great friend of the police in his court and would frequently disallow evidence which he thought had been obtained unfairly. In my case I hoped to persuade him to disallow a confession which the prosecution relied on. I submitted there were strong grounds to show the accused, a youth of 19 or so, had been ill-treated. Thus the confession was not made voluntarily and should be ruled as inadmissible. I was surprised and a little hurt when Henry allowed the statement in and convicted my client. When I got home I expressed my disappointment to Diana. She wisely said: Of course he was your friend he can't look as if he favours you. Thus my client had come to the wrong counsel.

I have no diary or notes now to reliably recall my memory but it is likely that during my early time at practice, the first 8 years, I was often instructed by a clerk Aaron Yip of K.Y. Woo and Co. Aaron was an efficient reliable clerk and we did some interesting cases together. It was with Aaron that I got involved with my first and only Privy Council appeal: 'Ng Enterprises and The Urban Council'. Ted Drew who was introduced to me by my best man Steve Stephenson was one of the owners and the manager/operator of Ng Enterprises which ran the Mister Softee ice cream business. I recall he had 12 or13 vans which could be seen all over Hong Kong selling their soft ice cream.

In 1994 the Urban Council decided to issue no more itinerant hawker licences. This would have meant putting Ted's ice cream vans out of business as they were licensed, with a huge annual licence fee, as itinerant hawkers. It always appeared to me that itinerant hawkers were those who were on the move with their two baskets and a carrying pole. Clearly ice cream vans who had to park for lengthy periods to sell their wares to people around public transport places should have had their own licensing regime. There was a general presumption of a freedom to trade albeit under appropriate and lawful licensing conditions. I had helped Ted when his vans got prosecuted for obstruction and had on one occasion persuaded a magistrate to dismiss the charge: on the basis of how were they suppose to sell their ice cream on the move.

I needed a more senior counsel to challenge the refusal to licence the vans and Aaron and I approached Phil Dykes a relative newcomer to Hong Kong but one who had obtained a good reputation in the Public Law field. I recall our case against the Urban Council was first brought before High Court Judge Raymond Sears, which we won. This must have been when we applied for leave to seek an application for Judicial Review. Then the judge was sympathetic and considered that there was a presumption in regard to freedom to trade and Mr. Softee should be able to be licenced to do so and in any event the huge licence fees were ultra vires; licence fees should only cover the costs of their issuance.

There was however a further case at the High Court before Judge Keith. This must have been the actual review hearing, where there our challenge was the Urban Council's abolishing itinerant hawking licences altogether and thus forcing Ted and Co out of business. Judge Keith found for the Urban Council, so we appealed to the Court of Appeal. In a judgement handed down on 5th December 1995 by a majority the Court found in favour of the Urban Council. I recall Judge Godfrey in a minority supported our free trade argument and allowed our appeal. So what were we to do?

The next stop was the Privy Council in England, Hong Kong's court of final appeal. We were approaching 1997 and the handover; Ted was anxious to get the viability of the business sorted out. We got leave to appeal from the Court of Appeal on the 1st February 1996: the only matter left in issue was the validity of the by-law eliminating the category of hawkers who traded itinerantly.

It was off as a family to England in June of 1996. Alfreda, I would pick up from her School in Reading. It must have been she had come to the end of her two years at Queen Anne's and was waiting on her A level results. She would have been starting to think about her next step: University. We were to stay at Ted Drew's place at Long Ashton, just outside Bristol. He had a really delightful home set in 2 acres, in what was the old club house of a golf club. The golf course was still there, situated on the hill above. We were there for a holiday, but more importantly, for Ted and I, was the Privy Council appeal which was set down for the 17th June,1996. We were however to come to London earlier: Counsel and Instructing Solicitors were to meet Leading Counsel in his chambers on the afternoon of 13th June, 1996.

It was to be one of the last appeals from Hong Kong, as after the change of sovereignty the final court of appeal for Hong Kong would be the Final Court of Appeal for the Special Autonomous Region of the Peoples Republic of China. We had been suggested a number of Queens Counsel to conduct the appeal and Ted chose Lord Michael Beloff. It was quite an outing: Ted and his daughter Carol, who had been my pupil/summer student for a few months, myself and the family.

We all came to London by National Express Bus. It took us to Victoria Coach Station and it was not far from there to the Court in Downing Street. It was an experience for all us. Ted was a typical old fashioned Englishman, proud of his heritage and knowledgeable on British history. He had served in the Parachute Regiment in Palestine after the war and had been a NAFFI manager for some time in Malaya. His wife was Chinese and our two families got on well together.

We had a lovely holiday together in Bali sometime before the Privy Council appeal. It must have been 1995. Ted and his wife accompanied us throughout although at the end of our stay they flew of to Java for an extended holiday. In Bali we stayed at a beach hotel but it was not that sort of holiday. Ted is an educated man with a keen interest in the history and culture of that uniquely Hindu based Island. Hindu in a sea of Islam and in many islands still animist beliefs. We really explored Bali and visited the home – really by chance – of the traditional ruler: the Rajah. A splendid fellow who showed us around his humble, and I mean humble, abode. We hired a driver and minibus which took us all around including up in the hills to a lovely lake

The Judges in the Court, I recall there were at least five, were not with wigs and gowns. They wore ordinary suites. We wore our wigs, our gowns and best barrister uniforms. There were three of us for Ng Enterprises: me, Beloff and Phil Dykes. And two for the Urban Council. Our instructing solicitors were the well known firm of Norton Rose, London EC1. They were to charge an arm and a leg for doing, what I thought, was very little. I recall they did provide a sandwich lunch! The Lords of Appeal were what you would expect: courteous, polite and sympathetic. No 'judgeitis' here, as one could often experience in Hong Kong. But in the event the learned Lords found for the Urban Council, on a point which had not be raised by counsel of either side. I forget what it was; but they did say some helpful things about Mr. Softee and the new by-law abolishing itinerant hawking licences.

Our efforts must have caused some impact back with the Hong Kong government. Because as far as Ted's vans were concerned the new by-laws were never promulgated and to this day Mr. Softee vans are alive and well on the streets, parks, playing fields etc of Hong Kong supplying their own produced soft ice cream and biscuit cones. They are now in competition with 7/11 shops on every corner selling ice cream, and must be finding it ever more difficult to keep going. My friend Ted alas, passed away 5 or so years ago. I know not if his son Jeffery or daughter Carol have taken it over.

Ted was a generous man who used to say running a business like his was one battle after another against the Urban Service and the Hawker Control Authority. There was always the problem of over officious staff who would chase the vans and report them for obstruction offences. Then there was his ice cream factory at Fo Tan, which also made his crispy cones, and the visits from the health and hygiene officers. I sympathised with him. It always seemed to me that you were better off being totally illegal in Hong Kong. Once you were seized with a proper licence you became fair game for the scores of different government servants who had to justify their posts and salaries. I recalled unlicensed restaurants that ran for years before being prosecuted. They would then change hands and continue to operate until they attracted the next interference from officials.

As a post script my son Alexander had a few days, or was it longer, on one of Ted's vans, helping to sell and sample the ices.

We must have stayed at least three times at Ted's place in Long Ashton. On one occasion he even left me his car to drive for our two weeks or so holiday. I unfortunately dented it whilst parking. Ted never murmured: 'no worry David'! He was a dear friend, a total gentleman and one of Hong Kong' s assets, always willing to give more to the place than receive. I think the last time we stayed at Long Ashton our friends Barney and Marilynne Humphris joined us and we had many a good yum cha lunch in one of Bristol's many excellent Chinese restaurants. Sadly I was sending Ted Christmas cards some time after his death. Before I learnt he had died in England.

The end of the 20th century began on the 1st July 1997 the end of Colonial Hong Kong.

For my children it meant the end of school and the beginning of university. In early summer of 1996 Alfreda received her A level results from Queen Anne's School followed by the beginning of three years at the University of Sussex studying for a Bachelor's degree in Geography. And for Alexander the end of summer of 1998 saw him taking his A levels at Island School Hong Kong followed by a start at Portsmouth University for a Bachelors degree in Business and Management.

Alfreda was quite happy with Sussex. I had met, in Hong Kong 1996, a senior member of one of the faculties during a UK Universities Fair at the Convention Centre. In our discussion he was confident that with our background and connection with the UK Alfreda would be regarded as a home student for fee purposes; I still had a property in Shrewsbury. This would help significantly with expenses. Sussex was also on Alfreda's choice list.

Alexander however had put down for Liverpool University as he was a fan of Liverpool F.A. The university had also told us they would regard him as a home student for fee purposes. Unfortunately Alex's A-level grades were not good enough to get into Liverpool so he had to go to his second choice, which was Portsmouth. They had refused to treat him as a home student, so the fees were heavy.

As we had done with Alfreda at Sussex we saw Alexander into his new accommodation at Portsmouth on his first day at University. I recall our friends Barney and Marilynne were with us. I must say I was more impressed with Sussex but in any event both children did their best to settle in and I was proud of them, especially Alex who I thought would have more trouble finding his feet.

I have often contemplated that our decision to move to Tai Wai, Shatin did not help Alex with the last year or so at Island School. It was time for A levels and the long bus ride must have added to his difficulties. I recall our first home there I rented from the brother of my pupil Franki Wu. It was at 19th floor Greenview Gardens, Chui Tin Street. Diana was in the early stages of Parkinson's disease and then was still able to cope without any domestic helper.

Why we moved from HK Island to Shatin I now cannot fully understand. But by selling our property on HK Island I was able to join Chris Grounds, Ada Chan our solicitor, and others to buy a property at Staunton Street, Soho. We collectively bought one half of a building; each having a share in the ground floor which was commercial and each buying a domestic flat on one of the floors above. I purchased the top floor and roof. It was a good investment; we sold all, five or so years later, at a good profit.

Our move got us going again to an Anglican Church which met at the Sheng Kung Hui, Tsang Shui Tim Secondary School at Wo Che. We would still occasionally attend our old church at Wanchai to see our friends. Wo Che was nearer and we made new friends with the minister, an Australian Stephen Durie and others when I joined a cell group for bible study and fellowship. One of those Brenda Liu is still a dear friend and was especially supportive when my Diana was going through her pain and suffering. We must have been living at Shatin for 10 years. It was the time of the handover 1997 when we moved and I moved to Discovery bay in 2007 after Diana died. By then we were living at quarters attached to the Prince of Wales Hospital. Shatin Church was very much our spiritual home during the terrible suffering of Diana; more of that later.

I see from my children's Cathay pacific log books, which have brought back my memories of many trips and adventures, that we went to the USA in the summer of 1989, flying via Seoul to Los Angeles on the 1st August. In the USA we hired a car and I drove along the California coast to San Francisco but first spending a couple of days in Disney Land. After a short stay there we flew to Hawaii where we spent a week on the big island of Hawaii. Our visit there was memorable only because Alfreda' s purse was stolen from her hotel room. A report to police did little to interest anyone and the purse remained missing. We landed back in Hong Kong after a short stop at Narita in Japan.

We flew North West Airlines! It must be one of our worst airline experiences: on the way out we stopped at Seoul and remained on the plane for about 6 plus hours because they could not get the door open. Well, something like that!

On the 24th July, 1991, with Alfreda at 13 and Alexander 11 we went as a family with a delegation from our church to attend the World Methodist Conference in Singapore. I recall it lasted a week during which time we attended activities in the large Assembly Hall in one of big centres and in a number of smaller rooms attached. On the first day each country's delegation put on a display. Our group of about 25 sang a song in Cantonese. There was plenty for me to do: attending group studies and meetings during which time Diana and the children went off on outings. After the conference finished we drove up into Malaysia and I have visions of visiting both the Cameron Highlands and Kuan Tun on the East coast. I am not sure now whether we went to those places on separate holidays or if it were on the one. I do have a recollection of driving up to the Cameron Highlands and driving across from the west to the east coast. I remember the hotel and the beach on the east coast

I note from my records that I took the family to Kota Kinabalu, Sabah for the New Year in January 1989. We stayed for a week. I recall we went there again in the Christmas of 1993. It was a memorable trip because our friends Barney and Marilynne Humphris joined us at the Tarung Aru Resort. We had a great time together. I have a recollection of me annoying Barney with my moaning at the staff about the quality of our dim sum at the 'yum cha' at the resort's Chinese restaurant. I also have a photograph of someone buying salted cuttle fish. Barney is the sort of man who relishes anything no other European would eat: chicken feet, would you believe it? I also have a treasured picture in my mind of Diana holding hands with an orang-u-tang. This was during a visit to a reserve at Sandakan on the eastern side of Sabah. We had flown there the short 30 minute flight. As we walked through the jungle Diana said Dave look; I turned around and saw that a young ape had come down from the trees and had attached his hand to hers as they both walked along.

August of 1992, most of the month saw the whole family on a holiday with our friends the Halters. Willie was from Germany who had come to Hong Kong in 1965 as a missionary. He had worked for a number of years amongst the ex KMT soldiers and their families who had settle at Rennies Mill, over the hill from Kwun Tong; now the area is called Tseung Kwan O. He had married one of the girls from the village there and they had one son Christen (he was born on Christmas day). The two families had known each other since 1985 when we first joined the Methodist Church in Kennedy Road. As the years progressed we joined Willie and Sandy with their friendship with Ian and Dorothy Brown and their children. The three families, sometimes joined by others from the church, would go on picnics in Tai Lam Country Park where the Dads and the children would play football. Other days we might go cycling at Cheung Chau.

The first part of the August 1992 trip we toured Wales. I hired a minibus and drove us around. We went back to Aberystwyth where we visited our Chinese friends the Chung family. We all went cockling at the Dovey estuary and drove over the hills to the Elan Valley Reservoir and then followed the Elan river to Rhayader. I have photographs of us exploring black currents and the associated sheep. I recall we had a stop in Shrewsbury to explore along the River Severn. Then it was a night in London and a decent yum cha at a Chinese restaurant. The following day we all bundled in a taxi, all 7 of us, to the airport where we flew to Germany.

In Germany it was Willies turn to drive. We flew to Frankfurt and then made our way to Hanau where Willie has a home. I recall that we drove south down to the Black Forrest stopping on the way at that famous University town of Heidelberg. In case you are wondering how I can remember all this I tell you that I have some photographs of the holiday, which have dates on them. I have also traced our route from memory and the help of a map. I have a memory that we spent the night at a zimmer frei (B and B: free room) near Dinkelsbuehl. I recall that the inn-keeper bewailed the near total destruction of the town by the RAF during the last day of the war. I like to think I said to him: Well you lot started it! but I am not sure if I was so impolite. My reading has since shown either he was telling porky pies or I have remembered it all wrong and he was taking about somewhere else, because records say the town suffered little or no damage in the war.

This was unlike Freiburg, a Black Forest town, not far away, which was flattened by bombing. From the Black Forest, I have a vision of walking through trees with the children, we travelled

339

east following the north shore of Lake Constance. We were now right in the south of Bavaria which was once the fiefdom of King Ludwig II. He built that fantastic fairyland castle: Neuschwanstein (the spelling!), set on a small mountain but dominated by the southern slopes of the Alps. We visited the castle and I have a few photographs showing us there on the 19th August 92. We visited the highest mountain in Germany, the Zugspitze, not too far from Ludwig's castle. I recall saying goodbye to the two families as they boarded the cable car to take them up the mountain. I was too chicken and stayed down at the cafe below awaiting their return.

We visited Munich and, of course, had a session in one of the beer halls. I recall we also visited a museum there. I have a photograph dated the18th of a Dornier aircraft which I think was on display in the Deutshes Museum in Munich. The dates on these and other photographs show our route might have been south from Hanau then west along Lake Constance to the Black Forest then up again via Freiburg to Hanau. But I realise to any reader it does not really matter.

I could have taken the photographs up to see Willie last Tuesday (13th August, 2013) when I went to see him at Chung Shan in China. But sadly he suffered Parkinson's disease about the same time as my Diana and now lies on a bed in hospital motionless, unable to speak just looking at the ceiling. He has tubes to feed him and has to have someone by the bed all the time. For most of the time he lies like this also at home. Sandy has bought a house just outside Chung Shan and is assisted by a Filipino couple. He was in hospital because of breathing problems. He has been like this for at least two years and really for the last five years has been an invalid. I felt so sad when I saw him and so sorry for Sandy who has cared for him for so long. He is not in a vegetative state and seemed to know my presence and did display a 'smile' when I attempted to raise everyone's spirits with a joke.

The photographs show us at a number of those lovely south German town with their cobbled roads, walkways and squares. The building with the red roofs and green shutters and the small town churches and the grander churches and cathedrals. One picture shows water, a lake or a river? It brought back a memory of swimming in the invigorating cold water. Where was it, only dear Willie could tell me. After the southern tour I have memory of spending some time based in Hanau where the Halters had a home during which time we visited Frankfurt where Willie took me to a typical English pub!

In 1995 we had holiday to Lombok, in Indonesia. I recall we stayed at a quiet beach hotel but thoroughly explored the Island with our own car and driver going everywhere along some hair-raising roads in the highlands.

Apart from that lovely picture in my mind of Diana and the young ape holding hands, the holiday which gives me the strongest reminiscences is the one we took on the Bali Sea Dancer.

It must have been the summer of 1997, the year of the handover to China. Alfreda was home after her first year at Sussex university. She had with her Chris Dennis, as far as I was aware, her first boy friend. I had booked us on a 7 day cruise on board a lovely small ship: the Bali Sea Dancer. It sailed from Bali, in Indonesia, eastwards to Flores and back to Bali visiting along the way Lombok, Komodo and the terrible dragons and Sumba. Memorable were: the snorkelling in the crystal clear water with all the wonderful creatures of the sea; the dragons on Komodo, awful things, and then there was the welcome ceremony on Flores or was it Sumba where we saw the native horsemen and their small horses.

Alfreda, Chris and Alexander seemed to get on, all bunked together. I liked young Chris and was pleased Alfreda had a pleasant boy friend. Diana was into two years of Parkinson's disease and although she had uncomfortable days I recall she was able to move around and enjoy the cruise. I found it simply delightful sitting in a reclining chair on the top deck of the ship looking into the gorgeous sun set, a glass of beer in my hand. I did not want to come down to the dining room for dinner. It was the start of a romance for Alfreda and Chris. I recall we also had some time on Bali after we finished the cruise. It was then at the end of summer back to University for Alfreda and for Alexander back to Island School and a long trek there from our flat at Tai Wai, Shatin. Alas I can find no photographs of this really lovely trip.

I recall that our family spent a lot of time on different occasions, when we were in London, staying with Barney and Marilynne Humphris at their nice home at 81 Byng Road, Barnet. I have a recollection of using their home one year (1993) as a base from which to explore London and the home counties. And from there one week we took a Cosmos package coach/channel ferry tour to the three capitals: Paris, Amsterdam and Brussels. I have little memory of what we did apart from having a rotten lunch in a Paris restaurant. I do remember coming back to England and paying the coach driver to drop us off, miles away from the usual London stop, at the top of Byng Road, where Barney welcomed me with a glass of his home made beer.

Barney and Marilynne have been very good friends and were particularly so during the children's time of growing up: the 1990's and early 2000's They kept an eye on them when both were in the country at school or university. And since adulthood – when living in England – both children, Alfreda in particular, have visited and stayed with them.

I also must have stayed with them with my family and, since Diana died, by myself a number of times. I have no record of the dates now but I know Byng Road the house and Barnet so well that posit that over the last 25 years I must have stayed with them at least 10 times in their comfortable second bedroom. On one of my more recent visits since Diana died, I guess around 2005/6 I was persuaded to go up in Barney's aircraft. I must admit I was afraid, although it was nice to be able to fly over Barnet. No it has to be a big plane for me, notwithstanding Barney was a good driver.

I saw them last in 2012, but sadly only met up with them for a short weekend up at Buxton Spa.

They attended the wedding, on the 27th July, 2003, here in Hong Kong of Alfreda and her ex-husband Chris. Alfreda has also visited them last year (2012) at Byng Road with daughter Isabel.

I went on holiday with them in the late autumn/winter of 2006. This was a memorable trip on 'The Khan' the Darwin to Adelaide cross central Australia train. It was a three-day trip, two nights on the train with a one-night stop at Alice Springs. There was excellent food and service and good accommodation for doubles but for a single it was OK for midgets but not for 250 pound lumps like me. Once in the cabin it was hard to get out, but the lounge and bar was nice with a couple of 'Cooper's' Sparkling Ales from Adelaide. A particularly fine brew, and may I say the only fine brew in Australia.

The start to new century was to be traumatic for us as a family as Diana's brain stimulation implant went wrong and she became a total invalid.

# 22. Sadness before Sorrow

2001 was disaster year for our family.

The **5th of February, 2001,** was the day fixed for Professor Y Poon to lead the operation at the Prince of Wales hospital to place the brain stimulation implant into Diana' s brain. I had taken her there from our rented flat at Parkview Garden, Pik Tin Street, Tai Wai on the afternoon of Friday 2nd February. We had moved there from Greenview Gardens in 2000. Diana was very confident and Professor Poon had spoken to us in the ward re-assuring us about the operation and how it was 99% risk free. The ward was comfortable and all manner of friends were there to wish her well on Saturday and Sunday. At church we had prayers for her and our cell group with friends like Brenda Liu, the minister Stephen Durie and others met at my house for more prayer. Sunday evening I stayed with her telling her to be strong and not to worry. Alexander was back in England at University, Alfreda was here in Hong Kong living with her boy friend from University days, Chris Dennis. They had married in a registry office in England, the purpose primarily so that Chris could work here as a dependent of Alfreda, a Hong Kong belonger. They would have a nice little flat next to the Happy Valley race-course. Chris would get a job with Volvo Trucks.

The operation was to be performed on the evening of the Monday. Diana would be resting and preparing for the operation in the day. I have no recollection if I went to the hospital on the Monday and why I was not at the hospital during the operation. I have some memory of contacting Professor Poon on the phone and he telling me to go home and wait. I went to work in the morning and returned home and went to bed.

The most terrible news our family has ever had was when Professor Poon rang me on the early morning of Tuesday. He said that Diana had had a stroke and was in a critical condition now in the Intensive Care Unit (ICU) of the hospital. There was a massive haemorrhaging of the brain and this would have to be removed. They would have to open the brain for a second time to be done soonest. The news was awful. She might die or be terribly injured. Poon explained they were probing the brain to ascertain the best location to install the electronic stimulator when she suffered a severe haemorrhaging. One minute she had been joking with the theatre staff and the next she was unconscious. I learnt that she had been conscious during the initial stages of the operation and was cheerfully assisting after they had opened her skull to place the implant; then for whatever reason they struck a blood vessel causing her to black out. She did not regain consciousness until the 10th day in ICU when she came off the ventilator and was transferred to a General ward. And from then on she was a chronic invalid. She had limited speech and movement requiring for the most part a wheelchair.

From the time she was in ICU until she was moved via the General Ward of the Prince of Wales Hospital to the Cheshire Home at A Kung Kok Shan, overlooking the Shatin race-course, we were at her bedside. Mabel our helper was great assisting with the bedside vigil at ICU. We had employed her, our first helper since coming back to Hong Kong in 1985, about year before. She had come because Diana was finding it too much to cope herself. I mention this to show that as she had managed so long by herself perhaps she did not need the implant. I also discovered later, that although the Chinese lady patient we saw months before the operation had evidenced in testimony and actions its success, Professor Poon and his team had only performed a few such operations. This was unlike Hospitals in the USA where the surgical procedure was common and where her neurologist and advocate of the brain stimulation here, Dr. Vincent Mok had witnessed many.

Back in the General ward we continued in shifts to watch and pray over her. Alexander came back from Portsmouth to be near her in March. Improvement was slow at the Prince of Wales. She didn't for a long time seem to be able to focus with her eyes and made no sounds except moans and cries. Towards the middle of March there was an improvement when a particularly lovely Sister, Edith Wong, managed to get her alive again. She started to show recognition and say at least the children's names. She also started to use her hands, could eat small amounts and do short assisted walks.

On the 22nd March she was transferred to the Cheshire Home and was there for well over two months. There she had occupational and speech therapy. She was always confused and in my view then was almost like a child. She was still in nappies and had to be washed. A thing which improved slowly over the months ahead. Her speaking was very limited: there were irrational answers to 'Yes' and 'No' questions and she could not tell colours or numbers. She could not read and could only do a swiggle for her name. The biggest problem of all was her unsteady movement. She was allowed leave from the Home sometimes at weekends but on two occasions fell from her bed whilst sorting things out. The first of a number of times when she fell over.

She left the Home at the beginning of June and returned home. And was unable to continue long with outpatients because of the SARS scare.

The year 2001 had also been a busy professional year for me. On the 28th April 2001, Diana was still in the Cheshire home, I had visited Mr. Fu Mo at Lai Chi Kok Remand Centre. He was one of seven accused charged with Murder and Arson to be tried at the High Court later in the year (High Court case number HCCC 6 of 2001). A pre-trial revue had been set down for August but before then there were a number of conferences with Fu Mo and other lawyers in the case. There were also preliminary procedural matters to deal with before the case was set down before Mr Justice Tom Gall, a very respected and experienced judge, for trial to start on the 8th October 2001 to last an estimated 90 court days.

The case arose from events which took place on the 2nd August when a number of Mainland claimants, seeking the right to live in Hong Kong, went to Room 1301 in Immigration Tower without an appointment, apparently seeking to achieve a face to face meeting with the Director of Immigration. The group refused to leave when ordered to do so and there was a confrontation during which bottles containing highly flammable thinners were thrown causing a senior immigration officer to be severely burnt which lead to his death 9 days later. One of the claimants was also injured when the thinners were thrown and he also died in hospital.

There were issues regarding the admissibility of confession statements and offers to plea to the lesser charge of manslaughter to be ruled on by the judge before the jury could be empanelled. They were so on the 16th October, the trial continued with breaks, including for Christmas, for 66 days when the verdict was delivered late afternoon on the 2nd February, 2002 all most a year to the day since I took Diana into hospital for the implant operation.

Only one of the seven accused: Sze Kwan Ling (D1) was convicted of Murder. The others were convicted of manslaughter, the offence which Fu Mo had offered to plead guilty. He was sentenced to 12 years imprisonment, the 5 years sentence for the arson charge was to run concurrently with the 12 years for the two manslaughter convictions.

It was a heavy trial, with site visits, legal arguments and numerous witnesses. All accused except Sze Kwan ling gave evidence in the witnesses box and were subject to cross examination. There was considerable interest in the case as it concerned a polemical issue: Immigration. D1. sentence was later quashed on a appeal and replaced with a manslaughter conviction and sentence.

The case certainly took much of my time but there were plenty of free days in which I could take Diana out. It also helped with our finances.

Alfreda and Chris were in Hong Kong until 2004 when they went back to live in Worcester, England where Chris got a job working for a subsidiary of Rolls Royce and Alfreda a teaching job at a local junior school. They were able to visit Diana and keep an eye on her when I went off in April 2002 to visit the South island of New Zealand and stay with an old chambers mate: Luke MacGuinity. He had a delightful home at Amberly, 12 miles north of Christchurch where he grew grapes and reared his four children. I stayed with him for a week or so and then toured the South Island using trains as much as I could.

I took the train along a really scenic route over the hills from Christchurch to Greymouth. There I visited the Monteith Brewery and tasted some of their really fine ales/beers. I then went south by bus and explored the west coast before stopping off at the Westland national Park to have a look at Mount Cook. A night here then on further south-east to Queenstown that lovely town set by a lake complete with steam boat. The town was famous as a winter sports resort but being early autumn down under the season had not got under way.

After a night at a guest house by the lake it was off south-east to Invercargill the most southern city on the planet, or is that Ushuaia in Argentina?

In Invercargill lived old friends from our days at Aberystwyth: Brian and Linda Batson. They had three children of similar ages to our two and had emigrated to new Zealand way back in the late 80's. Brian was biologist boffin, especially into things in the sea. I stayed with them, I forget how long, but long enough: to go with them to a brass band competition; for me to find the most southernmost brewery in the world, the Invercargill

Brewery; and to catch the ferry on the bumpy crossing to Stewart Island.

The Brewery was not easy to find; it was out of town on what seemed to be a farm with the brewery occupied in a barn. They had a bottling plant and I tried the Pils which was light. The trip from Bluff (famous for its oysters) to Stewart Island came later. The Island was small, you could walk around it in a day. I stayed one night at the small hotel/guest house, went to Church and recall it was a husband and wife team who were the clergy. The husband ran the Anglican church and the wife the non-conformists'. They would take it in turns at whose church each week the regular Sunday service would be held.

As you find all over New Zealand and most of the old British Empire there was the local cenotaph with names too numerous for the tiny population of Stewart Island. Then I recall my study of the history and visits to museums: the population of New Zealand at the start of the First World War was about one million, over one tenth of the whole population volunteered and signed up to support the 'motherland'. Of these well over a tenth were killed: approximately 60,000 killed or wounded.

It was back from Stewart Island and farewell to the Batsons then off on the bus north to Dunedin where the eldest Batson boy was at University. Dunedin the Kiwi Edinburgh of the Antipodes, here for a couple of nights and for some decent beer from a boutique brewery, a visit to thank God at the fine Cathedral and a 60 kilometre scenic rail journey on the Taieri Gorge Railway.

The main railway system on the South island only goes from Picton south along the coast to Christchurch and from there on another line to Greymouth. I did the trip North on the Christchurch to Picton train during the holiday on a separate occasion. I recall getting off the train at Marlborough where I visited wineries and stayed the night. I have a recollection of taking a dip at the hotel's pool there; goodness it was icy cold. It was a return trip on the train this time after having a couple of days on the North coast visiting Nelson, Picton and Blenheim. Back south and farewell at Amberly to Luke and co a night at a hotel, in Christchurch, such a lovely green and garden city, and the off in the plane back to Hong Kong.

Diana had a fall in the Autumn of 2002. She was unattended at the time. I recall that Mable had not renewed her contract and we had hired a new Filipino helper Marivic. She was admitted into hospital for one day and was OK afterwards. Her condition was not improving other than she could use her hands to eat. She was prone to Parkinson' s involuntary movement and it was this that caused her to dislocate her shoulder in July 2003. She was greatly distressed and I took her to the Union Hospital where she was for three days and was seen by Professor Poon. I realised that she needed someone with her all of the time, so I hired also Nina the sister of Marivic. As another precaution, to be nearer to hospital care, we moved to private quarters attached to the Prince of Wales Hospital. We were a stone's throw from Casualty. I hoped we would now have 24-hour coverage. Nina would sleep next to Diana and we would always have a relief for the helper's day off.

But alas on the 14th march, 2005 in the afternoon whilst unattended (you can guess my displeasure with the helper!) she fell off a chair as she was trying to get into the fridge to get some chocolate and was found laying face down outside the kitchen. She was conscious and crying and had a black eye. I rushed home from Court and took her to Casualty. A brain scan revealed no damage and, as I knew she hated hospitals, I took her home. She was unsteady for two days and with one of the helpers on long leave I had her re-admitted. She was detained for a short while. Her movement after was noticeably worse and the Parkinson's sticky feet a problem. She had difficulty standing and even when sitting she would slope off. One day – it was the 19th March – I was too slow to stop her falling of the chair onto the floor. I have a record that I wrote to the Hospital and asked them to keep her in for observation and do another brain scan. Í understand that there was no further damage. She saw Professor Poon who reported that as far as the stroke was concerned she was 'as good as she was going to get.' At this time she seemed able to understand what was said but would say only simple things: Shut up, Yes No! She was totally dependent on the helpers for washing, dressing and going to the W.C. She needed help also with feeding and drinking. After the last fall she had got worse and at one stage even had trouble taking her pills for her Parkinson' s condition.

It was not long after the stroke that I asked Professor Poon – his title was: Chief, Division of Neurosurgery, the Chinese University of Hong Kong – to write a certificate stating Diana's condition and prognosis. This was to assist in any claims I might want to make and to obtain a disability allowance to help pay for extra help with her care, although I note from my records I that did not apply to the government for Disability allowance till the summer of July 2004. I did so only because without a Disability allowance I could not apply for tax relief on my income. Strange that the Government pressured me, in effect, to get two benefits.

He wrote:
"The patient with Parkinson's disease went for surgical treatment on the 5th Feb, 2001. She developed per-operative complications of a major brain haemorrhage, resulting in 'cognitive' memory and mobility deficits. She does not understand enough to make major decisions concerning herself."

I did consider taking action against the Hospital for medical negligence. I realised that Professor Poon had done all he could and I was grateful. But I had the impression that the neurologist and others at the operation may have with their inexperience got carried away with placing the implant. I did take legal advice as to whether to sue. I had a barrister colleague who specialised in such cases and was ready to help. But my daughter was against the idea. Diana would have to appear at Court and, goodness knows, made to stand in the witness box. I was at the time earning in full time practice and would be able to care for her. I realise today (August 2013) that perhaps we should have sued but the dear soul has passed away and really what good would it have done?

But it was not all gloom and doom during those invalid 5 years 6 months from the stroke to her death in August 2006. In the early days she was able to stand up and shuffle around the flat. That she was able to do so was evidenced with the fall mentioned above. The poor soul had the problems of the stroke and the Parkinson's so she suffered from the symptoms of both: depression and agitation for her sinemet drugs; locking of the joints caused by muscular contraction; speech difficulties, she could say very little, from the stroke and the disease; drooling; swallowing difficulties, although there were 'switch on' times when she could eat quite well; then there was the mask like face. I mention just a few, as the disease progressed so she got worse. She was unable to tell us towards the end if there was something in particular wrong with her. Therefore when she got cancer of the gut in the spring of 2006 it was not until she could not keep down food that we took her to the hospital.

I have said not all gloom and doom so I must say something about good times. In the first few years she was able to shuffle around, sit and stand up. She was able to get in and out of her wheelchair, so we were mobile in that sense I could get her on and off buses (those with the ramp) and taxis. In the years up to 2005 we were out a lot together.

I had plenty of free time as practice as a barrister depends on the amount of work around at the time and the fickle disposition of those who brief you; whether they be the Director of Public Prosecutions (DPP), the Director of Legal Aid, or the solicitors in private practice who know you or have seen or heard about you in the press or in the courts. In the early days as mentioned above I was often briefed by Aaron Yip of K. Y. Woo and Co. Some months you could be in court every day, particularly if you had a long trial, other times you would have more days off in a month than those working.

I would take Diana along the Shatin River, sometimes as far as Ma On Shan; we would walk there or go on the new KCR line there. Other days we would walk to Shatin bus station and get the bus for that lovely ride to Sai Kung, then it was some nice seafood there. The airport bus was another ride, from the stop just around the corner from the our quarters at the hospital. I kept really fit getting her in and out of the wheelchair onto the transport. I can recall no occasion when the bus drivers were not helpful lowering the ramp and helping us on, likewise the taxi drivers would nearly always get out and help us with the wheelchair. I really enjoyed our outings and the meals that went with them. I could sense that Diana was always eager to go although the Parkinson' s mask didn't show much. There were grumpy times, but of course the disease plus the stroke did affect her moods. I recall that even before the stroke she was always a quiet withdrawn young women who kept things inside and now ponder the fact that this personality may have contributed to her disease. I have read much about this terrible disease and its causes. Some say those who keep their problems and hurts inside are more prone to succumbing to it. She also attended the occasional lunch, dinner with friends from the church at Shatin, the Methodist church at Kennedy Road and colleagues from my chambers. I have a picture of her, bless her, tucking in to some seafood (is it a fish head!) at a restaurant in Sai Kung. Christmas of course was a joyous time when we all got together; I can't recall at time when the whole family were not present.

My involvement with the home cell groups, which started early at the Methodist church way back in 1986, continued with the Shatin Anglicans. Our home both at Tai Wai and latter the quarters at the Prince of Wales was the meeting point. The average attendance was 8 persons: our friends Brenda and Trevour Yau, Tammy, and Susie Young to name some. Before the stroke Diana would join us but after it was just a question of her occasionally, in the early days, just sitting near us, later she would have been put to bed with a helper. We always prayed for her and the group was of great support to me. I still see Brenda today.

The big event was Alfreda's marriage to Chris which took place on the 26th July, 2003; purely out of co-incidence that it was the birthday of Diana 26th July, 1948! The wedding was at our church in Kennedy Road and was conducted by John Illsley the minister who was to baptise Diana at the Prince of Wales Hospital a few moths before she died. The church marriage was to 're-enforce' the promises they made at an earlier ceremony at the registry office in England. This was when they were living at Cheadle in Northamptonshire at a charming cottage which I visited in 2000. Diana I recall did not come with me, she was already finding long journeys too much.

I was delighted with the church wedding and there are pictures of me giving my beloved daughter away at the altar. Diana was there with the two helpers Marivic and sister Nina and we all went off to the Hong Kong Cricket Club for the reception. Barney and Marilynne came from England, all our friends from both churches, friends from my Chambers and the Bar, some old police mates plus Ah Keung (Diana' s brother) and his family attended. I have a photograph of Diana smiling through the Parkinson' s mask. The speeches at the reception were memorable especially as Barney almost shouted: 'Off Off' to me for rabbiting on too long with jokes and not saying enough nice things about my daughter.

I recall now it was only after the fall in 2005 that Diana' s condition seem to worsen. I am not sure now if I was still able to take her out, although my memory and a picture tells me I was taking her out in 2005.

The year 2006 saw perhaps the longest prosecution case that I ever dealt with: HKSAR and Li Wai-kwong and 15 others DCC 856/2005. The brief came to me in March 2006 and did not conclude until six of the accused were convicted and sentenced on the 20th October, 2006. The actual trial lasted 44 days and there were eight counsel representing the 16 defendants against me. Three of them: Acton-Bond, Surman and Raffell being extremely awkward opponents DPP saw fit to have just one counsel to handle the case notwithstanding there were three charges and that the issues legion. My records show apart from the trial time there were preliminary issues to be decided in court and two pre-trial revues, plus hours of conferences with the police and written replies to demands and enquiries from defence counsel. One of whom Acton-Bond esquire did everything possible to make it difficult for me to conduct the prosecution. As a barrister I have always followed the rules; I defend as well as prosecute. I have never considered that all is fair in love and war in a criminal trial; you are not rude to your opponent nor do your utmost to wind him or her up. The trial proper started on the 12th July, 2006 before His Honour Deputy Judge Dufton (as he was then) It finished, as stated above, with breaks, 44 working days later on the 20th October, 2006.

The prosecution relied much on identification evidence and as I did fairly bring out there were doubts as to the reliability of the Identification parades. Judge Dufton did not rely on them. He clearly was not happy how witnesses and accused had been made to wait around the Station all day perhaps sharing common areas, thus seeing each other before the attendance at the particular parade. He rightly, in my view, threw out the first charge and all accused were acquitted of this. The six remaining accused were found guilty of the two remaining charges and sentenced to up to 4 years.

I mention this case here because it was on the 5th May, 2006 that I took Diana over to the Casualty section at the Prince of Wales Hospital for her distress and inability to keep her food down. Plus she had not been to the lavatory for days and we were concerned. Extensive cancerous growths were found in her gut and liver and the poor soul was operated on the 15th May, to have them removed. It was a major operation and must have taken what strength she had. The doctors told us she was not expected to live and I should take precautions to alert the family and bring them back. I also was concerned that she needed help from Stephen Durie our priest at the Shatin Anglican Church. Unfortunately he was away so I asked John Illsley to come from the Methodist Church. He came over straight away and baptised the comatose Diana in the Hospital. Clearly she was tough and was not ready to go because with prayer and bedside vigil she got stronger, so much so that she could be removed to the Bradbury Hospice at A Kung Kok Shatin. A place there was obtained with the help of Professor Poon.

Here she remained until she died at 10.30pm on the 15th August. Only a week or so before we were looking for nursing help so we could take her home. The Hospice, we were sympathetically told, was generally only for those with just weeks to live; Diana was hanging on for three months. She did get stronger; it seemed the cancer was dormant, not moving, then it started again and the feeding tubes inserted again and dosed up with morphine she passed away. I was at her bedside for nights of the last three days: the Sunday to Tuesday. I sang love songs to her accompanied by Diane Krall singing those lovely old-fashioned songs from one of her CDs.

Her death occurred on the 23rd day of the trial. So perhaps it was not strange I was not at my best during the trial and not more of the sixteen were convicted. I defend myself here saying I prosecuted fairly in the face of a constant barrage of demands and complaints from some of my fellow counsel for the defence. I was not given anyone to help me and for three weeks had to pay a colleague a refresher for assisting me. This from a fee from the DPP that could only cover a trial with six defendants. The remaining ten, apparently were not covered or allowed for. Such was the flack I was getting from my 7 opponents and those instructing them that I persuaded the DPP to give me a 'bodyguard' to see off the attacks in open and closed court. Thus David Mackensie-Ross was briefed to assist me. He proved not much help with the examination of witnesses; to be fair to him he came into the case very late. He did, however with his known pugilistic, aggressive manner keep my opponents off guard and shut up.

The judge got it right and his written judgement was sound. Judge Dufton can display episodes of good judgement, but like many with their eye on the upward ladder and promotion he can sometimes give the impression of being the 'company man'.

The funeral was on the 24th August, 2006, at the Methodist Church, Kennedy Road. John Illsley was away and Stephen

Durie conducted the service. It was a full house: our friends from both churches were there together with colleagues from my profession, including those from the trial, and old mates from the police. Diana's friends and family were there and of course Alfreda, Alexander and Chris Denis. Alfreda read from Romans 6.3-9 and our friend from the bible study group Susie Young read from the Gospel of St John. My friend from chambers Willie Allen read the eulogy which was interpreted by Tammy Lam. Stephen Durie delivered a long sermon, which alas went on too long, especially as there was no interpretation in Chinese for Diana's family.

Alexander had had to return again from the UK. He had come back in answer to our call in May when we were told her death was imminent and now less than three months later was back again.

The service continued with cremation and the committal at the Cape Collinson Crematorium.

So ended 29 years of marriage, 27 years of motherhood, both states done as dutifully and lovingly as it was possible to do. Oh! what a credit to her are her two children today. Oh! how she would have loved and fussed over dear Isobel and Alexander and Michelle's baby to come this Christmas.(2013). The 5-and-a-half years as a chronic invalid were so undeserved. I must say for such a good and healthy living woman it was so unfair and was the reason for years I had my doubts about the Loving God. But it taught me the meaning of true love and I do feel compassion much more now for the sick and needy. I hope if she can somehow hear me now say: 'I am sorry I could have done better'.

I took Diana' s ashes home in a jar and placed them on a table in my bedroom at the quarters at the Prince of Wales Hospital where they were until I moved to Discovery Bay the next year.

I had intended to move soon after Diana' s funeral but the government leasing department insisted I give them the proper notice. I had taken out a new lease at the beginning of 2006, not thinking that Diana would pass away so it must have around the Spring of 2007 that I started to look for somewhere to live. In April I purchased in my son Alexander's name my present address 12 A Woodgreen Court, Discovery Bay. It certainly complicated things putting it in his name and later buying back off him in 2012. I did this so he could purchase a home for him and his wife Michelle in the USA. At the time I wanted to appear fair as I had helped Alfreda earlier on put a deposit on a house in Worcester.

I moved the ashes to my new home and decided they best be put somewhere more permanent where we could go and visit, especially at the Chinese festivals of Ching Ming (April) and Chung Yeung (October). So on the 27th July, 2007 at a simple ceremony conducted by John Illsley we placed her ashes behind a stone at a resting place at the Pok Fu Lam Christian Cemetery. As it is hoped these memoirs will provide a helpful record for my family I include the location: No.502. A.2. Level 8, In Area 4. block 3. The entrance to this part of the cemetery is opposite Scenic Villa. The man who supplied the stone and manages the grave is Mr.Tam of the Kwong Lun Kei Stone Factory which is near the entrance, telephone number 6337 6220. Our dear friend Dorothy Brown so kindly arranged things with this gentleman.

Our family moved on with our lives and I with my new home at Discovery Bay.

I include the eulogy read at her funeral, with a brief photo album, in the Appendix.

# 23. Work and the World

The case with the 16 defendants, (DCCC.856.2005) which I have mentioned before, resumed after the funeral in September 2006, when it was adjourned until October when a verdict was delivered early in the month. I then went off to fast for a week at Spa Samui at Koh Samui in Thailand. I needed to bring the blood pressure down with all the stress from work and poor Diana's suffering and funeral. I returned 12 days later 10 kilo lighter only to put most of it back in a months or so.

The end of the month of October saw me prosecuting an immigration case at the District Court. This ran for 8 or so working days and ended with three convictions and sentences of up to 9 months. As mentioned before I had to stay at the Prince of Wales quarters until the lease allowed so it was not until 2007 that I moved.

My practice continued after I moved to live at Discovery Bay.

I was still with good friends and colleagues like Chris Grounds, Willie Allen, Lorinda Lau, Patrick Tsang, and others and our dear clerk Cindy Yip, working from Convention Chambers at the 28th floor of Office Tower, Convention Plaza, 1 Harbour Road, Wanchai. We moved Chambers from Office Tower, Harbour Road to the 18th floor of the Chinese Overseas Building, 139 Hennessey Road, Wanchai at the end of 2008 but kept the name: Convention Chambers. By this time we had all been together at this and a location at Yip Fung Building in

Central for a long time; it seems for at least 10 years. Chris Grounds continued to be a low profile head of Chambers although there were occasions when he was not listed on the Bar List; fickle and temperamental as the good chap could be.

As indicated in the last chapter I acquired 12 A Woodgreen Court, Discovery Bay in April, 2007 when I bought it for my son with the understanding it would be my home. I spent a lot of money thoroughly renovating it and I recall this was finished around June 2007 when I moved in from the quarter at the Prince of Wales Hospital. Alfreda and Chris were really helpful with the move as I was busy with court work. Perhaps I could mention here that for the years 2006 to 2008 I was involved with enough work, some of the cases were most stressful and not easy on the blood pressure. A quick mention here: blood pressure depended much on who was sitting on the Judges' throne and also how the case had been prepared for trial. When prosecuting it was not infrequent that the charges didn't fit the evidence or there was much of it that was unnecessary and would only prolong the trial and hurt everyone's brain. The government lawyers of the DPP (Director of Public Prosecutions) were, apparently, putting nearly everything from the police file as case papers in the prosecution bundle. Certain police units were better than others and the Customs and Excise cases often needed the most scrutiny.

The ICAC's were a class on their own; unlike the police who could win one and lose one, with them every accused had to be convicted. They relied much on the evidence of witnesses who had been given immunities from prosecution. Their witness statements were so obviously more the work of ICAC officers than the witnesses themselves, to an old policeman like me they often looked so perfect, so contrived. Both the cases that I can remember prosecuting for the ICAC involved convictions; one involved the standard 'perfect' statements clearly written by the officer with his mind totally on the case and not on what the witness said. The other involved a senior fire officer where there were four ICAC officers sitting behind me scrutinizing my every move and giving me instructions about the conduct of the case on a daily basis. They nearly got apoplexy when although found guilty and in my view given a proper sentence he was not sent to prison. They ordered me to complain about the conduct of the judge who had ordered the four, whom he thought were clearly affecting my performance, to leave the court. I advised the officers concerned it was a matter for them. My duty was to write a report and pass it on to the DPP. You may rest assured I didn't get any more prosecutions from the ICAC.

I still have some of the papers in regard to the cases I was briefed to prosecute or defend and will look at these as we go along but I will try to continue to keep the memoirs in some chronological order. I do note from these that I was not short of briefs during the years 2006, 07 and 08 either in the District or High Courts. A reminder here that trials in the District Court were by judge alone, in the High Court it was before judge and jury. The outcome in the former could often be determined just by who the judge was, this was true to a much lesser extent with a jury, who would sometimes be contrary towards a judge who was telling them to convict.

In November 2006 I was off to Australia where I joined my old friends Barney and Marilynne on the Darwin to Adelaide, Trans' Australia train: The Ghan.

I flew from Hong Kong to Darwin via Perth(!) and stayed for a few days there exploring the Botanical Gardens and a museum. Then it was on the train, Barney and Marilynne had a nice cabin: a double bed and room to move around. The single cabins were very different, once the bed had been folded down and the sink made to appear out of the wall there was hardly room to get in and close the door. The dining car and the food, drink and service was good. Barney and I got stuck into that splendid, in my view, only proper beer made in Australia: Coopers of Adelaide, South Australia. They brewed in the old tradition and their Cooper's Sparking Ale was/is a connoisseurs beer. The company also make a fine stout and pale ale.The first stop, where we had a half day to look around was Katherine. Goodness nothing there except a road, like 'the old west', a couple of real outback pubs and stores and Australia's original people wandering around like ghosts. Back on the train, dinner a sleep and then Alice Springs.

Alice Springs started first as a relay station for the overland telegraph that eventually joined an undersea cable to Asia and onward to Europe to the centre of the Empire in London. What a lonely life it must have been, a couple of men operators stuck in the heart of the Red Desert of Central Australia. The overland telegraph and Alice Springs must have been in a similar state right up to World War Two, when the population was only around 500. By the time of my visit the population was over 25,000. It was a large town, the third biggest in the Northern Territories, complete with a shopping mall, nice hotels, restaurants and the Todd River on which was held, in the dry season when it had 'no' water, the Alice Springs Regatta.

After a day in Alice and a visit to the Overland Telegraph Museum it was back on the train to continue the second half of our journey; Alice is nearly equidistant from Adelaide and Darwin.

It was another night on the train, again some good food and drink. Barney as ever keen on the foods that normal people would not eat, got stuck in, this time with Marilynne as well, to crocodile and emu steaks, I had the roast lamb. The country as we got further south became less red and more green and then there was Adelaide a really beautiful city with parks, gardens and river walks. It certainly, sorry Aussies, has an English feel to it. We had a trip by coach and ferry over to Kangaroo Island where I have a memory of a beach where we were told 'Tasmanian' Aborigines were killed by Irish convicts. I realise that does not make much sense, perhaps I am losing my marbles! We flew back from Kangaroo Island. My other memory of Adelaide is the pie stall which was outside our 6 star hotel. A pie in a float: an Aussie pie (loads of gravy) floating in green pea soup.

I then got the train to Melbourne a day there then on to Sydney where I caught up for a day or so with Barney and Marilynne. I have no recollection of being on the train with them from Adelaide so presume they flew to Sydney. Melbourne and Sydney are like Adelaide: great cities with their botanical gardens, parks and river or harbour views. My trip on the Manly ferry and one up the Paramatta river, in particular, sticks in my mind, with its beautiful expensive properties. It was three days in Sydney then off back to Hong Kong and more briefs.

I mention here what a great cities those three are and the quality of life within them. I would recommend any young couple, with children especially, to migrate to Australia and the healthy style life there. Poor England now with its rapidly changing culture, life styles, attitudes, and prospects is not, I feel, for the folk who want better for themselves and children.

I mentioned earlier defending a police sergeant who was caught at the airport with two rounds of ammunition. My success must have got around the police. At the end of November I attended a pre-trial revue to be conducted later next year 2007 where I was defending, this time in the magistrates court, another policeman. He was a detective who had passed on unlawfully information on a case to another police officer who was under investigation for some other matter. I was surprised as, it seemed to me, it was more something to be dealt with under Police Disciplinary Orders. In the event he was vigorously prosecuted by counsel Hayson Tse from the DPP for abusing his office. The trail lasted a week and I was surprised at the determination of Mr Tse to get my client convicted and locked up. I conclude he had been the advising counsel and despite the more in-house nature of the 'crime' he was anxious to justify bringing it to a criminal court. He was convicted by a young deputy magistrate and sentenced to 5 months imprisonment. I managed to get him bail pending appeal, which I didn't handle, perhaps understandably he had lost confidence in me. It was one of many cases that I have handled; that I can remember it now shows how perturbed I was with the conviction and the way the case had been prosecuted.

Later in the year (2007) I was in the District Court prosecuting a false trade description case before Judge Rickie Chan. The goods in question were Birds Nests! Delicious but not real birds nest. The defendants were nice enough: A limited Company and one of its Director/Managers. The company was fined $20,000 and the manager got a suspended sentence. Judge Rickie Chan was always nice to be before whether you prosecuted or defended; he always seemed to try and get it right with parties leaving court without any seething grievance. 2007 saw me prosecuting an ICAC case at the District Court, and at least three drug cases at the High Court. These were before Judges Peter Line and Ester To, both of whom I respected as usually correct and eager to do it right.

In May of 2007 was to be another 10 day visit to Spa Samui at Koh Samui in Thailand. I seem to have gone there on an almost yearly basis since 2000. I would either go to the spa on the beach or the one, 15 minutes motor bike ride, up the hill at what was called the Spa Village. I would follow the diet regime rigidly : No food at all, apart from supplements and a four times a day flush which contain some fruit juice. It was gallons of water and nothing else. I would routinely lose anything up to 9 or 10 kilograms each time; my energy would not be affected and was able to swim sometimes up to two hours in the sea. I was walking well up from the village resort up the steep climb to the top of the hill also every day, at least until I had my hip replacement in 2009. Unfortunately the weight did not stay off for long and with months was often back again, although in the early days I seemed to keep it down to 240 pounds; now alas it is often 270.

In September 2007 it was off to New Zealand to visit my old school friend Evelyn and her husband Roy Evans. Evelyn was the sister of Marilynne my old flame. She had visited me twice with Roy when Diana was alive and we were living at Shatin, once in 2002 and again in 2004 when she came with two of her grandchildren. Evelyn drove us around and I recall we went up to the Bay of Islands where we stayed for a few days and visited their friends Claire and Eddie Sammons at Russell, Kororareka.

I went off to the Cook Islands for a week enjoying myself by hiring a motorcycle and swimming and snorkelling every day. On one day I took the hour or so flight to Aitutaki a coral island with a huge lagoon. It was most of the day on a boat with about 10 other tourist enjoying the stupendous reefs. We landed at 'Onefoot Island' where I got my passport stamped. The runway on the Island was built by the Americans in the last war and the lagoon was famous as the place that Pan Am Cross-Pacific flying boats would refuel. I recall there was a picture of Marlon Brando standing by one of the flying boats displayed in the little drinks place that stamped your passport. It was back to Raratonga then Auckland for a day before the flight back to Hong Kong.

It was on the 19th February, 2008 that I was admitted to Princess Margaret Hospital. I was admitted via the 999 system after I had been almost paralysed with acute lower back pain. I recall I answered the door to the ambulance men on the floor of my Discovery Bay flat. It was diagnosed as 'sponderosis. I was released on the 29th February but was still having standing up for long periods. Consequently I had to send a number of cases back to The Director of Legal Aid. It seemed it was the start of back and joint trouble, because almost a year later, on the 12th February, 2009 I had hip replacement surgery conducted by Doctor Peter Ko at the Adventist Hospital. I still

(September 2013) have acute pains in my lower back and right hip and expect these to get worse.

My first worry case in 2008 started in January when a case to be tried later in the year at the District Court was assigned to me. I was representing a bright, educated Chinese graduate who had allegedly assaulted a young French girl near the beauty spot: Brides Pool, just up from the Plover Cove Dam. He wanted to see me on a number of occasions but was unable to give me any proper instruction. The rules of the Bar say a barrister must take instructions in a case from the solicitor employed by the client or in legal aid cases assigned by the Director of Legal Aid. The facts of the case was that a young French girl, age 19, on holiday in Hong Kong was allegedly assaulted by the young man and had her camera stolen. He is supposed to have lead her to the remote Brides Pool where the crime took place. The facts certainly did not ring true. Why should a perfectly respectable young man entice a girl all the way there and steal her camera. There were no sexual imputations alleged. All the young man could say was he was confused but must have done it. He had no idea why he had the camera.

The trial eventually was set down for my birthday the 29th April, 2008 but was adjourned because the French girl could not come, it was then further adjourned until July when the accused pleaded, hardly unequivocally, not guilty with the trial lasting over a week (8 days). It was a difficult trial made so by the accused and the attitude of the trial judge. There were attempts to reduce the charge from Robbery to Wounding Section 19 (Wounding without intent), although the wound was minor. The prosecution eventually offered Assault Causing Grievous Bodily Harm (also section 19), but there was no such harm involved. They eventually came 'down' to Wounding 19, which under the circumstances on a plea may prevent a prison sentence. The accused agreed to this and pleaded guilty but the judge was not happy with the facts, and said he would not accept the pleas unless the accused agreed that he was conscious of what he was doing and had the necessary foresight that some harm was likely to be caused. The judge, not generally liked, seemed determined to convict the accused somehow. After a lengthy conference the accused could not agree to this so asked me to apply to the judge to change his plea to not guilty. Thus the original charge of Robbery remained.

I called a forensic psychiatrist who submitted a report and gave, what I thought was cogent and valuable evidence: "that the accused was in a dissociative state at the time of incident such that he could not have been fully aware of what he was doing and had no conscious intention to perform the action and thus could not form the intent of violence or stealing." His evidence was useful in that it persuaded the prosecution to add a Wounding 19 charge as an alternative. The judge adjourned the case until August when he found the young man guilty of Wounding. He was sentenced a fortnight later after I had presented over 20 good character references from just about everyone: senior staff from HKU, The University of British Columbia, friends, and neighbours. He was certainly a young man who should go to prison only as a last resort. The victim had only sustained minor cuts from falling down and the camera was not permanently taken. In the event I was amazed when the Judge gave him 15 months immediate imprisonment! Totally wrong, undeserved and excessive; I was really upset with the result. I feel the truth was he was overwhelmed somewhat with the pretty girl and wanted to make friends. He had no real nasty motives and was truthful when he said he had become totally confused. I advised in my report to Legal Aid that he should appeal against sentence.

He was not given legal aid to appeal against conviction and I learnt that he did this himself, acting in person before the Court of Appeal. He was successful, the appeal, against conviction was allowed. Cynic though I may be, I ponder whether if I had represented him he would have won the appeal. A bright young man standing alone before the three Appeal Judges does create more sympathy that an old hack who must have upset some of their Lordships over the years.

The year 2008 saw quite a busy professional year for me. About the time of the one mentioned above I was in the Court of Appeal representing an armed robber who had fled to China years before, it may have been before the handover to China, and had been arrested at the border as he returned to Hong Kong. He was in effect surrendering to the authorities here. I had represented him earlier in 2007 when he had been sentenced in the High Court by Mr Recorder McCoy who had given him a total of 23 years imprisonment after he had pleaded to the five robbery counts on the indictment. I had mitigated before the judge and clearly he was way off with his sentence. The man had surrendered and pleaded guilty. Clearly criminals should be encouraged to return to face justice and not overly punished for doing so. Mr. Justice Stuart-Moore Vice President and Mr Justice Lunn reduced the sentence to a total of 16 years.

Perhaps one of the most interesting was a fraud case involving the use of forged Barclays bank documents. The trial was at the

District Court before Deputy Judge Bernadette Woo and there were two defendants one of whom had jumped bail and was in China; he was in touch with his solicitors but was refusing to come back, the other was a female who worked for him. It was not an easy case in that the woman was defended by Jim Chandler, counsel often a difficult opponent and the fact that there were overseas expert witnesses from the bank involved. After me showing the appropriate authorities the judge agreed to proceed to try the case in the absence of the male accused. In the event she found him guilty and sentenced him to 30 months imprisonment, she acquitted, correctly in my view, the woman. This was at the end of September 2008.

Another case of interest in 2008 was one involving a Brazilian man who had been used by international criminals to launder millions of dollars through accounts with Hong Kong banks.

It was, again not an easy case and involved 15 box files of documents that needed sorting out into relevant/useful material or just paper wadding. The judge was the pleasant and able Bernard Whaley and the trial was to last 12 days. The case was the tip of the iceberg in that it showed the ease in which a person, with no connection to Hong Kong or any country with which it has strong commercial and legal links, could incorporate a company and open a bank account. The case involved a Lebanese (not arrested) acting for six Brazilians, each operating three corporate accounts. Approximately $30 million went through the accounts, the accused Brazilian being only a mule to open the accounts.

The case involved West Africans, Iraqis, Lebanese and Hong Kong residents. Australian, South African, Hong Kong,

Spanish, UK and US banks were all involved. There were companies who specialised, apparently legally, in setting up companies and opening bank accounts. The mule an unemployed man from Equatoria Province of Brazil, and described as a small cog, was sentenced to 3 years imprisonment in September 2008.

I recall I wrote a report at the end of the case stressing the need for the particulars of all those who were involved to be circulated through the international police community and suggested that because of the wide international implications consideration should be given to reviewing the sentence as manifestly inadequate.

I had a number of other cases which I either defended or prosecuted. I seem to have been favoured by those from Africa as I had at least two cases involving gentlemen from there. One involved cannabis from South Africa and the other heroin from West Africa. I had at least another three drug cases involving Chinese, these were cannabis and two cocaine cases. I was very much a legal aid and prosecutions counsel. It was unusual to get a brief from a firm of solicitors. In my case most of these would be Magistrates or District Court cases. There was an interesting case that came at the end of 2008. This concerned a police constable who had been charged at the magistrates Court with five counts of making persistent phone calls. It was a private brief and I mitigated on his behalf. A lady was involved. Probation reports were called which were favourable and he was eventually given heavy fines. He also had his phone confiscated!

Easter of 2008 saw a visit to Borocay in the Philippines. It is a small island with a delightful beach which despite the debris, left behind by hundreds of visitors and the Philippines' general lack of proper governance, is kept clean by a helpful tide. I never worked out the magic of how it took all the junk away. It was rarely a case of swallowing a paper bag or worse when I did my daily swim across the bay. I chose the break there because I knew Alfreda would be there with some friends from the British International School in Shangahi where she worked.

She had started there in 2007 and I had been up to visit her there. I was impressed with the campus and her quarter near the school was nice. Her friends at Borocay were all ladies and a lovely bunch they were. Unfortunately a wee bit too young for yours truly.

Her ties with Chris Dennis were sadly broken up at the end of 2005 and she had been alone whilst she continued to live and work in the City of Worcester. I had helped buy a small terraced house at 8 Camp Hill Avenue and had hoped it would provide a start for both of them.

It was not to be; he had apparently found someone else to please him and went off with a really great sounding job with a subsidiary of Roll Royce in the United States. Alfreda continued working at her Catholic primary school until she went of to teach in China.

The end of September 2008 saw a trip to Canada with Chris Grounds, my chambers mate, and his wife. After a couple of days in Vancouver we went over to Vancouver Island to the city of Victoria by bus which was carried over by one of the large well run Tsawwassen to Swartz Bay ferries. The trip lasted just under two hours and was enjoyable, the ferry making its way around a number of interesting Islands skirting the International Canada/USA border. We returned to Vancouver similarly by bus and ferry and I don't recall now if it was going or returning when all the passengers were alerted on the tannoy system that there was a grey whale to be seen in the sea near to the ferry. What a delightful site. There is something almost spiritual to such creatures, enormous animals that have been on the planet long before us. They have brains bigger and probably just as complex as ours.

At Victoria we stayed in a small hotel, perhaps one star. It was OK and was only a short walk to the sights like the harbour, the regal and elegant Princess Hotel, the old Parliament building with all it historical treasures and the fine restaurants and bars. There were at least two home brew pubs which brewed some very fine ales. But alas for me with my gout, they are highly hopped, too much for my liking. I prefer the more mellow malty Banks's beer of the English Midlands. There was definitely a British feel to Victoria.

We took a trip on the South Railway of Vancouver Island. This ran about 150 miles north up the east coast of the Island to Courtenay. We did the day return but I forget now where we got off; it was half way. My only memory of the stop is that it was a one platform halt in a small town. We had lunch and then walked down a hill from the town to the coast where we had a drink and waited for the train to return to take us back. I recall that the train was more of a rail car with only the one carriage.

I really like Victoria and it was no wonder to me that many British people, including retired Hong Kong civil servants and policemen e.g. Police Commissioner Sutcliffe (a good man who tried his best to clean up the force) settled there. Then it was back on the ferry to Vancouver for the next leg of the holiday.

We were to travel on the Rocky Mountaineer: The Most Spectacular Train Trip in the World. But first a stop in Vancouver where we stayed for a few days and spent some time with my friend Malcolm Bell and his lady, who has a really lovely place up the coast overlooking Lions Bay. The Rocky Mountaineer was a five-day trip on board a really ritzy train. We ate lunch in the dining car, which was served by really good looking young Canadians who were also our guides to the wonderful scenic sights along the way. The food and drinks were first class, cooked on the train by chefs with imagination; all the dishes from delicious local fish, meat and fruit and vegetables. There were also excellent Canadian wines.

The route was from Vancouver east with four stops where we would stay for the night at hotels and, if my memory serves me correctly, for evening meals. The stops were 1.Kamloops. 2.Jasper (In Alberta). 3.Quesnel (really in the back and beyond). and 4. Whistler (Canada's winter sports resort). I remember little of the stops other than 3. and 4. At Quesnel we went to a local pub/bar, it had locals who were real locals! They would have talked and looked the same in the 50's or even before, nice friendly folk. A bus had been provided to take us to the hotel from the train station and I remember the driver was part time, doing seasonal forestry, or was it mining work. At Whistler it was already cold but there was no snow. I walked up to the chairlifts for the skiers and gazed up at some of the ski runs.

We also had a pleasant walk around a Lake. I recall a fancy hotel where we stayed. The fifth day on the train was a shortish ride down the four or so hours to Vancouver. Did we change to the "The Whistler' train? It may have been only four days on the 'Rocky Mountaineer.'

Then it was back again to Vancouver and a few more days staying with my old friend from City Polytechnic days: Malcolm and Nini at their place further up the coast overlooking Lions Bay. It was a splendid time with them enjoying their home and outings with some great food and booze locally and down the 20 miles or so in that lovely city of Vancouver. Chris Grounds had few days with us and was then off with his wife to Alberta for further exploration. I re-joined them when they came back for our Cathay Pacific flight back to Hong Kong. It was a really awful flight: economy seats at the rear of the plane. They were supposed to be new technology seats made to give greater comfort. Sorry they were made to create more seats on the plane. They wouldn't adjust back and any attempt to improve the sitting caused you to slide down nearly castrating yourself as you touched the floor. It was from that flight, it seemed to never end, that my earlier lower back pain problem really took off and it has got steadily worse since. I wrote when I got back, as did Chris, to complain to Cathay, only to be told that the seats had been designed by experts. I wrote back saying: experts who had never sat in their seats. I go business class now if I have to fly long distance

I have gone back over my notes and find that 2007 appears to have been a busier time than 2008. I was certainly doing less as my years progressed and 2009 started with me in such pain that I needed to try and get relief so I could at least be able to stand

and perform in Court. I was told was the only option: a hip replacement surgery. But the best place to talk about this would be in the next chapter when I continue with events from January.

# 24. Buggering On

For much of the end of the end of 2008 I was suffering from pain in the back and right hip. I mentioned before how the economy flight back from Canada in those awful Cathay Pacific seats seems to have started the problem, although to be fair I had back pain problems before which had occasion for me to dial 999 and be admitted to the Princess Margaret Hospital. I have mentioned this in the last Chapter. I had after that got better by regular exercise in the swimming pool and going off again to Spa Samui to lose weight. And had gone off with the Royal Asiatic Society, of which I was a member, on a visit to he historical sites of interest in Shanghai. We had stayed at the slightly run-down but delightful historic Astor Hotel, built in 1858 and the first to have running water, electric light and a telephone system in Shanghai. It was neglected by the communists and used as a government building but renovated in the 90's and popular now for those with a feel for old Shanghai. It was here that Alfreda first introduced me to new boy friend Drew. My was I pleased, such a fine chap.

But the pain got worse and it must have been in November when through the help of one of the congregation of our church, who was a government doctor, I was admitted for tests to government hospital. They did a scan and did not find any evidence of the thigh bone pressing on the pelvis which would have accounted for the acute pain, but I was referred to a specialist over at a hospital at Chai Wan. This Doctor, an orthopaedic surgeon said that any surgery required would need a wait of at least 12 to 18 months. The pain was so bad that I went back to see Doctor Peter Ko an orthopaedic surgeon in private practice. He sent me for a further scan and tests at St Paul's Hospital up behind Causeway Bay. Here they put me to lie down on a steel slab whilst I was X Rayed. After this was done I had to remain laying there and told not to move. As I did so the pain in my back already bad, which I would register on my pain scale at 5, steadily rose to 9, at which point I was screaming in absolute agony. The staff seemed indifferent to this and just told me, rather abruptly, to stay there. I don't think I have ever experienced such pain. When I was allowed to get off the slab the pain reduced down to level 6. I left the hospital vowing never to go back there.

I returned to see Doctor Ko and he advised me to have a hip replacement operation. I said the sooner the better. He arranged for this within days at the Adventist Hospital on the 12th February, 2009. A hospital which charges a fortune but is sensitive to its patient's needs. Alfreda and Drew, her new partner, were at my bedside, as were our friends Iain and Dorothy Brown and Bose Mathews from our Church in Kennedy Road, before I was knocked out with the anaesthetic. They were also there when I woke up in the same bed about four hours later. I don't remember any thing about the operation and suffered no pain at all. Dr. Peter told me it was successful and I recall he said he had seen some infection at the top of the thigh bone which had been the cause of the pain. I now had a new bit where my old bit was. I should have researched more and found out exactly what would be installed and why, as later I started to have doubts whether I should have borne the pain a little longer and got a second opinion. But at the time I felt relieved. My family and friends were there and I thought how fortunate I was to have such loving and caring people around me who had patiently waited whilst I lay under the knife. I stayed in hospital for about a week. The wound healed well and I was soon walking around with the help of a crutch. The pain had gone although as the time went on my lower back pain returned and I felt as if my right leg was a little bit shorter than the left. Doctor Ko said that this was not so. In any event I was back in my Chambers after about a fortnight as very soon the wound had healed and I was functioning OK.

I did some work in what was left of January and February. I was still not so good on my pins and realised it would help if I could get my weight down. I did some preparation work, duty lawyer at the Magistrates courts, and some pleas at the District court; nothing to put too much pressure on my already too heavy body. I decided to go off again to Spa Samui to starve myself and get to looking more like a Greek God again. I left the last day in March and came back my usual 10 or so kilos lighter. I recall this time when I was riding my hired motorcycle around the island of Koh Samui my vision got a little blurred. But it did not worry me and I had plenty off energy and was able to swim in the sea. If my memory serves me I went off one day on an excursion to the Island to the North: Koh Tao, great for snorkelling but not without a few stingers, which were OK once you realised where they were. I returned to Ko Samui the same day and was back to Hong Kong on the 10th April and time to prepare my next High Court trial case.

It must have been around the beginning of March , 2009 that I was briefed by the Director of Legal Aid to defend an African man for trafficking in five (5) kilograms of cocaine. They had been brought into Hong Kong by a Malaysian from Surinam in South America. The drugs were found in four brief cases hidden in a suitcase by customs officers at the Hong Kong International Airport. These officers had then gone with the Malaysian man, in what was called a controlled delivery, to a guest house in Jordan Road, Kowloon where the man was to assist them in luring someone from the "other side" to come and collect the brief cases and drugs. My client was the man who the prosecution said came along to collect the drugs.

The case was a serious one to be tried at the High Court where sentences for such large quantities of drugs were huge.

The papers arrived in my Chambers and as usual with such a case involved plenty of reading, the documents being in numerous of box files. I had a number of conferences in March and April with the client at the Lai Chi Kok Remand Centre. His instructions were that he was innocent of the charge and was visiting the guest house where he had a room and had been lured into the room where the other man and the customs were hiding. The prosecutions case was he had been to the room before and said to the other man: "Are you the man from Malaysia". And that he had said things when he came a second time, did implicate him in that he knew what was in the brief cases.

The trial started at the beginning of May (2009) at the High Court before Deputy Longley, a judge who doesn't let many away.

Both men pleaded not guilty. The Malaysian man said he thought he was carrying diamonds. A defence version well known at the time for explaining possession of drugs. But 5 kilos of diamonds! The total weight of the substance containing the cocaine was over 7 kilos! My client said he had never been to the room before and only went the second time because he was lured in and then asked to help bring down a suitcase that was on a high shelf. He had not said any of the incriminating words alleged, by the customs officers hiding in the room.

During the trial there were surprises: Phone records which had not been part of the Prosecution case, and were not included with their case bundle of documents, were produced. There were two mobile phones involved. The evidence that a call had been made just before the bag containing the drugs was collected should not have been referred to as there was no record supporting it. I argued much about the fact that there was another black man staying on the same floor of the guest house when the first visit to the room was made and that the quality of the identification of my man was poor.

The quality of evidence in customs cases is usually inferior to that of the police and I drew attention to the jury that there were important inconsistencies in the statements given by the different officers both in court and out. There was a lack of contemporaneous records, in particular, of what my man was suppose to have said. There were no plans to indicate where the various officers were placed. As an old Detective of at least 10 years investigating serious crimes I could always smell when a piece of evidence came as an afterthought to tidy the case up and add that extra bit to plug the gaps.

The judge did not really deal with our defence case and made sure that even pieces of evidence that the prosecutor didn't rely on, was emphasized to the jury.

The trial lasted 12 days which, with weekends meant almost three weeks. The judge summed up to convict both but the jury, at least some of them were not sure beyond reasonable doubt as the Malaysian was found not guilty by two of the seven jurors and my African was found not guilty by one of them. They were out deliberating for most of the day as they came back with their verdict early evening at around 7.00pm. The judge sentenced the next day: the Malaysian to 24 years, two years off for helping the customs with the trap, and my African to 26 years.

I saw the convict in the cell that evening. I told him the sentence was unfortunately correct but whatever my own views on his guilt I felt he had not got a fair trial and that there were some grounds of appeal. I prepared these with my case report to the Director of legal Aid.

I note from my records that I appeared before the Court of Appeal about a year later in May, 2010 when the appeal against conviction was dismissed and that against sentence which I did pro bono (i.e. the Legal Aid had not so instructed me and so I did on my own) at my client's desperate entreaties. I realised it was a hopeless task but tried to persuade their three Lordships to show some mercy. Alas as my experience told me, there were now so many Africans involved in this sordid drug trafficking business, that it would require something especial for a reduction in sentence.

Another drug case soon followed in the last week of May (2009). This involved a young Chinese woman who had been caught with a significant amount of "Ice" (crystal methamphetamine). I saw her at the Tai Lai woman's prison. She was later convicted on her own plea and sentenced to 13 and half years imprisonment. The judge took a starting point of 21 years and gave her the usual one third discount for the guilty plea plus a further 6 months for her personal circumstances. I mention this case just to show how severe are the punishments for drugs in Hong Kong. Sentences are based on tariffs and there is little counsel can say in mitigation to reduce them. The only way to get a discount is to plead guilty: one third off or to give evidence against a co-accused or supply evidence to convict another trafficker in which case a discount can go up to fifty per cent off.

I have handled numerous cases where accomplice witnesses has been involved and you can never be sure what sort of discount over the usual one third for a plea of guilty is going to be allowed for the "grass." It depends very much on the Judge. Again being an ex-policemen, as much as the general dislike of such people, a judge who gives a good bonus for squealing on others (dishonour amongst thieves), does in my view help to make it difficult for brothers and sisters in crime.

I have been amazed when sometimes a reward for something substantial is only 40% off (5 plus % over the one for the guilty plea) when I have experienced a person who has given evidence for the crown which really has helped a co-accused and yet is awarded a full 50% discount. I have had cases also where discounts have gone up to two third discounts; but admittedly the super grass is a rare animal in Hong Kong. It does not make a lot of sense and the Judges can be fickle to say the least! Sadly it seems, in this greyish area, it depends if your face fits the one on the bench.

July 2009 saw me off to Cairns in Queensland, Australia. I was to stay with my old school friend again Evelyn and her husband Roy. They had hired a self servicing flat not far from the beach at Townsville Australia. I recall my friendship with them before; sadly it would be the last time I saw Roy as he died a year or so later in very trying circumstances for poor Evelyn. I flew to Cairns and then got the train down to Townsville. Evelyn hired a car and we had a few day tours. I recall we drove west to Charters Towers an old gold mining town which had a museum where they showed us how to pan for gold. Here we met a lovely old real Aussie couple who lived the outback life. We met whilst having our lunch. They were not afraid to witness for Christ, perhaps unusual now, and told us of their simple lives where they still used oil lamps for lighting. They could have come through a time machine. Another day we drove south to Ayr where I recall there was a centre for some of Aussies birdlife, black cockatoos was it, in any event they had flown. We were told they only come out in the rain! I have a memory also of us driving up a scenic route to a small village high amongst forest and waterfalls. I have spoken to Evelyn recently and she has no memory of this. I recall we had a meal at cafe near where the mountain road seemed to come to an end. I remember the trip because of the hairpin bends in the road and how well Evelyn drove the car. I can't find the place now on the map.

Another day we took the ferry over to Magnetic Island where we took a bus to show us around. I recall a nice beach and a

390

place we had a meal. I do recall that on the Townsville side our ferry shared a pier with a ferry to Palm Island which is home to many Aborigine folk many of whom we saw waiting there. I was able to do plenty of swimming in the sea off a long sandy beach and a managed pool on the sea side. On one of our Sundays there we went to St James Anglican Cathedral for the morning service which I thoroughly enjoyed together with the pleasant chat we had with the locals at coffee afterwards. I had two weeks with Evelyn and Roy which flew by then it was time for me to make my way north back to Cairns, this time I took a bus. It must have taken about 4 hours to do the 350 kilometres.

I stayed at Cairns at a hotel right on the seafront and did some exploring in the town and did a trip along the river looking for crocodiles. We saw three on the 2 hour trip. I also visited a crocodile farm: thousands of them all sizes. There was no beach at Cairns only a delightful seashore walk. Perhaps the highlight of my stay was the 90 minute, 34 kilometre journey on the Kuranda Scenic Railway. Which winds its way up from Cairns through a World Heritage listed tropical rain forest, ravines, waterfalls and spectacular scenery to the village of Kuranda with it quaint little café's, shops and a delightful railway station. I went up on the train and came back on a bus. I was five days in Cairns then it was off back to Hong Kong.

The rest of the year was work wise largely uninteresting. I had cases in the District Court and High Court – mostly drug related – for which the various accused pleaded guilty. I did have a confiscation of assets hearing under The Organised and Serious Crimes Ordinance, Chapter 455. I recall the hearing followed the trial of a group of people for offences involving the vice trade. The case papers had come to me from the

Director of Legal Aid in the Spring (2009) and the hearing for various reasons didn't start in the District Court until late in October (2009) where I appeared before the pleasant and understanding Deputy Judge Amanda Woodcock. There was one defendant, who I recall, was the moneyman in the group previously convicted. The hearing lasted 5 days after which, towards the end of November, the learned judge ordered over 2 million dollars to be confiscated from his assets.

I recall he said he wished me to tell the prosecution he wished everything to go to the government except his car for which he would pay them the market value to be returned.

As an aside I have noted that over the years the legislature has given the investigating authorities and the courts more powers to trace, find, and confiscate illicit funds. Actions against money launderers, even when there has been no conviction for any substantive offence have been successful. I have already referred in a previous chapter to a case I handled involving the man from Brazil which showed the extent of how illicit funds from all over the world are laundered.

The following month December saw a brief from a private solicitor and probably the best paid in respect of time spent and work done that I had for a long time. I was to represent an alleged senior office bearer of the Sun Yee On (SYO) Triad Society. He and five others were supposed to have taken part in a meeting of that society in a room in Kowloon. A police officer operating, I understand what is called in police jargon as 'deep cover', had been present at the meeting posing as a member or potential member. This officer had been undercover for many months and had collected much information about Triads, not only the SYO. His evidence had resulted in convictions of others in the magistrate's courts but clearly the prosecution were anxious to nail the four, who they thought were more important, at the District Court. I had spent some time interviewing my client whose instructions were to challenge the undercover officer's evidence. The meetings were not triad meetings and nothing nefarious took place at them. He, whatever he did in his youth, was not doing it now and in fact ran a successful restaurant business in Shanghai. The prosecution relied very much on this key witness being allowed to refer to a log book he kept of all the things he did and saw each day. He had an undercover job, I recall, working in a restaurant. All of us, there were five other counsel involved for the other accused, spent much time examining this record. And of course when he got in the witness box he faced detailed and lengthy cross-examination. I like to think I showed that his evidence was not consistent with the record and that he was embellishing what was said and done by those attending the meetings. I learnt from contacts that my client had come down from Shanghai not to disturb the peace but to prevent a certain SYO new blood for causing trouble in Tsim Sha Tsui. There had been some violence between the SYO and other triads and battles over turf. My client and another of the four accused: an elder senior brother had come to reign in the hooligans and restore order in the area.

In the event the officer did not impress the Judge a lady from our Portuguese community who had her finger on the pulse and could see that there had not been a triad 'meeting' and the words said, if said, as the officer stated in the witness box could not be relied on to convict beyond reasonable doubt that they were senior triads or at all.

The trial finished on the 12th day, there had been a break over Christmas after which it continued with my client's defence case. It was then adjourned further for verdict. The judge found all the Defendants not guilty. Clearly she wasn't satisfied so that she was sure they were guilty of the charges laid against them. There were many judges who would have convicted on the evidence but in my view she got it right (OK I would say that!) They were less than guilty! I had two conferences with my client and he struck me as a decent family man who – whatever his past – now was a respectable man doing his best to use his influence over the more unruly members of the SYO. Interestingly known, I might add in criminal legal practitioner patois, as the Sydney Youth Orchestra! I add he had no criminal record as far as I remember. The fees for that one certainly helped pay for Christmas 2009, presents, booze, food and all.

I have been going over my notes and see that my activities in 2010 to 20012 do warrant a separate chapter. I close this one with the observation that I was starting to feel the effects of the pains in my lower back caused or, at least, aggravated by the hip implant. But it did not appear to be slowing me down such that I couldn't continue with my work in court and enjoy trips abroad.

# 25. Grandfather's Footsteps

I'll start this chapter with the observation, from looking at my passport and records of my cases, that I was away from Hong Kong for a considerable part of the year. I recall after taking our family friend Brenda Liu up to Chiang Mai to stay at the Spa for a week in early spring 2010 (March/April) I decided I liked the place so much that I would rent a bungalow there for the summer. The trip with Brenda was just to show her the place and to rest and look around. There was no romance, unfortunately, and we had our own spacious flats with balconies. I didn't fast this time as I had already earlier in the year in January spent two weeks at Spa Samui where I had worked really hard to lose weight and I note from my diary that it went from a terrible 280 pounds to 260 pounds in 12 days. I had coupled the break with more sightseeing on my motorcycle and on a trip on the ferry up to the islands to the North where I had snorkelled at Koh Tao Island. Plus a visit to the dentist for a crown to be placed on a bad tooth. Thai dentists are first class and dollars cheaper than those in Hong Kong.

My rent at Chiang Mai was very reasonable and the lease was for three months: June through to August. In the event I spent three weeks there in June and July and did not use the place in August. When I left the spa at Chiang Mai at the end of July I was 234 pounds. This was after fasting during both of the months I was there and doing regular exercises and saunas.

From the beginning of the fasting I was losing weight and getting fit. Despite pains and the new hip I was walking regularly up a steep hill behind the Spa Chiang Mai village. I was also out on my motorbike exploring the really lovely countryside. I was really impressed with how good, even the small roads were. Which would be B or C roads in the UK. I visited one of the elephant centres and enjoyed these simply beautiful creatures performing apparently quite happily with their handlers. It was about 30 minutes drive from the spa village and beyond the elephant camp the road extended to Royal botanical gardens, also worth a visit. The town of Chiang Mai was about 35 miles from the Spa a journey troublesome with the traffic and really hot weather. I only used the bike a few times to visit there.

I took a bus one day up to Chiang Rai which is near the border with Burma and Laos and not so far from the borders with China. I stayed for two nights at a small hotel in Chaing Rai where I hired a car and driver to take me up to Mae Sai and the Golden Triangle, famous not so long ago for the opium trail on which mule trains lead by people from the hill tribes would take the opium down from Burma into the Mae Sai Province of Northern Thailand. Gone are the days of ex KMT soldiers from China with their leader Khun Sa, protecting the opium trail. He, at one time, had a contract on his head set by the US Drug Administration. My reading told me Thai Rangers and Burmese guerrillas had once instructions to assassinate him on their behalf. I also learnt that drugs were still found in the area and were being grown across into Burma. It was a good couple of days before I returned to Chiang Mai when after another few days swimming in the spa pool and having relaxing massages it was time to get the direct flight back to Hong Kong.

But surprisingly the weight lost over the two months soon came back on and when I returned again to Thailand to Spa Samui on the 30th November I was 265 pounds. I was not very sensible this time as I took a really nice girlfriend with me. She was supposed to enjoy herself, eat healthily whilst I performed my fast for just few days and the colonic irrigation that goes with it! Clearly soon afterwards and on reflection I realised that it was not the best thing for a pre-Christmas break with a new girlfriend. Sadly also the weather was bloody awful and we couldn't get out much to enjoy trips on my motor bike or go on the ferry to the other islands so we curtailed the holiday and flew back a couple of days early. She was a lovely lady however and we did enjoy some of the time together. Clearly these fasts were getting the better of me as I had a bad attack of gout during the last few days and had certainly didn't feel as good as I did during longer fasts I had done when unaccompanied. I did perhaps still foolishly consider it was a way to lose weight and would come again in future.

I note from a diary that I flew KLM to Norwich in England via Amsterdam on the 28th August, 2010. I visited my sister who lives with her husband George at a village called Saham Toney which is outside the market town of Watton, about 15 miles south of the city of Norwich. Her daughter Belinda is a solicitor who has her office not far away at Hingham, Norfolk. Belinda at that time was living in Norwich but she owned a delightful 18th century windmill which was just a 10 minute walk from her mother's place. She was renting this out at the time of my visit but moved back there the following year. I stayed at pleasant hotel a 15 minute bus ride out of Norwich which, good for my regular exercise habit, had a 20 yard indoor swimming pool. Belinda booked me in there and she was also a member of the swimming club. I saw a lot of my family and visited some full of character pubs: in the city of Norwich (15 at least real ales!), Saham Toney (the local quiz night!) and Watton (good food). Norwich is a really lovely City and I explored it and visited the Norfolk Regiments' museum. I also attended matins at the Cathedral.

I took the train across country to Bridgnorth in Shropshire where I stayed with my friends from Discovery Bay: Bob Sones and his wife Helen. They have a home in Discovery Bay but seem to use it to avoid the harsher UK weather spending time in each home every year. Bridgnorth is a quaint old Salop market town situated on the River Severn with its own cliff railway. I forget how long I stayed with them. I visited them again the following year again. On one of these occasions – it must have been over a week – I suspect I may have overstayed my welcome. I went with Bob one Saturday to watch Wolverhampton Wanderers football team at Molineux their splendid ground. There was also the Severn Valley Railway, not one of the mainline companies, but run by enthusiastic amateurs. It runs the 30 or so miles from Kidderminster in Worcestershire to Bridgnorth in Shropshire and follows the river through some lovely English countryside. There is a railway pub at Bridgnorth which serves some excellent ales and is only 15 minute walk from Bob's place.

I wanted to visit my old friends Barney and Marilynne Humphris who live at Barnet, North London and I travelled south to see them intending to stop on the way to see my old mate Ted Stevenson. But Barney and Marilynne were unavailable. Why didn't you give us more notice? Well I did say a month before I was coming to UK; Oh well!

Ted was on the plane with me on the 28th February, 1962 when we flew off to join the Northern Rhodesia Police. I have mentioned him before as the man who lost his leg. I stayed at his place at Bishops Stortford, Hertfordshire for a few days and remember I was there during the Pope's visit to the UK. Ted is devoted catholic who did some time training for the priesthood, so we both watched the programme of some of the visit on the TV. I call myself a Christian and support most of our brothers and sisters in Christ. The Mormons, with their covered wagon history and theology including Jesus revealing himself to early immigrants in America (apparently in ancient times), and who will found a new Jerusalem there, I find difficult. So I empathised with Ted and enjoyed the programme with our old Governor Chris Patten showing His Holiness around. I think I have mentioned before him attending the 100 anniversary service at our church in Kennedy Road (the English speaking Methodist church). Governor Patten would attend St Joseph' s Catholic church in Garden Road.

A few evenings in the local pub with Ted then it was back by train to Norwich to say goodbye to Jill, George and co then on the plane from the Norwich airport back in a nice comfortable business class seat to HK.

I recall I also went up to Shanghai to stay with my daughter on more than two occasions in 2010. I can't get the dates now from my passport as the chops are not readable. It must be I was up to Shanghai at least once, sometimes twice a year during the time (2007 to 2011) she was up at the British International

School teaching. I was there to see the new baby Isobel after her birth in November and again I was there for a week over Christmas, (2010) although alas I have little memory of that time. I have some recollection of attending the International church in what use to be the French concession.

I say here I like Shanghai, unlike Hong Kong, it has kept much its the old character. The buildings on the Bund remain much as they were after the foreign concession finished and the communists took over. Other old buildings like the old Police Headquarters remain standing although not in use by the police (the PSB: Public Security Bureau). The famous racecourse is now a park with the green bits carefully chained off from the public. The old French concession has kept its tree line pleasant avenues and large low rise buildings, which must have been very grand in earlier times, but to be fair they are all in good order and used for private and commercial purposes.

There are some good restaurants and bars, a couple which produce their own German style beer on the premises. Shanghai which has certainly awoken from its communist slumber, is alive with plenty to do. I can see it regaining its supremacy over Hong Kong soonest.

The Shanghainese were Chinas' natural entrepreneurs and capitalist who brought their skills and businesses to Hong Kong after 1948, helping it become the marvellous place it is today. Napoleon is supposed to have said: "When China awakes the world will quake." Well it has certainly awoken and looks to becoming the major world power in a decade or so. China has the energy, the skills, tenacity and general conservative sense to advance and continue to improve the material lives of its people.

But history has shown that it can descend into disorder when the centre loses control namely: The 'war lord' days and lack of strong central government, when there were short, mainly local attempts at democracy, which lead to demands for independence from a national government. It is so easy for the west to urge freedom, human rights and democracy in the form of one man one vote. But is this right for all countries?

If one looks at India: the world's biggest democracy! A place where the lower castes and poor have no influence on their lives at all, where their votes are bought by the locally powerful and often corrupt politicians. They have no enforceable rights and no freedom. There were 600 reported rapes in Delhi with one person convicted (BBC news September 2013). It is said you can buy absolutely anything in India. Another example of democracy: Look across the South China Sea to the Philippines! Corrupt government votes for sale and rights and freedom only with money or connections.

In Hong Kong we have freedom and human rights with no, or little, democracy. Is the western way the answer for all, China in particular? Should they not find their own way to have good governance and representative government which ensures freedom and human rights. This begs the question what is freedom; what are human rights? Are they really universal? I understand there was a time in Sicily, Italy, when the population elected Mafia gangsters. In our present time Islamists are being elected on a platform which wishes to bring sharia law and non democratic government. Madness! You vote to have no democracy!

I see I am getting carried away and must get back now to look at some of the professional work I did in 2010.

The first case in 2010 was with me prosecuting a young Chinese man for trafficking in cocaine. His defence was: it was not for trafficking but was for his own consumption. I called evidence from an expert to give an opinion as to current doses for an addict. This showed the drugs involved, 30 large packets and they way they were packed were indicative of being trafficked. The judge considered that with all the circumstances: the place where the drugs were, which was inside his car and the time of day and location, plus the way they were packed and the quantity, she could draw the irresistible inference that he was trafficking the drugs. He was convicted and sentenced to five years. He had many similar convictions for trafficking. I mention it to show the heavy sentences for drugs in Hong Kong, in the UK a sentence for such a case would probably not have involved such a time in prison.

With much time away 2010 was not a very busy time. There were, however, a few noteworthy cases, one in particular, shows justice was not done and in my view was not seen to be done. In March I was briefed to defend a young African, like many he had 'lost' his passport and thus although an illegal immigrant who could not easily be deported. He was a bright young man, who at one stage appeared a juvenile and should be tried as such. But he had no document showing his birth day and so when he realised that far from helping him being sentenced as a juvenile it may be worse than as an adult, he said he was 18.

The court ordered test to be carried out and an expert scientific opinion was given that he was an adult. He was charged with others with Trafficking in a large quantity of herbal cannabis (over 30 kilos).

The drugs had been brought in by a white couple from South Africa and as is often the case they co-operated with the customs with a controlled delivery. The collection of the drugs, at hotel room in Kowloon, was caught on camera by the customs officers in ambush positions. The third accused a Nigerian man came and collected the drugs.

My client the fourth accused was seen following behind the Nigerian. The only evidence of his possession of the drugs was his moving it to the doorway of the room. The keys to the suitcase had been given by the male South African to the Nigerian. The customs allegation was that the key to the suitcase was found in his possession, which was, as just mentioned, contradicted by the unchallenged evidence of the South African male. There was no evidence that the key was then handed to him in the room by the third accused.

At the end of the Prosecutions case I made a submission of no case to answer. For those who are not familiar with the criminal trial process such a submission is made when it is submitted that there is no or no sufficient evidence on which a jury properly instructed could convict an accused of the charge/s laid against him.

The prosecution counsel was a Cantonese speaking 'Gwai lo' against whom I have been against both as a prosecutor and defence counsel. He is a man who is always looking for justice, extremely fair and old fashioned. It would not be unfair if you thought sometimes that he was impervious to the slings and arrows that were being hurled at him from the bench. I recall hearing of a case he dealt with in the High Court where despite being knocked down time again by the judge for his questions or submissions he eventually won over the jury with an acquittal to the admiration of the trial judge involved. As you imagine he can be hard work.

He agreed with my submission and instead of saying nothing in reply, as is the general practice in such cases, he stood up and gave a reply supporting my submission. He went on to submit in writing, at the request of the Judge, a submission explaining his reasons and authority for not seeking a conviction against my client in view of the weakness of the evidence. Unusual to say the least, but if the prosecutor who knows every thing there is to know about the evidence and those involved is asking the Judge not to convict what more is there for me to do, other than to reply to his submission by way of adopting what he said in support of my submission.

The judge was a lady with whom I had crossed swords before, although to be fair she was the one who did acquit the police sergeant with two illegal bullets case I referred to earlier. I was surprised when she came back after the submissions without addressing the points raised and ruled a case to answer. It is the practice in Hong Kong that a judge does not give reasons at this stage for ruling a case to answer, but under the unusual circumstances I felt she should. I was in predicament what was I to do?

Should I call evidence, I already had evidence that the key was handed by the South African to the Nigerian, there was no other evidence adduced and relied on by the prosecution for a conviction. Putting my fellow in the witness box was a risk and was it really necessary; at the end of the day how could she convict. How would he impress the judge: as a young tearaway illegal immigrant with no passport? I didn't put him in the witness box.

She convicted him and hammered him with the sentence: 5 years 7 months, significantly more than the other three who had pleaded guilty, the Nigerian only after the case had started and evidence given against him by the white male. I was saddened by the result especially when I heard how she justified the conviction: she seemed to have based it on what the Nigerian had said in the room when he described my fellow as his brother from South Africa when he was describing, in fact to those in the room, a man he was talking to on the phone as his brother from South Africa.

I saw him in the cells afterwards he was a chirpy young man who thanked me for my efforts! And asked for my help with an appeal which I advised we did against conviction and sentence. Legal Aid supported the appeal and I appeared before the Court of Appeal who made short work of my appeal against conviction, we can't have prosecutors supporting no case submissions with more than the usual: "I have nothing to say or I don't think I can help the court." They did however reduce the sentence by 6 months to five years. I saw the young fellow in the High Court cells afterwards and he was delighted. I fancy other convicted people may have complained about me, in any event it left me feeling somewhat jaundiced with the whole system. This boy was less than guilty!

Julio, there was a character! A Eurasian Portuguese young man who I defended years back in the High Court when he was charged with his brother who was defended by my friend and chambers colleague Chris Grounds. Julio who would proudly boast that his younger brother was a more senior triad than he was! They were charged with false imprisonment, blackmail and assault. I recall we had an excellent Judge who is still around but deals more with civil cases now. The prosecutor was Ian Polson who was my chambers mate when I came back to Hong Kong and started my career as a barrister. A grumpy miserable old sod in later years to be against but then pleasant enough. He was one of Hong Kong's 'Iron Men': They that run a marathon, swim five miles then bicycle for 50 miles, well something like that. I recall his joints were later to complain, requiring surgery.

In fact it was an enjoyable trial, with as much humour as a serious criminal matter can allow. Julio to his astonishment and gratitude ended up only being convicted for common assault. His brother also had the most serious charges against him dismissed and received a modest sentence under all the circumstances.

Julio never forgot me, for late in 2010 he instructed me through legal Aid to defend him for Trafficking in heroin. He was going to plead guilty but the case was complicated by the special mitigation involved. Julio was anxious to have the considerable assistance he had given to the Police recognized and rewarded with a further discount beyond that allowed for his plea of guilty. I needed to do much work to persuade those in authority that he had assisted the police with information to break up two trafficking gangs. There were initial denials of his help and I was forced to write to the DPP and talk directly with the counsel instructed to prosecute the case. Eventually through the good offices of one of the government counsels information that he had helped in the arrest and conviction of one of the traffickers was confirmed and warranted a reward in the form of a discount. They refused to admit, however, that he had helped in another case, even though we were able to supply the name and the conviction details of that trafficker.

There was a special hearing in the chambers of Judge Wright, an able and respected judge who had been on the bench for years, first as a magistrate then rising through the ranks to High Court judge. The particulars of the assistance Julio had given were supplied to the judge under a confidential cover; to those interested the procedure is called a SIVAN HEARING. In the event he obtained a third off for his plea plus an extra 10 months of for the special issue making a sentence of 4 and a half years.

I saw him in the cells and advised him to take care, criminals don't like a grass, that is, if they found out what he had done. Hopefully the 'Sivan' procedure gave him protection. Julio by the way is not his correct name.

The last quarter of the year saw me with four cases: one defending and three prosecuting.

The defence case involved a 16-year-old boy in the District Court for Trafficking in Dangerous Drugs. The drug was ketamine hydrochloride was becoming a worry in Hong Kong and across the border in Shen Zhen as it was popular with such young people some even school children. The evidence against the boy was largely in admissions which I challenged as not being admissible because they were not voluntarily given, but he was convicted by an ambitious deputy judge keen to be a substantive District Court Judge. Despite favourable Training Centre (places for young offenders punishment and reformation, away from adult criminals) reports the Judge sent him to prison for 4 years 6 months. Something which would be unheard of in the UK and, believe it or not, in China across the border. I advised an appeal as he was after all a young, at worst, street pedlar with no criminal record; surely rehabilitation/reform in an individual sentence was the proper one. (Note. I see from re-checking my notes that this case was heard in May/June 2011 not 2010)

The prosecution's cases were all in the District Court: a burglary involving two professional but not very clever thieves who had entered as trespassers in a commercial building to steal and were caught in the act by alert patrolling police officers. I note rather cynically that, unlike London, we still have officers who actually patrol the streets on the ground.

The other two were noteworthy in that they were, for Hong Kong, not commonplace. They both involved cruelty.

The first was a Filipino who had caused serious harm to his son by shaking and gripping him when he had lost his temper. It was our case that he had caused the child to suffer injuries including a fracture arm. The defence was conducted by a man I had previously been against and had always called – in my mind – Mr Muddle. He contested the injuries and seemed to indicate there were medical reports from the Philippines that contradicted those relied on by the prosecution. I must admit that these detailed reports from specialists including a paediatrician from Queen Elizabeth Hospital only came when ordered by the Judge. There were difficulties also in that the child was not in Hong Kong and the mother had no money to bring her back to Hong Kong for the trial. As you can see, a right pigs breakfast!

Eventually the medical evidence was agreed and the trial proceeded. It was clear once the child came to court that both father and child loved each other and both had a good relationship with the mother. I felt sympathy for both and could not see under the circumstances that lengthy time in prison would do anything but harm to the family. In the event the Judge took all this into account plus the fact that the child's overall prognosis appeared good, and sentenced the man to 16 months imprisonment.

I was saddened at the end of the case to find that the poor mother had been criticised at QE Hospital when she could not pay for her son to be examined again. She also had to pay for his medical expenses in the Philippines and his airfare together with a carer back to Hong Kong. I asked the woman police officer in charge of the case to assist her in seeking help from the Criminal Injuries Compensation Scheme.

The second concerned a young man infatuated with an ex-girlfriend who had spurned him for another. He violently, using a cutter, had imprisoned her in a flat for 9 hours. He had assaulted her, albeit causing superficial injuries. He was charged with False Imprisonment and Wounding with Intent. But I could see from the evidence that there was not enough evidence to prove the intention required. A simple wounding charge with the false imprisonment would properly indicate the degree of criminality involved. He was sentenced by an always pleasant and helpful lady Judge to 18 months imprisonment. I thought – under all the circumstances – this was an over lenient sentence and that the DPP should apply to the Court of Appeal to review it. But they never did. I did write to the DPP expressing my concern for the young lady victim in the case. He would be out from prison in a year as it was the practice that he would be given a third discount for good behaviour in prison. Such was the record of violence towards the victim that he should be monitored by the police on his release.

I finish this Chapter with Christmas with the new family: Alfreda, Drew and Isobel in Shanghai. I have managed to decipher my passport chops and see I was there from the 22nd December, 2010 to the 2nd of January, 2011.

# 26. Final Caseload

2011 certainly saw me fully occupied both professionally with prosecuting and defending in the District, High, and Court of Appeal Court and privately with trips abroad.

In March I was defending in the High Court another West African man, for trafficking in cocaine. I had seen him twice in conference at the Lai Chi Kok remand prison and he had told me he was guilty of the offence but still wanted me to fight the case basing his defence on an untruth. He had also, unusually (I had never experienced such a course before), written a letter to the Judge, set down to hear the case, saying he had accepted responsibility for the whole matter. And had signed admitted facts saying the same. Under such circumstances I was in difficulties in putting the defence case he now instructed me. I was of the view that I could only put the prosecution to proof which would be limited to me challenging any confessions he had made as not being voluntary could not put him in the witness box and relate a defence which I knew to be a lie. The judge a well respected and experienced man understood my predicament: I could not properly follow my instructions and he allowed me to withdraw.

I mention this case to show my readers that at the Bar we have strict rules to follow and a code of conduct. British and Hong Kong barristers are not allowed, as may appear to happen, from the 'movies' in some jurisdictions, to knowingly be used to present false evidence to a Court.

April 2011 saw what should have been the holiday of a lifetime. I was to go South Africa, Botswana and Zimbabwe. I was to have a travelling companion: Ms ....... who I had known since I started using the Shatin Anglican Church that met at the Tsang Shui Tim Secondary school at Wor Che. I use to combine going there with going to our old and familiar church in Kennedy road, Wanchai. She did join a bible study group that met once a week at our home at the Prince of Wales Hospital. I did not want to go alone on the trip which would last all of April and would entail a stay at the Cape; a trip on 'Rovas Rail' up through Botswana to the Victoria Falls in Zimbabwe and then a week in Botswana and again in South Africa on 'safari'. I hasten to emphasize **looking** at as much game as possible, perhaps giving the odd bun to an elephant but no nasties done to the animals or our guides!

I said should have been the holiday of a lifetime but alas my companion never stopped complaining and showed no gratitude to me for paying for everything: flights, fares, hotels safaris etc. I was keen to go and needed someone to accompany me as I was getting bad on my pins. She was a burden with a long face most of the time, but to be fair perhaps she expected more from me. We did not unfortunately click!

We flew on Quatar Airlines, a newish airline with all new planes, to Cape Town where we were met at the airport by Chris Maltby and his wife. I had come to know him through my membership of the Northern Rhodesia Police Association. I had never met him during my short time in that force but had seen his name in the bi-annual NRP Association journal, NKHWAZI in which he does place a regular advertisement for his travel agency business. It was he who organised our trip, everything from our flights to our hotels, the rail trip and the safaris in Botswana and South Africa. He had booked us in Cape Town at The Commodore, situated in Portswood Road not far from the Harbour and the centre of good restaurants and Mitchell's Brewery; a home brew pub/restaurant with some splendid ales.

We organised some local tours ourselves, two with the help of Chris were guided and the others we took buses on 'get on get off' tickets. We toured vineyards and wineries in the Cape Town area and also took a guided tour further out as far as that lovely Afrikaans town of Paarl where I found it strange that there were not many black Africans doing the service work in the shops and restaurants. I visited the local Dutch reform church. I forget the names of the vineyards, although we visited several which went back to the days of the early Dutch settlers. The buildings and old wine making equipment certainly brought you back to another time. It was amazing what these early people had done bringing modern farming as well as the harvesting of grapes and wine making to Southern Africa. We did, of course try the wines both near to Cape Town and the Paarl area.

It was on the Paarl trip that we also stopped at a prison where our guide told us Nelson Mandela had spent some time after Robben Island. This was the Victor Vorster Prison where in 1988 he was given a more comfortable stay in a cottage during his 27 years of incarceration. We were not allowed into the prison but outside the main gate there was a lady hawker where I was able to buy a Nelson Mandela t-shirt, or was it three for the price of two?

413

Another guided tour was on a Sunday when we were escorted around the African Townships. We saw how the people lived and also viewed a service at a local church. The homes were certainly not very special and I was surprised that even our guide, a man of some substance with his own smart vehicle, lived in something little better than a concrete shanty. He further surprised me by saying that a significant number of the residents in this township and others were from outside the Cape Province. And have homes in their own Provinces, often much better than those they used at the Cape where they work. We observed a lady making African beer, something I was familiar with from my time in the NRP.

We took a hop on bus along the east coast out from the City. I have looked on the map and cannot now remember where we alighted half way; it was right on the sea front and there was a roadhouse selling burgers/refreshments and the like and some people in the sea. I believe it must have been about 30 miles or less out from where we got on in Cape Town. We didn't go up the famous Table Mountain cable car but did have two really special days one when Chris sent a driver to take us to his 'Fred Flintstone' outdoor barbecue which was situated a good fifty to sixty miles west along the coast road to Yzerfontein. I have looked at the map; it is marvellous how on the internet you can zoom on to a photographic view as well. The restaurant, which would have blown away in a Typhoon, was on a sand dune up from a beach facing the Atlantic Ocean was called Standkombuis. It was run by Chris and his family. The food was seafood, fish and all manner of other creatures from the ocean plus plenty of local beer. It was a lovely day and my companion got on very well with Chris's wife. It was then a fast hours drive back to our Hotel along a good road but through a dry sandy landscape.

Chris himself picked us up another day sand took us out in the sticks to a small family owned winery and restaurant where there were to meet us were a group of ex NRP fellows, Chris, Martin Linette, Mick Robson, Mike Wright and their wives. One of those Mike Wright, still a large friendly Rhodesian (Zimbabwean now) that he was, who you may recall from my mention of him in my days as a young cadet at Ndola, Northern Rhodesia. When he had pulled the South African, Danny Robinson off me as he proceeded to throttle me into oblivion (Chapter 5). It was really pleasant to talk about old times and to enquire the present state of Southern Africa. It seems that in the Cape Province the State ruling party: the ANC, do not have a majority and the provincial government was run by the able white South African lady, Helen Zille of the Democratic Alliance. The local budget balanced and there was good governance.

Perhaps the highlights of our trip to South Africa was our journey on Rovos Rail, the visits to the Okavango in Botswana and the Entabeni Game Reserve up in the Limpopo, South Africa. I wrote a short article in Nkhwazi, the journal of the Northern Rhodesia Police Association (Newsletter No.83 Summer 2011) under the heading 'African Odyssey'; alas now I see there is a misspelling: should be another 'd'. I have re-read this to help my memory.

We caught the train at station at Cape Town, but first enjoyed snacks and cocktails at a place opposite, where the man with the most expensive train set in the world: Mr Rovos, introduced himself and explained his railway: its routes, history and objectives. We then moved across and boarded our train. It was indeed a luxurious train with classic 20's Orient Express type carriages. Our cabin had two bunks and its own shower/w.c. The bunks pulled down to make comfortable sofa benches. The food served in the dining car, again a gem in itself, was fantastic served with all manner of wines by really lovely young South Africans, dare I say white folk; as was our cabin stewardess. There was a separate bar, where all the booze was on the house, with a viewing platform at the end where you could watch the countryside and hopefully the game as you went along. The train was pulled by two powerful diesels locomotives although I understand that Rovos Rail did run journeys using historic steam locomotives. The train moved over through the Cape mountains and on to the Karoo with its flat semi desert plain.

Our first stop, after about four hours and about 180 miles on the train, was Matjesfontein just into the Karoo on the Hex river. It was a perfectly preserved Victorian railway village which hadn't changed much or at all since the Boer War. There was the Lord Milner Hotel which looked as if it still had gas lights and was waiting for Lord Milner's return. We were met by a mixed race gentleman who drove an ancient bus that could have been from the 40/50's. He took us around in a 15 minute view of the 'acre' or so of the sights. There was ancient bar next to the hotel where we had a drink and again with the decorations and pictures on the wall it could have been 1900.There was talk that a ghost of a Tommy from the Boer War was still around. It was then back on the train and on over the Karoo with a marvellous dinner, then a few drinks in the lounge car before bed in our sleeper. The next stop was

Kimberly famous for Cecil Rhodes, diamonds and De Beers, the mine he controlled back at the end of the 19th century with its famous Big Hole. We visited the Diamond museum and the Big Hole. I recall I bought a small stone for my daughter but nothing special. I would have liked to see 'Long Cecil' an immense gun with a 300 metre barrel that was made in the De Beers' workshops named after Cecil Rhodes and used against the Boers in the Seige of Kimberly. It had a range of 5000 yards.

After Kimberly our next stop was to be Pretoria where Rovos Rail had its headquarters, own station and railway works. But it was back on the train, dinner, and a second night on the train as the train continued on the 550 odd miles to Pretoria. Here we left the train to stay one night at a hotel. But here a calamity which certainly added to the bad mood of my lady companion. We had been told by the train staff that it was safe to leave our belongings in the cabin as it would be locked and the train secured. Valuables, cash, passports etc we had locked in a safe, but things like clothing, bags shoes and my lady's charger for her camera we left in the wardrobe or in our cases, as advised, in the cabin. We returned the following day after short tour of Pretoria, the State capital of South Africa, of which I have no memory. We returned to our room and then it was off to re-join our train.

I went off for to the buffet carriage for breakfast whilst my friend returned back to the cabin. She joined me soon after with a long face, she couldn't find much of her property and thought it must have been stolen. We both returned to the cabin; sure enough, missing from the wardrobe were: some NRP ties I had bought from Chris, a pair of new Chukka boots

417

and nice holdall I had bought at a shop by the Cape harbour, and my Nelson Mandela Tee shirts. My poor companion had fared worse: her charger, some CDs and necklaces bought at the harbour shops, her high heel shoes and a smart dress for evening wear.

There were no signs of breaking and I learnt afterwards that some cleaners had come on the train at Pretoria. I reported to the train manager who couldn't believe what had happened, apparently we were the only ones to lose anything. Our poor cabin stewardess looked very upset and I hastened to tell her I had no suspicion in regard to her at all. Why? because it didn't make sense. I was told that I should ring the boss Mr Rovos when we came to a place called Deke further up the line.

This I did, to be told in an angry voice, that 'Africans don't steal things like that. ' So who took them? He clearly didn't believe me. I told him I was a professional man who did not tell lies. He seemed to reject any responsibility for the loss and told me to write a letter confirming what we had allegedly lost and reported to him (Rovos Rail). I was unhappy with his attitude which was accusatory and created an atmosphere amongst my fellow passenger, some of whom had become our friends, and the staff of, if not hostility, then unfriendliness. I wanted to report to police but by the time we were in Deke we were in Botswana, perhaps that is why he told me to wait until then. I see it is my old police mind working: He didn't want the South African Police involved?

The train crossed the border into Botswana during the night. We had given our passports to the train staff so we were not conscious of entering that country or leaving the next day when we crossed into Zimbabwe. We had one stop in Botswana when we got off the train. It was not a regular station but just a halt where there was a cattle station which we visited and met the stock men and some of the family who ran it. I have not been able to find the name of the halt and cattle station. I was impressed; it was run by a family of white Botswanans who had been there for four generations. We saw some of the stock which were the humped cattle, able to exist on the limited water supply in this largely semi desert terrain. We were there a morning before going off north again towards Zimbabwe.

It was one more night on the train until we crossed the border again into Mugabe's Zimbabwe. Travel into Zimbabwe required a US$50 visa for me, for my Chinese companion it was free! The Victoria Falls were magnificent: God at his best. In 1963 when I had visited last, as young colonial police officer, a view of them both sides of the border: Northern or Southern Rhodesia, was free, then April, 2011 it cost US$30 just to walk along a path in a small roped off area. We stayed for two nights at a posh hotel which unfortunately lacked the polish expected of its four star status: the lifts didn't work and it had that run down, grubby feel. Most of the people who attended us were Shona (Mugabe's Tribe), which I thought was strange as we were in Matabele land.

We left as planned the hotel and spent another two days at a camp in the bush run by a white Zimbabwean. This was well run with good food and the staff Endebele. Where we learnt that Zimbabwe was now very much run by Mugabe, his family, friends and tribe.

We visited a local market where there were some really nice African handicrafts but sadly no customers. The stall holders looked so poor and were anxious for us to buy. I bought a beautifully carved wooden statue of a Kalahari bushman, which I have displayed in my flat. Then it was goodbye to the Falls and off by car into Botswana.

It was about 50 miles to the border to a point near where the mighty Zambezi and Chobe rivers meet and the countries of Zambia to the North, Zimbabwe to the east Botswana to the south and Namibia through the Caprivi strip to the west all converge. All have borders there but despite the close proximity of the other two countries there were only Zimbabwe and Botswana customs/Immigration. For me with my British passport it was entry fees free; for my companion who had a Hong Kong SAR passport there was a problem. Unlike Zimbabwe which was British passport unfriendly and Chinese passport very friendly, Botswana was the reverse. I had great difficulty persuading the Botswanan lady immigration officer to let my companion in. I told her that it was in fact a Hong Kong passport which we had cleared with our agents before as OK to enter Botswana visa free.

We showed her hotel bookings at a nearby hotel on the Chobe river and the details of our later and further trip into the Okavango. She let us both through visa free with a: 'Oh I don't know'. I had met in my time far more unpleasant border officials. Perhaps I could mention here that I found Botswana well governed and the people with happier faces than I had seen in Zimbabwe and South Africa. From the border it was about 15 miles to the Kebu lodge which was our Chobe riverside hotel, situated just a mile or so from the town of

Kasane. The lodge had lawns which went right down to the river and there were warning notices about hippos coming up out of the river especially in the hours of darkness. Their foot prints could be seen on the grass and from our beds in our room you could certainly hear them; but shadows only by the time you had got up and gone to investigate. We had two full days there including a trip on the Chobe river where we did see hippos and elephant. I was interested to see on the north Namibia shore of the river a really ritzy floating resort. But I didn't see any one using it yet. Clearly development even in this remote part was on its way.

We were then off from the Kasane airport in a four seater plane with a gorgeous young black lady pilot to fly us over and to the Okavango Delta where we landed on an air strip with nothing there except a wind sock. There we had waiting for us a simply lovely Tswana man who said call me 'Bushman.' He drove us about an hour along a good dirt road, plenty of just tracts and across rivers (the vehicle a Japanese Jeep type vehicle with a snorkel) until we came to our tented camp. They were tents, we were under canvas, but believe it or not there were proper sit down flush loo's and showers. The water came from large buckets that were suspended above and operated by pulling a string. Every morning they were full for our use. Bushman was the camp chief and he had four other Tswana people working the camp. He almost gave himself apoplexy finding game for us to view day or night, driving over almost impossible terrain, crossing rivers and where there were no tracks in the bush itself. He would call us out in the vehicle sometimes in the dead of night waking us up to go and look at Hippos grazing, his assistant manning a powerful spot light. He did us well as did his staff at the camp. The food was really good, cooked by the lady cook. It was beautifully served with us at dinner sitting out in the open. On one occasion it was really special with the absolutely wonderful, amazing, breathtaking, stunning, unbelievable night sky above us. I can't find enough adjectives to fully express the sight: a myriad, myriad of stars, the sky brilliantly ablaze. We each had our own tent, loo and shower and regularly there was a giraffe family and two elephants watching us at our morning ablutions and sometimes at nocturnal cleansing.

The highlights of our stay in the Okavango was a night patrol when we saw the hippos grazing and when we saw in the early morning just after sun rise, just a few yards away, a lioness picking on an impala carcass. It was just bones, whilst her mate slept nearby with probably almost all of her kill in his bloated tum. Still no equal rights in the animal world, although it seems in the world of the elephant it is matriarchy.

The time flew by and it was goodbye to these good people and the animals, who we may have disturbed, and back in the jeep to the airstrip. It was then about an hour or so in the light plane again, this time it was a young white pilot, to take us to Maun, the centre for the Okavango to catch the plane to Johannesburg, South Africa. The distance was around 550 miles and the flight did not take long.

We were met at the Oliver Tambo airport by a car and driver, all very efficient as every thing was, as organised by Chris and taken for about three hour drive to the Entabeni Private Game Reserve up in the Limpopo. We stayed here at the real up market 5 star Kingfisher lodge on the lake, where we were put after I couldn't handle the steep walking at another lodge on the side of a ravine. It was excellent accommodation by the lake. The food and service with buffets and barbecues was great, although you had to pay for your own booze, but at R130 a bottle you couldn't complain. It was a 65,000-acre reserve, well managed with all manner of game. We had our own game guide who was a young white Afrikaner who took us out day and some nights and did his best to find us as many types of animal as he could. The highlights must have been three beautiful rhino: Mum, Dad and junior!

It certainly was different from the wild Okavango but the way the game were allowed to roam free you would not have thought you were in a private reserve. The sight seeing trips around the reserve were along some very rugged tracks. To go from the lower plain to higher one involved a mountain track which required much skill from our young guide in the handling of a four wheel drive vehicle.

Again it was soon over and we were back in a car to take us back to the airport for our return to Hong Kong. Sadly by this time my companion seemed to have had enough and I recall that the second half of the flight back: from Dubai she was sitting on the plane by herself. Oh well! She must have got something from this fantastic month in Southern Africa.

The end of May beginning of June saw me defending the young 16-year-old boy for the street peddling of ketamine in the District Court. I mentioned the case in the last chapter. You may recall I was unhappy with his 4 year 6 month sentence.

June and July saw me defending in the High Court a West African from Guinea for trafficking in over 700 grams of heroin. The drugs were in 66 pellets which were found inside his stomach, by X ray examination after he had been stopped by customs officers at the airport. His defence was I did not know they were there! He had no idea how they got there other than it may have been when he was in an unconscious state at a Hotel in Bangkok.

He was told in no uncertain terms that it would be difficult to persuade a jury that he did not know he had such a quantity in his body for such a long time. They must have been there for at least a day and half, not counting the time he was in hospital for examination. When he later said he must have been drugged the drug Rohypnol came to mind. This drug I had come across in regard to Robbery cases where visiting servicemen had been drugged with spiked drinks and then taken by escorts/prostitutes to ETC machines where they had been 'helped' to draw money.

I had an excellent instructing solicitor who was able to find an expert, a scientist who gave evidence as to the availability of Rohypnol and its effects. But this did not really help a total denial that he did not know at any time until discovery that he had the drugs inside him. They would have had to be swallowed one by one or similarly inserted through the back passage.

I told him again and again the defence would fail but he insisted on the pleading not guilty. He gave evidence. The jury were out for 4 hours and came back with a unanimous guilty. The lady judge sentenced him to 22 and a half years. I had to advise him afterwards in the cells that there were no arguable grounds of appeal. He told me that he wanted now to change his plea to guilty. A bit late now!

I had it in writing before the trial and signed by him, that his defence was extraordinary and would not be believed, but that I would defend him vigorously to the best of my ability. I was minded that he would complain about me for being negligent with his defence and had not properly advised him. It was not an uncommon ground in appeals before Hong Kong's Court of Appeal that defence counsel had been negligent in their defence and had not properly advised. Then there were complaints to the Bar Association. The availability of such avenues was, of course, a good thing in our society however irksome they may be to professional people.

The mention of complaining to the Bar Association about the misconduct of one of its members draws to mind the only complaint I had made against me during my nearly 30 years as a barrister in Hong Kong.

It concerned a middle age Chinese family man who could not get a job. He eventually got a job in a massage establishment. It may have been unlicensed, it was some time ago, when things may have been less regulated. In any event the man was alleged to have touched a young woman's breast/s, was it one or both, I think it was just the left one, as he gave her a massage. He was charged with Indecent Assault. The case was heard in the Magistrates' court before a magistrate who had previously been a physiotherapist. The victim, she must have been early 20's came to court dressed like a boy complete with cropped hair and a shirt showing no bra and a flat chest (the Chinese street slang for such a condition is 'Fei Kei Cheung', which translates into English as aircraft runway!).

My defence was he had not touched her breasts and if he had, he had done so accidentally. She had come to court with her friend who was very girlie and it was obvious, to me and all, they were a lesbian couple. OK nothing wrong with that, such homosexual relations for both men and women are today accepted, promoted, encouraged even, in all walks of our all-permissive and open society. I had one real defence which I am sure with a different magistrate, perhaps a lady one, would have succeeded. I cross examined her about her dress and asked her to stand up so we could all see that she didn't have any breasts to touch. I put this to her and she burst into tears. (You swine Tolliday-Wright! Is that what you are saying readers?). There was a cry of protest from the girl friend and the magistrate did not look happy.

I emphasized this man was on trial for an offence which from many of us draws opprobrium. For him a family man who had been out of work for some time it was worse. He allowed me to continue as to her disappointment that she was not given a particular female masseuse, although he clearly disliked my line of questioning.

I argued that on the evidence with no breast to indecently assault and the fact it occurred during a massage performed by a man who clearly was not a professional masseuse, to which course she had agreed by going in an illegal establishment, there was no case to answer. The magistrate, by this time looking askance at me, found a case to answer and after a short denial from the man in the witness box, he was found guilty and sentence of 6 or was it 9 months. The magistrate being before as a physiotherapist, involved with massage and bodies, took a dim view of what he had done and, if my memory serves me correctly, he refused bail pending appeal. I saw the man in the cells and advised about appealing. I understand he never did, it would have needed going to a high court judge for bail, then getting legal aid to assist him. I would have assisted him by doing the appeal 'pro bono': no fee.

It was one of perhaps a handful of cases which I have felt really bad about. And when I received a notice from the Bar Association to answer a complaint the victim had made about my oppressive and improper cross examining her I was ready with my reply. He was a decent man with no criminal record who had upset a young clearly immature woman who was looking for fault in him almost as soon as he started to massage her. She had made something nasty out of what she perceived an affront by me to her sexuality. She was trying to justify to herself what she had done to the poor man by raising the complaint against me. I replied in strong and vigorous terms to the Bar Council: I should have tried harder. I should not have stopped when she started to cry. As barrister we are to fight against the slings and arrows that come to us from all sides, the bench in particular. I add here that I recall that the prosecution was not exactly after his blood. The Bar Council was satisfied with the written explanation I had provided to them in my response to answer the complaint and no disciplinary action was taken against me.

The 21st July 2011 saw me arriving at Vancouver Airport on my way to Portland in Oregon, USA to attend the really joyous occasion of the marriage of my son Alexander to truly a lovely, intelligent, gifted, musical, culinary, professional and beautiful Michelle. Wah what a catch! It was not a relationship based on a short courtship; they had known each other to my knowledge, at least five years. The dear girl was present with Alex during the last months of my Diana's life at the Bradbury Hospice in Shatin. That she should have met her mother in law, albeit in terribly sad, heart-breaking circumstances meant a lot to me and I am sure to my son.

I recall the Department of Homeland Security, US Customs and Border Protection dealt with me in Vancouver, Canada before I boarded the short flight down to Portland. Always a performance going into the USA and you must be careful what you say and how you act: any feeling of annoyance as you are being groped could be met with the robotic invitation from the officer: 'Surrr, Would you like to be searched away from the public view?' What! and be strip searched with things put up my bum! No thanks do your worse, I'll grin and bare it.

I was met at Portland airport by one of Michelle's brothers. She has a large family: four sisters and three brothers; she is number five.

I forget the name of the hotel we stayed, it was not the one where the wedding and reception took place. Sharon, the daughter of Margaret, the caretaker of our Church in Kennedy Road had been on the same plane as me attended the wedding. I understand it was Sharon who had introduced Alexander to Michelle when she visited her in Hong Kong. They had been friends when Sharon came to study in Oregon years before. The ceremony was conducted in a room in hotel or was a large restaurant? The bride looked gorgeous and my son, well not too bad. No! He looked really smart and good looking. I was so proud of the pair of them.

*My family just after the wedding.*

Alfreda and Drew attended, leaving baby Isobel back at Bristol with her Grandma. The highlight of the wedding ceremony, perhaps I should say the thing that most sticks in my mind, was the 'wedding march' played 'heavy metal' style on the electric guitar by Michelle's youngest brother Mark. The baby of the family and a proud member of the US Coast Guard, serving then up in Alaska. All the siblings were present: four sisters and three brothers, only the husband of the eldest sister was not there. I made a short speech; I hope it was better than the one I had made at Alfreda's wedding to Chris Denis, almost 8 years before to the day, on the 26th July 2003. Then I had been slow hand clapped by my friend Barney for not saying enough nice things about Alfreda and going on too long with Tommy Cooper jokes. This time I had found some appropriate and, I hoped, amusing things to say about the happy couple and the institution of marriage in particular.

I had arrived in Portland on the 21st July and left the day after the wedding, the 23rd when my family were driven by Michelle down south to her Mum and Dad's place at Oakland. In those few days I had a chance to look around Portland and was impressed with the City, its fine buildings and the Umpqua river. On the second day there Jack one of Michelle's brothers and like me, an aficionado of fine ales, took me to a bar which had what must have been over a hundred draught beers from around the world. But of course like bread, beer has to be fresh and I feared that some of it had been in the kegs too long. The Americans are still learning about beer after spending most of the 20th century drinking fizzy p..s!

Their home was at 380 Yellow Creek Road (there were no lions, tin men or scarecrows so it was not the Yellow Brick Road!), Oakland, Oregon over 600 miles to the south of Portland. A really lovely house built, I understand, by Michelle's Dad. It was spacious indeed by Hong Kong standards and was situated on a lot of land about 3 acres, which ran alongside a small stream, a babbling brook, which drained into Willamette river about 1,000 yards away. There were trees all around and with no main road nearby it was idyllic. I explored around and one day we went to the river where I took a plunge. I had seen the young coastguard leaping over the rocks and into the river and thought I'd have ago but got the fright of my life when the current started to whiz me down the river. I caught hold of a rock and got out as fast as I could.

It was easy to see where Michelle got her culinary skills as her Mum, Charlotte was a talented cook, in fact she seemed good at most things and had educated most of her children herself, not trusting the US state school system. With her husband James (Jim) also being so good at doing things it was no wonder that my son had so much admiration and affection for them. His own poor old Dad was not good at much at all. As his Mum use to say: good at talking rubbish. Oh well! I think I am well read, history wise at least.

It was just a short stay at the Yellow Brick road and then off with Michelle driving into the forests and lakes of Oregon when we made for the town of Bend; the home of Jack, where he worked. There we stayed at a holiday house; it had about five bedrooms. Bend is situated on a pleasant river ideal for sport and fun. It is much used by holidaymakers and being the summer was at its best. I forget if it was on the way to or from Bend that we visited the Crater Lake National Park and Crater Lake and Devil's Lake. The former as you can imagine is situated hundreds of feet down in an extinct volcano's crater, Devil's was accessible and I did take a dip. Or was it at Elk lake I took the dip? The others didn't and when I entered the bracing waters I realised why.

Too soon it was time to make our way back to Portland where we stayed with Michelle's sister and her partner Brook, a lawyer, for two nights before he drove us to the airport. Alfreda and Drew were to go back with Michelle and Alex to San Antonio for a longer stay before returning to pick up Izzie from her grandma's at Bristol. For me it was a comfortable business class flight for me back to Hong Kong to arrive in time for me to prepare for an appeal to the Court of Appeal.

It was an appeal heard in the middle of August against conviction and sentence imposed on the young 'stateless' African who had been sentenced to 5 years and 7 months for trafficking in 30 kilograms of herbal cannabis from South Africa. I have mentioned his case in the previous chapter 25. You recall it was the case when the prosecutor took the unusual step of supporting my submission of no case to answer. The Appeal Court were not with me and clearly didn't like the idea of a prosecutor helping the defence. The appeal against conviction was dismissed with barely a word and we were given what is known in the profession as 'a hospital pass' on the sentence: an insignificant 6 months reduction.

At the end of August I was off again to Spa Samui to fast for 7 days. I lost about 9 kilo which I kept down for a month or so but this time on my second day back I noticed that there was numbness in my big left toe. I could feel pricks if I touched my feet with a point and there was still feeling in my big toes. I thought it may have been a trapped nerve and did not worry unduly but it remains with me today (October, 2013). It has never been conclusively diagnosed despite seeing private and government doctors. The most common view is type-two diabetes! I did see Dr Peter Ko who was the surgeon who installed my hip replacement at the Adventist Hospital in February 2009. He sent me for a scan of the left foot in which I see from the report mentions: Thickening around the ankle joint suggestive of underlying synovitis and underlying inflammatory atrophy is suggested! My local Doctor wrote a referral way back in June 2012 but that still has to be addressed properly by doctors at QM Hospital.

September. 2011 saw me defending an asylum seeker from Pakistan in the District Court charged with robbing a New Territories taxi driver. He was with three other culprits who had not been arrested. It occurred in the early hours of the morning and even though a weapon was not involved and the driver was not harmed the Judge sentenced him after trial to 5 years 6 months imprisonment. It certainly was not one of the worst type of Robberies. The driver made a report to police over his radio and the police were soon scouring the area looking for the culprits. I recall his defence was he had not stolen anything and was just with the others.

October 2011 was a High Court drugs case in which I defended a man from South America who was involved with a Nepalese man with trafficking cocaine in the Tsim Sha Tsui area. The evidence against my accused was strong whilst against the other man not so. I advised him that if he was willing to give a statement to the police and was willing to give evidence against the other accused it would certainly help reduce his sentence. He gave it some time to think about it. No one likes a grass and such people are always at some risk of harm within the prison, notwithstanding we generally have an efficient Correctional Service in Hong Kong. He agreed to make a statement and did so implicating his co-accused. The prosecution served, as they are bound to do, a copy on the co-accused's lawyer whereupon she asked for a short adjournment and came back saying her client would plead guilty.

It is well recognised by all involved with criminals and the criminal justice system that every encouragement must be made to get criminals turning on each other: the term is 'grassing them up.' My client was sentenced to twelve and half years. The amount of drug involved was 850 grammes and on the sentencing tariff for amounts 600 to 1200 grammes the sentence is 20 to 23 years. A full discount of one third is always allowed for a plea of guilty. Further discounts are given for those who assist the prosecution ranging from the more usual 40 to 50%, to as high as two thirds off the 'super grass'. I was thus disappointed when my man got only 40% off his sentence, which meant in effect a reward of only 6-7%, on top of the one third for his plea, for grassing up his co-accused. I advised him to appeal which he did.

Another counsel handled the appeal as I had already retired. I did however attend the appeal to hear it dismissed in a peremptory manner by the two judges.

My most important case of 2011 was the prosecution of gang of cocaine traffickers at the High Court. I had started to prepare the case in October and had a number of conferences with the OC Case, a senior inspector from the Hong Kong Police Narcotics Bureau (NB). The drugs: 70 kilograms of a mixture containing 57 kilograms of cocaine with a retail value at the time of 67 million Hong Kong dollars, were shipped from Paraguay hidden in a consignment of tiles packed together with thousands of others in a container. And sent via Germany on a Hapag Lloyd container ship to our Kwai Chung Modern Terminals. Here they were stored to be then loaded onto a vehicle and taken away. There were three accused to be tried: A Paraguay man whose name was on the bill of lading who had supervised the loading in South America and had come to the terminal to collect the consignment, a Chinese man who worked at Terminal as a loader/crane driver and the driver of the vehicle who had come to collect the goods.

As the preparation progressed it became apparent that only the Terminal man would plead not guilty. The other two had already pleaded guilty at the lower court and both were willing to give evidence to help the prosecution. As you may imagine the sentences with such a huge quantity of cocaine were going to be at the very top of the scale: 30 years! By pleading guilty and giving evidence they could expect significant discounts. (I dealt with this aspect above.) I didn't at first consider using either one or both of them to give evidence. But after discussion with those in the Legal Department decided to get proofs of evidence from both of them. The Paraguay man was able to help generally by describing to a jury how things were organised and how the drugs came here. I understand he also was able to supply intelligence to NB. The Chinese man was able to implicate the man maintaining his innocence by showing he knew what was in the crates of tiles and had been part of the plan before the consignment arrived.

It was not an easy case. I had no counsel to help me, and believe it or believe it not, instructing police officers sitting behind counsel were now not supposed to take a note for prosecuting counsel. It had always been the case, when I was in that position as a police officer and for most of my time at the bar in Hong Kong, that the police OC case, would, like a solicitor instructing counsel, assist by taking a note of the evidence. I therefore got a young first year law student to sit behind me and take as best as he could a note of the evidence

435

and things said in court by judge and counsel. The student was the son of a friend who I had been helping to make a start with the law. Sadly he was not going to make a go of it and was not much help in the trial. But a bad workman should not blame his tools. I know that a case like this in the UK would have had a silk (Queens Counsel) and one or two juniors assisting.

The trial started with a young Chinese lady counsel appearing for the remaining accused. I had never seen her before in the courts although I did recall she had sat as a temporary magistrate. She kept silent about her defence, as she was so entitled and gave no indication that she would object to any of the prosecution's evidence. She did cross-examine one of our key witnesses who was the manager of the Terminal and the direct boss of the man on trial. He clearly had been got at by the defence, answering all the leading questions put to him in the way she wanted. Which was to help his worker, distancing him from any guilty knowledge about what was in the consignment of tiles. I contemplated applying to treat him as a hostile witness, but such a course, in my experience, even if allowed by a Court, provides for the most part unreliable evidence. I decided to leave his evidence and to move on. The evidence from the Paraguay man came up to proof, was not challenged in cross-examination and helped the jury understand the background of the case.

The second tainted witness: the Chinese lorry driver proved to be an unexpected disaster for the prosecution. He came up to proof in his evidence in chief and did not stray from the statement he had made to the police. Whom he had approached seeking favourable treatment by giving evidence against the remaining co-accused. But a bombshell came when in cross-examination he was shown a letter which he agreed he had written at the Remand Prison. The letter was an exoneration of the accused's (the Terminals worker) involvement in the case. It accepted that it was he (the witness) who was the person who involved the accused not the other way round. The letter further said it was one of his friends who 'had' the batch of 70 kilos of coke which would be conveyed to Hong Kong and that he (the witness) would be paid $150,000 as long as he was able to arrange someone here to unpack the goods, show them to a foreigner and then hide them for about two weeks.

In re-examination of the witness he said he had copied an identical letter that the accused had written and then passed through a gap in their adjourning cells. And had then returned the letter and copy he had written to the accused. He said he agreed to copy the letter for no particular reason other than he was on good terms with the accused and had himself already pleaded guilty before the lower court. Sadly his evidence that the accused had said in prison on remand words like: "It cost $100,000 to take someone out in prison" was not supported in the evidence of the two police officers who had interviewed him in the remand prison.

This 'defence' was strengthened when a cellmate of the witness gave evidence as a defence witness saying that the witness had written the letter in his presence and had then given it to him to read. He said he had not read the letter because the same night he had attempted to commit suicide. It was not until later when he realised that the witness would give tainted evidence against the accused that he read the letter and came forward to help. I vigorously cross-examined this cellmate and put to him his substantial criminal record. He was in fact on remand awaiting trial for murder. At one stage he broke down in tears saying how could a man be so evil as to implicate an innocent man. That is my memory of it now, although alas I did not have much help with a full and proper note of the evidence when I was on my feet.

As can be imagined eyebrows went up from the judge on her bench to the jurors in their box. My blood pressure also went up a number of points.

The evidence certainly had the appearance of a contrived, clever, manufactured defence. The letter certainly looked as if it had been especially prepared for use in Court with terms like D2 (for Defendant 2). The fact that the accused had a brother who I understood was a serving police officer and importantly that the letter was never mentioned to the investigating team certainly added to my suspicion that his defence was recently manufactured.

The letter and the evidence of the cellmate was able to raise a real doubt as to the guilt of the accused and their verdict was 5 to 2 not guilty. Only 2 of them were against the verdict of not guilty.

The accused walked free and the two others were both given sentences with a starting point of 30 years but with a 50% discount for their early pleas guilty and for their assistance in giving evidence for the prosecution. Thus both were given 15 years imprisonment. I of course was not too happy with the full discount for the man who wrote the letter. But as the Judge said he did come up to proof and she was not prepared to make a distinction with the Paraguayan. Under the circumstances, I was of the view I could not say anything except advise his counsel, who came for the sentencing, as to what had happened. He mitigated for his client on the basis he had made a statement to the police and answered their questions and had given evidence against the accused as required by the prosecution.

At the end of day when I looked again at the evidence and the trial I realized that perhaps we would have won a conviction against this inside man at the Terminal without the tainted evidence of the Chinese accomplice. Should I have twigged that something was fishy? Should my instructing police officers have smelt a rat somewhere? I did feel somewhat depressed when I think of the investigative work across countries that must have gone into the trafficking of this huge and valuable consignment of cocaine worth: HK $ 67,000,000.

Hopefully NB gained intelligence on the syndicate involved in such an International operation with the Paraguayan in particular able to provide information. Two important members were locked up and the valuable consignment of drugs taken out of circulation. Although such a loss probably only affected the street price for a short time.

The week before Christmas saw me visiting an Asian lady at the Tai Lam Woman's Prison to take instructions regarding her trafficking in a half a kilogramme of heroin. She intended to plead guilty as charged. She came before High Court on the day before Christmas Eve and was sentenced on the tariff to nine and half years getting the full one third discount for a plea of guilty. I often wonder, rather cynically, as to why have counsel along at all for such cases. The Court of Appeal has stated often enough that such sentences are based on following strictly the appropriate tariff for the type and quantity of the particular drug. Perhaps understandably matters like: good character, youth, age, gender, background, health, foreignness and background are not grounds for mitigation. I have only known one case and one judge in all my nearly 30 years: Judge Joe Duffy who did not follow the tariff strictly and did allow for my plea in mitigation. For whatever reason I have since never been able to find that particular case in the Law Reports.

Christmas soon followed a time which has always been special for me with church, the message, the carols and music being a lovely part. Of course the best was Christmas day with Alfreda, Drew and baby Isabel, now 2 and full of fun. Boxing day was around at my friend Angus's place with his lady Pam and other friends.

# 27. From Yon Far Country Blows

The lease for Convention Chambers at Unit B, 18th floor, China Overseas Building,139 Hennessey Road was due to expire at the end of September, 2012 and I was starting to wonder how much longer I would be up to the stress of handling some of the professional work that came my way. A barrister's life does not get easier as you age. In fact the longer in the legal tooth you become the more difficult are the cases that are given to you; that usually means trials in the High Court and the District Court: prosecuting or defending criminal cases. In my early days I did dabble a bit in some non-criminal work but clearly my long time as a policeman catching criminals and my involvement in their trials directed me to a 100% criminal practice. You don't get nice little jobs in the Magistracy or simple short trials when you are a senior junior (if that does not make sense only a 'silk': in the UK a QC or here a SC, can be called a senior counsel). No, you get all the difficult ones, especially if your practise is largely funded by Prosecutions or Legal Aid. The highly paid private work usually goes to those with connections to the larger solicitors firms who have their favourite SCs who bring with them their own juniors. A recent criminal case involving a foreigner charged with murder which was privately funded, as opposed to one by the Director of Legal Aid, had two SCs, one a QC from the UK and three junior counsel. If it had been on legal aid it is likely one junior counsel would have been assigned. I suppose my practise involved rarely more than 20% private work. .

I was also becoming cynical in regard to my attitude towards some in my profession who sat on the bench. That cannot be healthy. You must have faith in the system you are there as an officer of the court to uphold. You must remember to 'Yes My Lord', 'No My Lord', to people who may glare down at you as if you are unclean. Oh the difference when you prosecute! The deference you are given in comparison to the scowls and frowns when there for the baddies. It may be that in youth you are stronger and the slings and arrows bounce off, especially so when you can turn them into amusing stories over a few ales with your brothers in law after work. But you learn over the years the terrible responsibility you have; often as a lone counsel, it is only you that can keep the innocent or the less than guilty for being put away for years. It was my observation in my time in the Police and at the Bar that Judges in the Colonial service in Hong Kong and elsewhere always had their eye on possible rebellion and disturbance in their colonies. Sentences in my police days and early days at the bar were lighter when our Judges were colonially grown i.e. did not come from English bench. The last 20 years saw much heavier sentences often, to my mind, coming from a few particular Judges from the English bench who seemed to have lost their compassion and humanity. This atmosphere has come down from the Court of Appeal. I am not alone when I note that there is a feeling that you get a better result from an all-Chinese bench.

As you may have realised that perhaps I have had enough. My health was deteriorating, what with my lower back pain, a permanent numb left foot and joint pain in the hip and knees.

Was I able, as I am supposed to do, to take like a taxi driver, all the fares that came along? We are not, as far as I am aware, professionally allowed to take only the cases we want. We are there for all to represent without fear or favour. Do I hear laughter? If I do then it is sad.

So I was not going to do much in 2012.

Despite my friends in the profession and the fun we had after work with a few drinks and the banter about cases and personalities and my liking and respect for many men and women on the bench. I decided that I would retire or greatly reduce my practice. I would not in any event join my colleagues in seeking a new lease.

I would do little this year. My notes show that I was assigned in February a High Court prosecution. This was another drug case involving two Urdu speaking Pakistani men. I had two conferences with the police OC case and gave him advice and instructions concerning the need to adduce at trial fresh evidence. I also passed on instructions from the Judge regarding the recorded interviews, with their translations, from the two men, which she had raised with me at a pre-trial review. Another pre-trial review was set down for August and the trial set down for 23 days on the 10th September, 2012. I did, however, return the brief in plenty of time to the Director of Pubic Prosecutions for re-assignment way before this date. I had decided to retire.

In February I flew off to Kuala Lumpur, Malaysia to stay for a week with my dear friends Ian and Dorothy Brown. They have been friends of my family for 25 years since they started going to our church: The Methodist International Church, Kennedy Road, Wanchai.

They introduced me to some lovely friends they had made in KL and of course there was no shortage of great food. Ian drove us around and there was a nice trip, which included a stop off at a Military Museum, to Malacca. Their home, with its own gym and swimming pool, is delightful. It is just down the road from the King of Malaysia's palace. An up-market area with a comfortable watering hole just a few yards walk away down a hill.

I was in the District Court at the end of April the beginning of May prosecuting a Filipina for a serious immigration offence. She ran an employment agency which had been charged with assisting others to breach their condition of stay and conspiracy to defraud, namely to submit false documents and to make false statements for visa applications.

Unlike the UK where I understand the Border Security Service is not fit for purpose, our Immigration Service seems to be on top of things and with firm but fair prosecution, together with sentences which deter, have stopped HK descending into the mire experienced there. That is evidenced by illegal immigrants, in figures of 100's of thousands living and working in the country.

There were two Filipina defendants before the court, one pleaded guilty and I used her to give evidence against the other. My opponent for the defence was James Collins who was my boss for the two years when I worked at the City Polytechnic. A decent and honourable man married to a Filipino court

Tagalog interpreter. I know he was involved with the church and charitable work with the Philippine community here.

I advised him counsel to counsel that the evidence was strong against his client and I had no reason to doubt the co-accused's evidence would come up to proof. He shook his head and I understood he had to fight on. The trial concluded and the Judge set a date down for the verdict and sentence of the other accused. I had to ask the Judge and those instructing me (the DPP) if I could return the brief as I was booked to fly to the UK before that date. This was allowed and I sent the papers back to the DPP. I learnt later that the first accused who gave evidence for the prosecution got a 50% discount and was sentenced to 1 year and 10 months. The other one who pleaded not guilty was sentenced to 3 years 8 months.

I went off to the England on the 13th May, 2012. As before in 2010 I flew KLM to Norwich via Amsterdam. As mentioned before I don't feel safe or comfortable arriving at Heathrow. I was met by my sister and her family; husband George and her daughter Belinda, the solicitor. They took me to the place I had stayed before: The Park Farm Hotel at Hethersett in acres of lovely countryside but not far from the City of Norwich. There was a bus stop not far away and a 20-minute ride took you there. There was an indoor swimming pool which I used every day. My niece was also a member of the leisure club that use the facilities. There was a nice bar with plenty of pleasant sit out areas. The food, for me the breakfast was great: kippers or smoked haddock or a cholesterol fry up.

Unfortunately I was only booked in for a few days and there were no bookings, at least at the rate I was given, for longer.

Also my sister lived at Saham Toney near Watton about 23 miles away on the Norwich road. Here my niece Belinda had moved back to live at her home which was a converted windmill.

I had a few days in the city of Norwich exploring around visiting the museum of the Norfolk Regiment and the Cathedral. Did I go to matins this time? I am not sure.

Scott is the husband of Belinda, an American citizen but English by accent and culture. It seems he has lived most of his life in England although one parent is an American. He suggested I move to accommodation at the Richmond Park golf club where he plays and is a member. This is situated between Saham Toney and Watton only about 20 minutes walk to the windmill. My sister's place at 5 Neville Close behind, St.George's Parish Church is not far away. The holiday apartments at the golf club were comfortable with a living room downstairs and bedroom upstairs. I slept on a divan downstairs the joints getting a bit bad for the climb, especially after a few jars of ale and or bottles of red 'plonk'. I also had a stove and fridge and it was 50% cheaper than Park Farm. I recall the previous time I had visited my sister I had stayed at the Broom Hall country hotel in Saham Toney but had been dissatisfied when the owner looked askance at me when I asked to check my internet. Don't you have a lap top, we have 'wifi' but there are no facilities for you to use our terminal.

I also have in my memory using two other places to stay when last in Norwich: I recall the small B&B Station Hotel, and across the river from it, on the other side by the bridge in Prince of Wales Street, the Premier Inn. Were they used this time or in 2010 or sometime before? Does it matter to my readers? I would suggest not, but all this memory testing does help me stave off early dotage! My stay in Norfolk this time was divided into two parts. The first was from when I got of the plane until about 10 days later when I went off across country to stay with my friends Bob and Helen in Bridgnorth, Shropshire. I was in Shropshire for another 10 or so days before I returned to Norfolk again via London to spend the rest of my holiday before flying back to Hong Kong from Norwich airport via Amsterdam.

My time in Norfolk was joie de vivre with the days fully occupied with trips to interesting places and some good eating and drinking in English pubs. I forget now in which order the visits were and whether they were made in the first or second half of the 30 day holiday. I did not keep a record and can only rely on my memory which, of course, is helped by the electronic memory jogger in front of me now: the Worldwide internet web. Some days I would go off by myself other times it was with Jill and George in their car or with Belinda and family in her larger people carrier. My base was the golf club.

One day after breakfast I walked down to the market of Watton to catch a bus to take me to Thetford which is to the south near the border with the county of Suffolk. Watton I would visit often, it had a nice pub and restaurant and a public library with free internet cafe, which I used to send and answer my e-mails. From Watton to Thetford it was only about 35 minutes on the number 81 bus. Thetford and the area around has an interesting history. It was the centre for the royal palace of Boadicea, Queen of the Iceni. Who in the middle of the first century Anno Domini (AD) took on the Romans, when the Governor

447

Suetonius was off with legions bashing up the druids on Anglesey, North Wales. She raised an army from her tribe and the one next door after the Romans had flogged her and raped her two daughters. She gave a good hiding to the Legio IX Hispana (recruited presumable from the bars on the Costa Brava!) whereupon Suetonius returned, with three legions from punishing the druids and their fellow human sacrifice adherents, to sort things out. There was a huge scrap at the Battle of Watling Street, where it is believed 70 to 80 thousand Romans and Celts were slaughtered, although one report written soon after says only 400 Romans were killed; trained and disciplined troops over savages! Boadicea and her girls fought well and it is reported that the Queen killed herself rather than suffer disgrace and further indignities.

There was further bloodshed there nearly a thousand years later when in the 9th AD wild Danish Vikings invaded the land of the East Angles and brutally slayed their King Edmund. He later became Saint Edmund as it appears a number of Christian rulers were so beatified after resisting and being slain by these heathens from across the sea.

I walked around the town and to be honest did not find that much to interest me. I walked along the Little Ouse river and the Thet which flows into it.

I have mentioned in other chapters the journeys I have made by rail and readers will have noted how pleasurable I find it travelling on the ground, seeing the countryside as you go, being able to walk about on the train and on some even to have food and drink. Norfolk is blessed with a number of small lines, some run privately by enthusiasts and two other by British Rail.

These are the Bittern line which runs from Norwich north, then along the coast to Sherringham. The other, the Wherry line goes from Norwich to Great Yarmouth and Lowestoft, both on the coast facing east and the North Sea. Both lines go through some delightful countryside and pass through or stop at some quaint little towns and villages. Cromer of the Bittern line has a nice beach and is more of a resort town. Much of the rest of the North coast seemed, at least to the western end, to be sand dunes and salt marsh with many furlongs, perhaps miles, to reach the sea. Where the breakers looked pretty rough. I took a trip on the Bittern train with Jill and George and we got off at Sheringham, it was only about an hours ride. We stayed there just a short while and got the train back to Norwich.

Another day we took the Wherry line to Lowestoft. The line divides at Reedham with one line going North to Great Yarmouth and the other South to Lowestoft. I recall a trip to Great Yamouth on my 2010 visit to Norfolk. Great Yarmouth is a large seaside resort with a beach and all the fun of the fair. It has a major shopping centre with some major department stores. Lowestoft which I did this time, was once the centre of a thriving fishing fleet This was when we were allowed to catch fish and the North sea and beyond had them to catch. There was still a harbour but I understand that now there were just a handful of fishing boats. There were no more the trawlers busy here up to the 1960s going up to the fishing grounds around Iceland and beyond. Although I did not see much evidence of it, Lowestoft has a tourism industry. There is a nice beach with all the facilities. But I did not walk down to the southern part of the town where these were situated. We stayed around the harbour where we found a place to drink on an old converted sailing barge. We also later found a place for fish and chips not far away on the sea front.

That raised the question with me: If we had no fishing industry any more where do we get all our fish. Our national dish may now be chicken tikka, but fish and chips (cod, haddock, rock eel, rock salmon, hake, huss, whiting even) is still a favourite with the old fashioned Brits like me. So where does the fish come from? I understand there are plenty of pirates, mainly from countries far from our shores, who don't seem to worry about rules and conventions regarding fishing.

There are stories of factory ships which scour the seas with 'fishing' equipment like giant vacuum cleaners that just suck up everything. Those too small or not liked as food are just dumped, dead or alive back into the sea. Then there are drift nets, especially in the Pacific ocean that extend for 10's of miles catching everything, from sea mammals like dolphins to creatures that probably have yet to be given a name by marine scientists.

I had my cod and chips, it certainly tasted like it used to when I was last a resident of Mother England. Perhaps it was the naughty Icelanders or Faroese who sneaked it into Britain for Billingsgate fish market, or has that gone as well?

Lowestoft is right to the south of the Norfolk broads with all their lovely rivers and lakes, most of them navigable. On another day George drove us around the Broads, but I can't remember the places we visited. I have looked at the map and pictures on the internet but they have not jogged my memory as to where we went one day for a boat ride and after had a nice pub lunch.

George also took us to Sandringham Estate, which comprises the House, 24 acres of country park and a museum. As you may have gathered I am a fierce supporter of the monarch and have great affection for our Queen. As daft as this sounds, on my leaves from the colonial police I would, as soon as possible after arriving back to London, go to Buckingham Palace. I would look up at the balcony, where the Queen and the Duke on important occasions would come out to give all a wave, and report back.

OK its time to take him away!

Sandringham has great vehicle museum and you are able to look at part of the house, including the place where HM keeps her few baubles, bangles and beads; gifts from heads of state and other worthies.

It is about 6 miles from Sandringham to Kings Lynn, another old town with a wealth of history. I am not sure if I visited there this time or before in 2010. I know I was very interested in the old police court, station and lock up and some of the buildings connected with the City when in the middle ages it was a the most important port in England. And was closely connected to the North European trading cartel: the Hanseatic League. The town still has two warehouses which are the only remaining Hanseatic buildings in Britain. There is also the Trinity Guildhall which dates to the 15th century and purports to be the largest and oldest guildhall in the country. Also there are the remnants of the old defensive wall that surrounded the town.

There was also a great lunch at the Globe, a J.D. Wetherspoon's Hotel, that had their usual splendid array of real ales and food at reasonable prices. Which are often 20% or more down on prices in other public houses. I recall the first Wetherspoons opening in Colney Hatch lane just down from Muswell Hill. I visited there, it must have in the late 70's or early 80's. The name and style of pub with its excellent real British food and Ale at fair prices became so popular that by the 2000s they were all over the country. There were few places where they didn't have a pub or hotel. Sometime they took over historic buildings, like the Globe which dated back to the 17th century, other times they converted premises that had been High Street shops, like the old Woolworth's store in High Barnet where I use to go with my friend Barney Humphris.

Belinda lent me one of her cars and I drove north to Hillington, not far from Sandringham, to visit my old school friend Roger Crouch. You may recall I had mentioned him earlier about our bicycle trip, as 15 year-olds, down to Lands End and back. I had not seen him for more than 30 years. I was impressed with his large bungalow and in particular his workshop where he repaired antique watches. I invited them for lunch and we went to a real quaint rural pub where the landlord was Chinese. I was so embarrassed when I found I had left my wallet in a hand bag in the car which I had left at his home. So Pip his wife ended up paying the bill.

I enjoyed driving Belinda's car. It must have been when we were living in Wales that I last owned or driven a car. I have never driven in Hong Kong since leaving in 1980 to go to study in Wales and the only vehicles I have driven since coming back to Hong Kong in 1985 have been the occasional motorcycle that I hire when I go on my fasting jaunts to Thailand. I enjoyed being back behind the wheel; it was a nice car, powerful enough to feel secure when overtaking. The drive to Hillington was along some pleasant country roads and I recall I went through the old Georgian town of Holt where they have a really splendid bakers with all those lovely English and local cakes and buns.

Belinda worked, usually and unless she had a case in London, a four day week, so during the long weekends she would show us around and join us for drinks and dinner at the various country pubs; many full of historic character. In Watton there was at the end of the High Street, the Willow House; a 16th Century Inn, serving really good food. If my memory serves me correctly I did spend a night or two there B&B. Nearer to home for Jill and George was the Old Bell at Saham Toney another old Pub selling good local ales, with a regular pub quiz, which we as a family took part. I recall that with many of the questions on pop music, band groups and films I was not very good. I think our team came third or fourth much to the surprise of my sister Jill who is usually good at these quizzes. Belinda took us to the quaint village of Hingham where she has her solicitor's office and showed us around. The place is convenient for her as it is only a few miles down the road from her home at the Windmill at Saham Toney.

One Sunday I was there at Saham Toney I attended the morning service at St George's Parish Church. Which is situated near the privately owned mere which has a history going back to the Ice Age. The church has parts going back to the 14th century. It was a pleasant Anglican service following the Book of Common Prayer, with which, despite my years attending a Methodist church, I am familiar. The congregation was small by Hong Kong standards, 40 at best, compared to 300 to 350 at each of two services at our church in Kennedy road. The vicar was a lady, who must have been a grandma. I was interested to note many in the congregation were retirees from London who, like my, sister had fled the new multi culture: my reading tells me now only 40% of London have English as their first language. A change which has been huge and so rapid to come about. I remember as a 9 year school boy going with the Church Street Junior School to visit the Tower of London. The class were photographed – which I have somewhere – all the children were white; today if the same class were photographed there would probably be only one or two white faces and they may be from Poland.

My mind goes to history of our Islands. The Romans left Hadrian's Wall in 409 AD and by the next year 410 had left the Provincia Britania (Roman Britain) entirely. They left behind a Celtic people romanised with many speaking Latin as there first language. Roman Britain was at its height in the middle of the second century AD (AD 150). There were cities connected by surfaced and maintained roads. The country was peaceful, prosperous and safe. It was protected by Roman legions, some of its men must have included replacements locally recruited. There was Hadrian's Wall to the North to guard against the wild and painted Picts. There were patrols on the East coast both by galleys and from shore watch-towers to guard against the Germanic wild men from across the North sea. The equally wild Scoti from Ireland were always a threat with their plundering and enslaving people in settlements to the West and South West. They were contained by garrisons at forts in North and South Wales and in the South of England at Ilchester and Exeter. The Provincia produced corn to feed Rome and there were hides and minerals to be exported like tin.

The Romans were here for over 400 years and there must have been times (I recall the words of Prime Minister MacMillan in the late 1950's) when Eppillus said to Antedios whilst they were in the stands of the Amphitheatre at Eboracum (York) watching the gladiatorial games. Eppy to Anty: 'Eh lad **we've never had it so good'.**' Yeh Eppy, But I thought that brown job from Syria should have clobbered that the big red headed bugger from Gaul in the first round.'

Within about 60 and no more than 100 years after the Romans had left the Saxons, Angles and Jutes had taken over all of the East and South of England. They were up as far North as Strathclyde and were pushing what was left of the Roman Britons into Wales, Cornwall and across the Channel into Brittany. The roads, so well built, soon started to break up and the villas and town dwellings were often broken by the pagan immigrants to use to build their own hovels. There must have been some miscegenation with the Britons who would have been enslaved. Although there is no great evidence that the indigenous people put up much of a fight against the invaders. There are the stories of Hengist and Horsa, Saxon mercenaries who were recruited by Vortigen, a Celtic chieftain around AD 450, to help fight the Pictish raiders. It would be years before Christianity and some culture returned, ironically from across the Irish sea from the followers of St Patrick who had earlier been taken as a slave from the West of England by Scoti raiders.

400 years of, for the most part good governance, some rights and some freedom. The invaders changed that in a man's life-time.

I look now at the country of my birth and see the British life, culture, civilisation and values similarly changing; not by violent migration but by massive immigration from peoples whose culture and values are as different to ours as those were between Roman British Celts and the pagan Saxons from across the North Sea. Our new immigrants, from the 1950s to now, come not with weapons to overwhelm but with babies. They have 4 to 5 children, whereas the average English family has 1 perhaps 2. A look at the schools and maternity wings of the hospital in the cities show what is to come. Should we be concerned? Apparently not. We are not even allowed to express any view on immigration. In the UK it is taboo. Quite ordinary folk who protest about some devaluing of our culture or the loss of their rights are branded fascists or as members of the extreme right. While our new people many with their beards, some with faces full of hate, regard anyone who does not believe in Jihad as fair game, for vilification at best and at worse, well I better not say any more at the risk of prosecution. Our police as agents of Satan are pilloried with verbal abuse and inflammatory posters and banners which to my mind, as a policeman and lawyer for 50 years, warrants at least arrest and prosecution for behaviour likely to cause a Breach of the Peace. That would be a start, but there are many other offences more serious that are on the statue books.

Did any of the Roman Britons follow their colonial masters to Rome? It would not have done much good as it was not long before Italy like Britain had been overrun by Germanic invaders, like the Goths, Vandals and Franks. But there was, at least, the Pope and the Roman Catholic church!

It does seem there are many now who see the writing on the wall and are leaving for the Antipodes and Canada. Politicians tell us there us there is no problem as immigration in is matched by migration out. Oh I see!

I see I have got hopelessly off tract and will get back to my late spring break in England.

After 10 days or so in Norfolk it was off by train from to Norwich across country west to Peterborough where Barney and Marilynne Humphris were waiting for me for a weekend up at the 18th century Spa Town of Buxton, set in the lovely Peak District. I mention that the train was packed with people standing. In my view – the way the carriages were designed – it was dangerously overloaded. I raised this with the Indian guard who, perhaps understandably said: 'Well what can I do?' This was not a commuter train.

The UK may have been the first with a railway system and was responsible for developing many of the world's railways. But alas was now in the Stone Age in regard to that best way of transporting people and goods. Look at China: a high-speed rail system covering the entire country in 13 or so years (2000-2013). The railway man behind this amazing development was so energetic in pushing his lines through mountains and everywhere that he was called Lunatic Liu. He is now in prison for corruption involving amounts which went beyond fair remuneration but were not huge in a western perspective. In England he would have been put in the House of Lords and in the US made so much that he would have been able to buy his way into Congress.

In any event I got to Peterborough and there was Barney waiting with his powerful Saab car. We drove up to Buxton through some delightful countryside and checked in to the Buckingham Hotel. Barney was familiar with Buxton and had already booked our room. It was a four star hotel with an old fashion restaurant serving a good British breakfast, not yet proscribed by Health and Safety laws.

I had not seen them for what must have been 4 years when I had stayed with them at their home in Barnet and we had a break up at Cheadle in Staffordshire. Where we had indulged ourselves with Barney's pastime of riding on small volunteer run railways, in that case the Churnet Valley Railway. I always try and see Barney and Marilynne when I come to the UK. As I have mentioned before they are dear friends and would keep an eye on my children when they were in the UK finishing their education. When I did come I would usually stay with them for while and these visits nearly always included trips out on railways, National or privately run volunteer lines.

So again at Buxton, after dinner at a Thai restaurant in the town, a comfortable kip at the hotel and a leisurely breakfast, it was off to ride on another railway. I forget the name of it. I do recall it went, albeit for a short distance, along a river and through some pretty countryside.

Barney then drove me South to Shropshire to Bridgnorth where I was to stay with my friends Bob and Helen Sones. Bob had been in the Royal Hong Kong Police, although we had never worked together. He had a home, like me, in Discovery Bay, Hong Kong and we often met, drank and ate together. He is a Midlander who grew up in Wolverhampton and proudly boasts of his time at that old and respected Wolverhampton Grammar School which I visited when I stayed with him in 2010.

His home is just a stones throw from the Bridgnorth terminus of the Severn Valley Railway. Which is one of the oldest and best of the volunteer run railways. It runs along the Severn about 30 miles, a joy of countryside, to Kidderminster where you can join up with National rail. At the Bridgnorth station there is a really great pub with a marvellous selection of beer and cider; a place for all the old real ale addicts. Barney dropped me off here, stayed for a pint with Bob and I before shooting off to London. Bob and Helen made me very welcome but I sensed that after about 10 days they were understandably looking for me to move on. Helen is Hong Kong Chinese, who like my Diana did, suffers from Parkinson's disease.

As I have appreciated with guests, it is not uncommon to have a sense of relief when they say it is time to go. Even easy old fart type guests who want nothing more than a good boozer and a good pork pie can get on your nerves when you and your family want time to themselves. But dear Bob and Helen made me really welcome. I went to the local Methodist church on Sunday with Helen. About 30 people in the congregation. Bob dares not go into church for fear of a bolt from heaven giving him one for all his sins. He, as he does with St Andrews Church in Tsim Sha Tsui, takes Helen there and meets her after. It was a pleasant service and I was able able to exercise my lungs with a few rousing hymns.

One day Bob drove me to the splendid RAF museum at Cosford. I love museums, especially any thing to do with our Empire history and its soldiers. I was there about three hours before Bob came back for me.

Another day he drove me to Shrewsbury, where I used to own a house, for some business he had to attend. Bob deals in stamps and memorabilia which he buys and sells from dealers at shops and fairs. He seems to do well, bringing them back to sell in Hong Kong. Chinese stamps are, he says, now the things to have, as the new China, with an emerging well off middle class, has the money to indulge in expensive 'hobbies.' Whilst there I looked at the museum at the Castle and I visited the church of St Mary the Virgin at the St Mary's Place, opposite the old Victorian hospital which is situated in the heart of Shrewsbury.

I returned to Shrewsbury again myself on another day, when I caught the 436 bus for the hours journey there through some interesting towns and country. I walked from the bus station up the hill to the Railway Station where I took the train to Ludlow. You will recall from previous chapters that my parents and I had a home there: At Westminster cottage, Bell lane; a listed property 300 years old. I visited the St Laurence Church which is a very large building and is purported to be the largest parish church in the country. It is as large as some Cathedrals. The ashes of my dear mother are buried there under a stone in the graveyard. It always takes a bit of gardening with a trowel to clear the grass from the stone and give it a clean showing her name and dates of life : 2nd January,1909 to 3rd February, 1977.

I laid flowers and talked to her giving our news of her grandchildren and great granddaughter. I sat in the lovely church for about 30 minutes, talked to God and thanked him, or is it her, for my life and Mum's and of those so dear to me. I just sat there, as I often do in an ancient church and pictured in my mind all the folk who had come through the ages to worship, seek help and refuge there, through civil wars, and wars with our neighbours across the channel. I am so conscious of the place our faith and the Christian church has, and has had, on our lives; the very essence of our British culture.

I had lunch at one of the splendid and ancient pubs in the town. I had a pint of Ansell's mild beer; mild beer still typical of the Midlands. I looked around the farmers market, who were fortuitously in town that day, before I caught the train back to Shrewsbury; another hour or so's pleasant ride by the Shropshire hills. Then it was a short break and a look around the Darwin Shopping centre before getting on the 436 bus for Bridgnorth.

A couple of days or more in Bridgnorth then it was off again to Shrewsbury on the 436 bus. There I caught a taxi to take me to the Mercure Albrighton Hall Spa and Hotel about 6 miles North of Shrewsbury. Helen had found the place and booked me in there, perhaps, after 10 days, eager to move me on! I recall that as a barely adequate thank you, I took Helen and Bob and their neighbours for a dinner in the local Chinese restaurant. An exceedingly pleasant evening.

Albrighton Hall was fine: an indoor swimming pool, sauna and steam, lovely grounds, a lake and gardens and typical, slightly dated, charming restaurants and bar. Oh! and my room, spacious, lovely bed and all 'mod cons' was not bad either!

I saw my old friend Richard Howse, another friend from the RHKP who I had got to know through Bob Sones. On my trip to the England in 2010 I had stayed with him and his lovely Okinawan wife at his home at Milton Keynes. Then we had gone down together one evening to a pub in London's West End for the monthly gathering of the RHKP Association.

Richard has connections with Wolverhampton where his father still lives and who he regularly visits. My recollection is he picked me up from the Albrighton Hotel and took me the 20 miles to the Albrighton Railway Station where I took the train to Wolverhampton and the fast train to London, Euston.

My purpose for coming to London was take the medals of my great uncle George, that lovely man I mentioned way back in Chapter 2 of these memoirs. I was given the medals by one of my great aunts decades ago and had kept them in the same ancient 4711 Eau De Cologne box ever since. My interest in medals and my membership in 2010 of the Orders and Medals Research Society Hong Kong prompted me to have these medals properly mounted. They included two Military Medals for Gallantry, which are only one down from the Victoria Cross, won during Western front in 1914 and 16, plus the Mon's Star with clasp and Boer War medals. I have always been very proud of these and decided to take them to the specialist coins, stamps, bonds, medals and orders people :Spink and Son,

462

founded in 1666 (They must have started dealing in fire sales!?) at the smart shop in Southampton Row, Bloomsbury.

I took a black cab from the Station. I knew it was only a mile or so away, but I was only in London a matter of hours and was not up to walking with all my joint problems. The taxi driver, who as black cab drivers are famous for their 'Knowledge test', must have been driving illegally because she had not heard of Spink and I had to tell her in which direction it was, then she managed to boost her fare by taking me around the houses.

Spink was impressive with a smart lady receptionist. You could feel tradition and history as you walked in. I stated my purpose and after a short time in the waiting saw a Mr Ian Copson who took the medals and told me they would be ready in about three months and would post them to me in Hong Kong. I was about thirty minutes in the shop. I caught a taxi outside who took me to Liverpool Street Railway Station where I took the train back to Attleborough, Norfolk where I was met by George – my Brother-in-Law – who took me back to stay at the Richmond Park Golf club for a few more busy and enjoyable days, before I went off back to Hong Kong, again on KLM via Amsterdam.

You note that from arriving at Euston to leaving at Liverpool Street I was in London just a matter of hours. This time, as also in 2010, I spent no time at all in London. My family are Londoners: my Mum and Dad were both born in London and spent all of their lives there, except for the short period during the war. My mother did, however, spend much of her childhood in South Wales where she learnt a fair bit of Welsh. Although I was born in Shropshire I was a Londoner arriving at the age of 4 or 5 and going to schools there. I had a cockney voice, which over the years I realised didn't help me much in regard to my image as Inspector in the Colonial police and a Barrister at the English and Hong Kong Bar. I am, however, a good mimic and can speak most of our Island dialects reasonably well. I can speak like a Jock, a Taff, a Mick or someone from Brummagem and also like an Officer and Gentleman. I can do the right thing with my vowels, from the clipped short ones of our Prince Charles and co, to the more longer sounds made with the mouth opened wider with the head raised above the lower orders to whom you are talking.

I mention this because if you go to London now you will rarely hear the London voice on the buses or Tube (underground trains). As hard on the ear as it was, Cockney English and its rhyming slang was London. As mentioned above I read in worthy papers that only 40% of London today have English as their first language. 60% identify themselves as coming from other lands, where presumably much of their culture and loyalty lie. The London Cockney is now extinct and is only seen in fantasy programmes on the television like East Enders, where attempts seem to be made to reassure people that those wonderful Londoners of the Blitz, like my great aunts, who stood fast against the Nazi menace, are still around. OK perhaps those portrayed in East Enders are hardly wonderful people and perhaps I am dreaming of people that were never there.

I arrived back in Hong Kong on the 12th June, 2012, in time to deal with defending a Chinese man for Trafficking in 63 grammes of Heroin which he had taken across the border. He pleaded guilty and admitted the facts of the case. There was little for me to do. The sentence was based on the tariff which was 8 years for that amount of drugs, plus an enhancement for bringing the drugs across the border, minus a third off for the plea of guilty. In fact as I have already said, rather cynically, there is little point in Legal Aid paying for a counsel at all in such cases. Whatever he says does not make any difference. I may have futilely remarked to the judge that surely the sentences are heavy enough without having any enhancement.

My last case after fifty years of dealing with criminals since I joined the Northern Rhodesia Police on the 28tth February, 1962, was another drug case. This time it was before Deputy Judge Mr. Justice Stuart-Moore. It was nearly half a kilo of ketamine found on a Chinese man on a train that had left the Lo Wu Railway Station. Although it would have been obvious that the drug must have come across the border the facts of the case did not state that. Accordingly I had the temerity to submit that if the prosecution had not bothered to expressly plead the cross border aggravation the Judge should not enhance the sentence. "Its obvious it did" says the Judge and enhances the sentence.

And that was it. What a piece of glory for me to go out with!

Sadly later as the end of the lease at Convention chambers drew near there was a misunderstanding with my dear friend Chris Grounds and I over subscriptions. I allowed myself to lose my temper to a degree which was not healthy for me and perhaps disturbing to Chris and our dear clerk Cindy who was within hearing. I am a person who always pays his way, dues and with my career coming to an end, the accusation that I had not hit a raw nerve and I flipped. I displayed a degree of anger that was totally wrong. I knew then, that decision to leave practice, as displayed in my resignation letter to the core members of chambers in May, 2012, was the right one. I did toy with idea of finding a door tenancy in another chambers but realized that I had been, with 20 years in Convention chambers, too long to start somewhere else. I sent my practising certificate back to the Bar Association in September. The outstanding pro -bono appeal I have mention before I gave to the junior who had helped me prepare it.

I sat behind him to assist some months later in the Court of Appeal only to hear him get hauled over the coals and the appeal thrown out by Mr Justice Lunn. Who seemed to glare at me as if I was wrong to have even contemplated an appeal.

Thank goodness this was all behind me now.

What was I to do?

I close this Chapter with a word concerning my health. As I have indicated, I have over the years tried to keep fit, or as fit as could be expected. I have drunk too much for most of my life and during the last 7 or so years in Discovery Bay have not gone many days without a few pints of cider or a bottle of red wine. During the last year or so and especially since I had my hip replacement operation in February, 2009, conducted by the orthopaedic surgeon Dr. Peter Ko, my walking has not been good and I have not been able to cover the distance I use to. Before I would, at least once a week, walk from Discovery Bay over to Mui Wo. I tried usually to walk up and down from my flat to the ferry and the Plaza; not a difficult walk but one requiring some effort going up the steep steps. Now I can barely manage walking down and usually wait for the bus for both journeys. I have, however been able to keep up my swimming routine: going at least twice a week to do 50 to 60 lengths at the Residents clubs here in Discovery Bay. But around August to September last year (2012) I found I was getting breathless on the tenth length. This really affected my confidence and I thought it must be that my motor was not working properly. I went to see the cardiologist: Dr Walter Chen, in private practice. He on the 11th September at the Adventist hospital, performed a coronary angiogram and inserted a stent where he found a blockage. I felt OK for a few days and my swimming resumed. However in November I started getting breathless again and was concerned about my heart. I had another coronary angiogram at the Queen Mary Hospital, a government hospital. Although you don't get much feedback as a government patient I understand the stent had not fallen out and that the heart was still working! Another test organised by my local GP: Dr Simon Siu, showed my lungs were OK. He prescribed a steroid puffer and my breathing improved. At least for a while but this last year I felt I was really slowing up and was getting unsteady on my feet. But I am 70 for Goodness sake or I was on the 29th April 2013 (I am writing this now Autumn 2013) and have not looked after myself really since Diana died. And old bones are not in my family: Mum was 68 and Dad 73 when they died.

Of course I have plenty still to do, places in this wonderful world to visit, concerts to attend and my family to enjoy. At the time of writing, although down in the dumps with my knees and back crippling me, I am full of joy for the granddaughter that comes on or about Christmas day this year when Michelle gives birth in San Antonio, Texas. And in March for Alfreda and twins, genders not yet known, due in March next year.

Wow what a lot to look forward to.

What blessings!!!

I suppose that wraps up: "Grandchild of Empire."

Over and Out!


PS They are twin boys. Praise the Lord!

Samuel David and Joseph Albert

Born 7th March 2014

Samuel: 7.43 am – 2.34 kgs
Joseph: 7.44 am – 2.65 kgs

PPS Not forgetting

Nathalie Charlotte, 27th November 2013 at 1.27pm, 2.31 kgs.

# Appendix

I dedicate these memoirs to my beloved wife Diana a woman I feel I let down as a husband, but who was a strength to me and whom I deeply loved and admired. She came to UK, landing at Heathrow in the Autumn of 1980, as a young Chinese girl, who was born, raised, educated and spent her working life in Hong Kong. I met her, a man to whom she had only been married for a little over two years, at the airport. She had our son on a sling carried on her front and our daughter in a sling on her back: a four month and a 27 month year old. She thus had born our two children in a very short marriage, without any of the freedom and pleasures that married couples, particularly today can expect before children. She was to be alone to bring the children for much of the time we were in Aberystwyth. As I was heavily engaged in studies and part time work and did not give my family the time most fathers would give. She also had the burden of working part time in a number of jobs to help the family budget. She worked in the local Wimpey Bar, one of the Chinese Restaurants and as a dinner lady at the local comprehensive school.

I was away in London for much of the Autumn, and spring of 1983 and 1984 at the Bar school in London and then again from the Summer of 1984 to the early summer of 1985 in pupillage in the Temple in London. Thus she had to bring up the children in a Welsh environment with little help from me, least in 1983/5. She did so with love but traditional caring Chinese firmness: in not allowing them to run free and do their own thing.

They are today a credit to her. I am so proud of them. Both even when away, were always back when their mother needed them. Her condition after the terrible stroke and her long time in the Hospice clearly affected them and could not have helped when they were involved with their work and studies. Alex in particular had to return whilst engaged in the last period of his finals at university and Alfreda was engaged in post university qualification. They were awful times, first Mum nearly dying in ICU at Prince of Wales Hospital in 2001 and then again the poor soul in a critical state dying of cancer at Bradbury Hospice for nearly 4 months in 2006.

I still cry when I recall how she suffered and I think it appropriate to include here some photographs to show how she declined. There is photograph of her in 1998 after she was diagnosed with Parkinson's, there are others to show her as she was after the 'implant' operation and some, towards the end, of her at Alfreda's wedding to Chris Dennis.

I nursed her with eventually the two sisters from the Philippines. I have described above, in the memoirs some of the 'mishaps' in their care. I would take her out often in the wheel chair around the Shatin river, going as far as Ma On Shan: a 5 to 6 mile hike. Other times we would have excursions on the bus to Tung Chung or Fanling. I mention here how helpful the drivers always were getting us on and off the bus. Alas with problems with my back and hip joints and the numbness in the right foot I could not do such exercise today. I hope I lightened her life a bit. She rarely complained although got terrible frustrated, with me and the helpers, sometimes. But perhaps no wonder!

We live in a Godless atheist age, particularly so in Europe, but can we not take comfort in the hope of the millions of believers who have found faith and courage in the message of the Gospels which says we will meet in the hereafter. If there was ever anyone who deserved life in heaven then Diana did. I only posit that perhaps she will enjoy the peace without me. We loved each other, but we were not holding hands forever love birds!

I include in this appendix photographs of Diana's early life. They show what a lovely girl she was. I include the few photographs I can find of her early days with her family. I hope they are of sufficient quality to to be displayed.

I also show the photographs showing her decline after the operation:

I include this appendix really as a post script for our family that comes after:

Diana would have been over the moon with Alfreda and Drew's Izzy and even more so with the twin boys coming in March, 2014, and Alex and Michelle's baby girl, Natalie which was due on Christmas day 2013 but decided to come a wee bit earlier on the 27th November.

To those dear Children and any that they may bring into this truly wonderful world I say on behalf on my Diana and I: honour your English and Chinese ancestors; do good, show love and compassion to those you meet. Don't despair when things in the world look glum. Do all you can to bring peace and harmony to those in your life wherever you are and to the world in general. You are fortunate in the genes you have: The Tolliday-Wrights/Cheungs/Potters/Newkirks.

For those interested: go back further and see where we all came from. It most certainly wasn't by chance!

**Photographs of Diana CHEUNG Yee-fun:**

*1. Baby Diana with her parents and elder brother.*

*2. Diana with Cheung Keung (Kau Foo) her young brother.*

虹光照相
九龍南山道一二二號二樓
電話八零五九六一

*3. Her two brothers and her mother (Poh Poh). A pretty girl 16(?).*

*4. Her and her old friend Ah May at her wedding.*

*5. In her late teens/twenties.*

*6. Older 20's.*

*7. In London 1978.*

*8. Family picture the two families Tolliday-Wright/Cheung at Siu Lungs 'moon yuet' celebration. (1989)*

*9. At a friend's wedding, 24/25 years old.*

*10. Diana a beautiful 50 year old at the religious retreat at Tao Fong Shan, Shatin, 3/98 Parkinson's was starting to show.*

*11. Mum and Dad in a restaurant for 'yum cha', after church 2004/5.*

*12. Mum and Alfreda on the sofa.*

*13. Mum and Alexander at Alfreda's Wedding to Chris.*

*14. Four Generations.*

I have a more recent picture taken later showing her at a gathering for sea food at Sai Kung organised by friends from my chambers. I have it in a frame as it is my last photograph of her. It must have been taken around 2006 and the poor soul had worsened.

Notes For Diana's Eulogy.

LAST FEW MONTHS
Born 26.7.48.
Certified dead 10.30 PM on Tuesday 15/8/06 at the Bradbury Hospice, Shatin
Admitted to Prince of Wales Hospital with problems digesting on the 6/5/06.
Extensive cancerous growths found in the gut and liver. An operation to
investigate and remove around 15/5/06. At P of W until 4/6/06 when transferred
to The Bradbury Hospice.

The operation to remove the growth was a lengthy one and very trying for Diana.
A few days after she developed pneumonia and we thought we would lose her.
Alfreda and Alex came back and committal prayers were said when we thought
we were going to lose her. She fought off the fever and got stronger, albeit for
short and irregular intervals.

At one stage the Hospice considered she was fit enough to come home but we
had difficulty finding appropriate nursing and/or a private nursing home. Alex
helped in this regard when he visited on the 5/7/06 for a few weeks. We couldn't
find anything suitable and in any event by the middle of July her condition had
worsened. The cancer had started to grow and she was in pain both from the
rigidity from the Parkinson's disease and the effects of the cancer on the
digestive and liver organs.

The last week or so of her life we were in close support. She was heavily sedated
with morphine and didn't seem to know much as to what was going on. We held
her hand, prayed and cried.

THROUGH OUT THE TIME AT THE HOSPICE THE STAFF WERE REALLY
AND EXAMPLE TO US ALL. NURSES AND ORDERLIES WERE TRULY
CARING AND COMPASIONATE. THE WAY THEY TREATED THE DYING
MEN AND WOMEN REALLY TOUCHED THE HEART.
I ASK ALL TO ENCOURAGE THE EXISTANCE AND EXPANSION OF SUCH
PLACES IN HONG KONG
The staff were true witnesses for Christ and/or Lord Buddha.


DIANA'S LIFE
She was born in Western District on the 26/7/48. Her father was a butcher and
the family were very much Hong Kong/Macau centred. Diana(Cheung Yee-fun)
had an elder half-brother who passed away 2 to 3 years ago. He often visited her
and was very supportive with her Parkinson's disabilities.
She has a younger brother, Ah Keung, who with his wife and two sons have
always been very loving. Diana's mother passed away 12 or so years ago when
the families all attended a traditional Chinese funeral very unlike to days.

David met Diana when he was in charge of the CID at Sham Shui Po Police District. He met her at Sincere Department Store in Shuen Wan when buying shirts at her counter. The courtship included taking her home to Ludlow in Shropshire to see David's mum. She was very pleased but I understand did warn her of the mess she may be getting herself into ( not really!!!) Seriously Diana impressed her with a kind, affectionate and respectful nature. In regard to her looks she called her little 'moon face'. An expression that later often touched her when repeated.

She married David at Yuen Long Registry Office on the 5th February 1977. He was then a Chief Inspector in charge of the CID at Yuen Long. The reception was in the Yuen Long Police Officers Mess. Sadly David had to fly off the next day to attend his mother's funeral in Shropshire. His old mate Steve Stephenson stood in at the Chinese wedding banquet. David continued at Yuen Long. It was not the sleepy hollow everyone thought especially with the development of the new town Tuen Mun. Alfreda was born on the 16/4/78. I have found memories of her in her cot by our bed standing up and gazing at us both cuddling in our bed beside her.

David's health started to deteriorate in 79 with a heart problem. After leave in England, when Alex was conceived he realized the cardiac neurosis that had developed was making it difficult for him to work. He would suffer irrational fears and phobias, which he realizes now was caused by his Doctor who told him that whenever his pulse was irregular he should report to the nearest Casualty Hospital. He was afraid even to travel on the MTR or go over 30MPH in a vehicle. Madness indeed. Poor Diana had to cope with this, Baby Alfreda and Alex who she was carrying. The confident, fear not, successful Chief of Detectives who she had married expecting an uncomplicated marriage, was now looking where to go.

Alexander was born on the 4/6/80 and a few months later David was off to Aberystwyth University in Wales to study law, hoping he would get rid of his heart and neurosis problem, and become a lawyer. He had seen barristers perform in HK and was convinced he could do as well. Diana was left with the two babies. Our Dear friends Grace and Steve Stephenson cared for them until she joined David in the UK in September/October1980. I recall that she got the 24 hour clock flight times muddled up and Steve had to make special arrangement to halt the take off!

David picked her up at Heathrow; Alex was in a sling on her front and Alfreda at 2 in another on her back. The other arms carried luggage and baby equipment. I felt so sorry for her, but so proud. What must she have thought?! But Diana was always one to take things as they came and was strong and determined to make things work.

We had five years in Aberystwyth. David was at the University for three years then two years away from the family whilst he stayed in digs in London doing his Bar examinations and then one plus years as a pupil barrister.

Whilst at University David was able to give time to the family and we have fond memories of outings in the Welsh Hills and coast. Cockling with Chinese friends from the local Chinese Restaurant/Take Away at the Dovey Estuary was always great fun.

The two plus years in London were lonely for all of us. David would only get home once every third week end. Our money was tight. David's income then was no more than $3,000 a month. Throughout all the time in Aberyswyth Diana worked to supplement our income. First cleaning then in a Wimpy fastfood restaurant. Later as a dinner lady at the local Secondary School.. I remember once she was told by her welsh lady work mates not to knock her self out. 'You don't have to work too hard my love'. It sums up Diana, who always wanted to do her best and would look out for others and try to help out as much as possible. She was always one to put others before herself and was a true and loyal friend.

Diana passed her driving test and was able to use our small car, although she disliked driving. Alfreda can remember one time when they were parallel parked on the side of the road and Diana getting very distraught because she couldn't maneuver the car out of the parking space. In the end a very kind man steered her out and she was very relieved. David remembers meeting one of the children on the platform when getting off the train from London during a visit back with the family. The other was hiding in the car. There was great excitement when David had his return breaks but when he wasn't around Diana did an exceptional job making the children feel comfortable and happy in their quiet Welsh town.

Diana was indeed a marvelous wife. Always loyal and never asking me for money. Even when things got better when we retuned to HK she never asked for more than an extremely modest amount for housekeeping. David was never asked to pay for clothes or luxuries. Indeed Diana was a bargin hunter and never liked spending a lot of money. When she did have a spluge it was only at Christmas time and then it was for others, never herself.

The family never had a servant/helper until 1999 when the Parkinson's disease was getting too much for her and she was suffering terrible cramps. It was these that made us decide to have the electronic implant operation in February 2001 which unfortunately resulted in a massive haemorrhage of the brain. She was in ICU for 10 days and never spoke more than very few words after. Also her ability to tell objects, colours/ people was severely restricted. Over the years she did get more comfortable and as most of you know she did attend Church with me and did enjoy your company and the Yum Chas after church.

Diana was a typical clean living chinese girl. She didn't smoke, drink( she would go red with a wine gum) and ate sensibly; fish, soups and vegetables. Wow did she love a fish head – never one to waste 'properly food'! It prompts me to say thank to my Chambers for all our sea food feasts in Sai Kung.

A great mum to Alex and Alfreda: Diana was kind but strict. Alex has recovered admirably from the numerous punishments he received, however the broken wood spoons have been less fortunate. And I hope Alfreda has forgiven her for trying to make her a right handed chopstick user and for putting bak fah yau on her thumb to stop her sucking it.

Poor Diana, she certainly didn't deserve the suffering she has had since the dreadful Parkinson's was detected those 8 years ago. She hated to be a burden and found the whole progression most distressing. However, she was brave and had a fighting spirit always.

We love her deeply. My love for her now is stronger that when I first met her all those years ago. When she was simply gorgeous. A lovely smiling face so petite and attractive.

She has installed in Alfreda and Alex strong family values and a sense of fairness and selflessness. Thank you to her.

May she sleep with Jesus until we all awake to share God's Heavenly Kingdom.

Printed in Great Britain
by Amazon